My Story

ANSON MILLS

BRIGADIER GENERAL, U.S.A.

Edited by C. H. Claudy

With a new introduction by John D. McDermott

STACKPOLE
BOOKS

Published by
STACKPOLE BOOKS
5067 Ritter Road
Mechanicsburg, PA 17055
www.stackpolebooks.com

Cover design by Tracy Patterson
Cover photograph: Anson Mills, page ii

Printed in the United States of America

10 9 8 7 6 5 4 3 2 1

FIRST EDITION

Library of Congress Cataloging-in-Publication Data

Mills, Anson, b. 1834.
My story / by Anson Mills ; with a new introduction by John McDermott.— 1st ed.
    p. cm. — (Frontier classics)
Originally published: Washington, D.C. : Anson Mills, 1918.
ISBN 0-8117-2481-6
  1. Mills, Anson, b. 1834. 2. United States. Army—Officers—Biography. 3. United States. Army—Military life. 4. Businessmen—United States—Biography. I. Title. II. Series.

U53.M57 .A3 2003
355'.0092—dc21
[B]

                                                                    2002030251

Hannah Cassel Wills —

INTRODUCTION

by John D. McDermott

Anson Mills was a remarkable man. His careers included those of surveyor, building contractor, civil engineer, army officer, inventor, American boundary commissioner, diplomat, and author. His origins were humble, yet he ended up well-to-do, valued for his opinions, and respected in his many fields of endeavor. Consequently, one might expect his life story to be something special, and it is. His book is much more than a recounting of achievements; it is full of insights concerning the United States Army in particular and nineteenth century values in general. There is no doubt that *My Story* deserves reprinting in this Frontier Classics series.[1]

Who was the man behind the book? As Mills tells us in his first chapter, he came from a rural frontier background. Born on a farm near Thorntown, Indiana, on August 21, 1834, he was the son of James P. and Sarah Mills, both Quakers. Despite his parents convictions, Anson Mills would become a professional soldier, bold in battle and unrelenting in war.

The Millses had nine children, six boys and three girls, with Anson being the oldest, a circumstance that caused him to assume a leadership role early in life. Mills was also accountable in his adult dealings, another trait often associated with an eldest child. Of his parents, he tells us that both lacked schooling, "but had the greatest of all endowments—strong hands, clear heads, and brave hearts, with which to enter their life struggle for existence."[2] Such behavior builds confidence, and Mills never lacked for it in himself, whether being only one of two people to vote against secession in El Paso County, Texas, in 1861, or in telling his father that because of his failed opportunity at West Point he would not ask for further assistance but would make it on his own.

Mills did not lack for schooling. He received an elementary education in Indiana, beginning instruction in the three R's at age six.[3] At the same time, Mills absorbed much at home. Like boys of his age living on the frontier, he learned to use firearms as a matter of course. He tells us in his book that he shot sixty squirrels one day while protecting the family corn field. No wonder he was one of the best rifle shots in his class at West Point. With a gift of a carpenter's bench and tools from his father, Mills also became an expert at making furniture and repairing farm equipment, the kind of activity that nurtured an inventor's mind. Mills tells us that after his mother died when he was fifteen, he assumed responsibility for the housework with the assistance of his thirteen- and eleven-year-old sisters. Here was another learning experience, one that encouraged a practical turn of mind, where utility was foremost.

Mills finally received a chance to reach a higher station in life when his father told the boy that a bumper crop would enable him to send young Anson and his oldest sister to Charlotteville Academy in Schoharie County, New York. While there, Mills took the opportunity to learn Spanish from two revolutionary refugees from Cuba whom he met in town. Armed with new knowledge and hopes, the young man obtained appointment to the United States Military Academy at West Point, where he reported on June 1, 1855. Now fully grown, he was five feet, ten-and-one-half inches tall and weighed one hundred sixty pounds. Mills remained at the academy for nearly two years. He tells us very little about his experience there, but either his studies were difficult or he spent too much time doing other things. Whatever the case, he learned in February, 1857, that he had been found deficient in mathematics, causing him to resign.

Never one to bemoan his fate, Mills decided to practice what he had learned at the two academies and headed for West Texas, eventually obtaining a position as district surveyor. It was there that he began to show his promise. Plotting civilian lands below Franklin and Forts Quitman, Davis, Stockton, and Bliss, he laid out the first plan for El Paso, giving the town its name. At the same time, he showed his versatility, constructing the new headquarters of the Overland Mail Company in downtown El Paso. Covering a square block, it remained the largest structure in the city for three decades.

Mills tells us that in February 1861, he was one of two out of 985 persons in El Paso County who voted against secession from the Union, his homemade ballot proclaiming "No separation—Anson Mills." To say the least, this made him unpopular, and after failing to talk the commander at Fort Bliss out of surrendering the federal fort to Confederate forces, he journeyed to the Nation's capital. There he became a sergeant in the Cassius M. Clay Guards, consisting of 150 Southern men awaiting military appointments in the Union Army.

In his autobiography, Mills does not make much of his service in Washington. His was an elite group, however, one of two units organized by District of Columbia Marshall Ward H. Lamon to provide security until Federal troops arrived. Every day, and particularly every night, the men expected Confederate raids from nearby Alexandria, Virginia. Lamon later declared: "No more timely and effective service was at any time done during the war. Not one of the men slept in a bed from the time of his enlisting until his discharge. There was never banded together a braver, more determined or desperate set of men."[4]

On May 14, Mills received his commission in the Union army as a first lieutenant in the 18th Infantry. He later revealed that he had obtained the signatures of the senior class at the U.S. Military Academy recommending his favorable consideration to the Adjutant General of the Army.[5] Notification did not come until June 22, however, when he left for Columbus, Ohio, to report to his new commander, Col. Henry B. Carrington.

A graduate of Yale Law School in 1848, Carrington had settled in Columbus, becoming adjutant general of the Ohio militia in 1857. When Lincoln issued his first call for troops four years later, Carrington hurried nine regiments across the Ohio River to save West Virginia for the Union. Shortly afterward, on May 14, he received an unsolicited appointment as colonel of the 18th Infantry. Carrington, however, did not join his command, remaining on special service for the duration of the war.[6] Unfortunately, Mills does not give us a picture of Carrington, who was to become the scapegoat in Red Cloud's War of 1866. As circumstance would have it, after the war Mills and several companies of the 18th were sent to Fort Bridger, Wyoming, where they missed the terrible ordeal along the Bozeman Trail. This disaster was punctuated by the death of Capt. William J. Fetterman and eighty men a few miles from Fort Phil Kearny on December 21, 1866.

Reminding us that his intent was not to write a history of the Civil War, Mills tells us about his battles but mostly prefers to discuss his own experience in surviving. In the process, he relates some fascinating stories about what men do under pressure. He tells us that he served with his regiment throughout the conflict, never missing a day of service for any reason, a remarkable feat.[7]

Mills is too modest in many respects. The 18th Infantry participated in several important engagements and complied an impressive record. Mills's first action was the Siege of Corinth, April 9 to June 5, 1862, followed by the Battle of Perrysville, Kentucky, October 8. A reorganization on December 25, 1862, assigned the 18th Infantry to the XIV Corps, and four days later the regiment engaged Confederate forces in the Battle of Murfreesboro, Tennessee. In a hard-fought, four-day struggle, nearly thirteen hundred Union and twelve hundred Confederate soldiers died.

The 18th held the center in this battle as part of Gen. L. H. Rousseau's Division, losing nearly three hundred men, or half its strength, in an hour of combat. Rousseau later stated that if he had had the power, he have would promoted every officer and many noncoms and privates of the Ohio regiment for their efforts that day. On June 25 and 26, 1863, Mills fought in the Battle of Hoover's Gap, Tennessee, and on September 19 and 20 in the Battle of Chickamauga, Georgia. He then saw action during the Siege of Chattanooga, Tennessee, from September 21 to November 4, and the Battle of Missionary Ridge, Tennessee, November 24 and 25.

In 1864, he participated in the last phases of the war, beginning with the Battle of Tunnel Hill, Georgia, on February 23 and 24, Buzzard's Roost, February 25 and 26. The 18th then joined William Tecumseh Sherman in the Atlanta campaign. From May 3 to September 8, Mills and his regiment formed part of the 2nd Brigade, 1st Division, the XIV Corps of the Army of the Cumberland. Included in the campaign were the Battles of Resaca, May 13 to 15; Dallas, May 24 to June 5; New Hope Church, May 29 to 31; Kennesaw Mountain, June 22 to July 3; Neal Dow Station, July 4; Peach Tree Creek, June 20, where he was slightly wounded; Utoy Creek, August 7; and the Battle of Jonesboro on September 1.

In the Battle of Jonesboro, which resulted in the fall of Atlanta, the 18th Infantry led the assault on the enemy's fortifications and enveloped the Confederate army's first line of defense. The regiment suffered heavy losses in this battle and during the campaign, because Sherman relied on experienced units to make initial contact in turning a flank or seizing enemy fortifications. On December 15 and 16, Mills ended his active fighting in the Battle of Nashville.

The 18th Infantry had a remarkable record during the Civil War. The regiment numbered 653 officers and men at the start of the campaign, but at the end only 210 remained. According to Fox's *Regimental Losses*, the 18th lost more killed and mortally wounded than any other regiment in the regular army. Mills does not tell us this, nor that his company, Co. H, had more casualties than any other in the regiment.[8] Nor does he mention brevets he earned for gallantry in action. Mills received three of them during the Civil War: captain, December 31, 1862, for gallant and meritorious services in the Battle of Murfreesboro, Tennessee; major, September 1, 1864, for gallant and meritorious services in the Battle of Chickamauga, Georgia, and during the Atlanta campaign; and lieutenant colonel in December 16, 1864, for gallant and meritorious services in the Battle of Nashville, Tennessee.[9]

At the end of the war, Mills had the permanent rank of captain. This was not unusual, as, for example, George Armstrong Custer, probably the second-best-known cavalry officer behind Phillip Sheridan in the Union Army, held the same rank. Like many of his peers, Mills decided to serve in the peacetime army. It was in this duty where he made his mark. While not formally declared, a war raged in the American West between frontier settlers and the Indians of the prairies and plains. Years of intrusion, mistreatment, and fraud propelled the latter, while hopes of independence, wealth, and revenge drove the former. Mills and his colleagues had to punish the Indians when they committed depredations, and evict whites when they appropriated reservation land. In many respects, it was a thankless task, undertaken in an isolated region with few men and supplies.[10]

During his long career, Mills served at and often commanded dozens of military posts in the hinterlands, including Fort Aubry in Kansas; Fort Sedgwick in Colorado; Forts Bridger and Fetterman in Wyoming; Fort Halleck in Nevada; Forts Whipple, McDowell, Thomas, and Grant in Arizona; Fort Bayard in New Mexico; Fort McPherson and Camp Sheridan in Nebraska; and Forts Concho, Davis, Bliss, and McIntosh in Texas; the Presidio in California; Fort Walla Wall in Washington; and Forts Sill and Reno in Oklahoma. Some of the most interesting passages in the book concern how Mills and his wife adapted to these frontier conditions.

Always the clear-headed man on a course, Mills decided in 1868 that he should get married and took a leave of absence to search for a bride. His quest took him to Zanesville, Ohio, where he had been a recruiter just after the end of the Civil War. His choice was Hannah Cassel, a vivacious, privately-educated young woman, who with her three sisters charmed eligible bachelors of the region. Married on October 13, 1868, Mills and his wife were mutually supportive and productive in their years together. Undoubtedly part of their success was due to the fact that Mills believed that women should have the same rights as men and that a man and his wife should be equal partners in all human endeavors.

The couple had two children later in life, Anson Cassel, born on November 1, 1878, and Constance Lydia born October 22, 1881.[11] "Nannie," as Hannah was called by her intimates, was a talented and spirited mate. Several letters that she wrote home to her parents from frontier posts, included in this volume, reveal her as energetic and resourceful, unafraid, and equal to the challenge. The Washington, D.C., *Evening Star* once remarked of her: "Mrs. Mills was known for her personal beauty, her charm of manner and her splendid philanthropic work."[12]

During the early 1870s, Mills began to receive special assignments, a testimony to the confidence placed in him by his superiors. In July 1870, Mills and two companies joined Professor Marsh of Yale and thirty students on a paleontological expedition in the Bad Lands along the

Niobrara River in northwestern Nebraska. In 1873, he escorted Lord Dunraven and three friends on a hunting expedition on the Loup River in the same region. The party included William F. "Buffalo Bill" Cody, with whom Mills became lifelong friends.

In 1874, an even greater challenge presented itself. That September, the Sioux raided the parade grounds at Forts Fetterman and Steele in Wyoming and killed several soldiers. Mills received orders to pursue with six companies, a total of 343 men and 15 officers. The plan called for the troops to proceed to Rawlins, Wyoming, by rail, march to Independence Rock, cross the Big Horn Mountains, and destroy a camp of hostiles believed to be near old Fort Reno on Powder River.[13] In his book, Mills tersely comments on the expedition, stating that, "Unfortunately the Indians discovered our movements, and moved north beyond our reach."[14]

Some, however, were critical of the expedition. A correspondent writing in the *Evanston (Wyoming) Age* reported that the value of Government property abandoned was ten thousand dollars, and that officers vied with one another in lightening their loads, exhausting their stock, and hurrying back to Rawlins. Mills, he declared, was finally reduced to a sack of bacon and a load of whisky, and rumor had it that the expedition would have continued longer had there not been danger of the failure of the keg.[15] Mills apparently thought this humorous, as he pasted the article in his scrapbook.

Mills was soon to experience some of the most exciting moments of his life. In April 1875, he was ordered to command Camp Sheridan in northwestern Nebraska, established a year before to watch over Spotted Tail Agency, the home of the Brule Sioux. On September 9, the agency and the camp had been moved to a better site on Beaver Creek, about 12 miles southeast.[16]

The Brules had been some of the most warlike of the Western Sioux or Lakota and had been partners in the Bozeman Trail War. Mills's job was complicated because gold had been discovered in the Black Hills, miners were entering the reservation illegally, and Indians were beginning to retaliate. Although the 1868 Fort Laramie Treaty had established a reservation and provided a general administrative framework, it had proved less than successful in changing the Sioux. The attempt to make warriors into farmers had failed, and, periodically, young men left the reservation to live the nomadic life of the Plains Indian warrior in the unceded Indian territory between the Black Hills and the Big Horn Mountains. This was a volatile situation, and Mills landed in the middle of it.

Mills's first real action with illegal entries came a few weeks after his arrival. In mid-May, a detachment of thirty troops from Fort Randall attempted to arrest a party of miners from Sioux City. When the group ignored the smaller force, its commander sent a message to Camp Sheridan, asking for assistance. Mills rushed to the rescue with seventy-six men and a gatling gun, arrested seventy-eight miners, and destroyed their wagons and other property. Mills sent John Gordon, the leader of the party and a well-known entrepreneur who had led the first unlawful penetration of the Black Hills in December 1874 to his guardhouse at Camp Sheridan, turned over another leader to the to the U.S. Marshall, and let the rest go. Mills's quick and decisive action soon became public knowledge and temporarily deterred others from attempting illegal entry.[17]

The next step in avoiding conflict was an attempt to purchase the Black Hills from the Sioux. On September 20, 1875, the so-called Allison Commission met at Fort Robinson, Nebraska, with Mills and his troops from nearby Camp Sheridan acting as part of its protective force. About forty-five hundred Indians had gathered to attend the council. Principal among the chiefs were Red Cloud of the Oglala, Spotted Tail of the Brule, Turkey and Little Wolf of the Cheyenne, and Black Coal of the Arapaho.[18]

The commissioners opened the session by offering $6 million for the Black Hills or a lease for $400,000 a year. They also asked the Sioux to surrender their hunting rights on unceded lands. When Little Big Man and others of the nonreservation Western Sioux circled the council and threatened to kill anyone who signed the paper, Mills and his colleagues prepared for the worst, but violence was avoided with the aid of Man-Afraid-of-His-Horses and other friendly Lakota. The disturbance, however, was enough to disrupt the council, so that in the end nothing was accomplished.[19] The commission recommended in its final report that the Sioux should be offered what the Congress determined was a fair price for the Black Hills. If the Indians rejected the offer, the commission recommended that the Government end annual subsistence allotments.[20]

On November 3, President Grant stepped in. Among those summoned to a meeting in his office were the Secretaries of War and the Interior and Gens. Philip Sheridan and George Crook. After discussion, Grant ruled that while the army would continue to voice opposition to entry into the Black Hills by miners, it would no longer take action to stop them. Furthermore, because the commissioners believed that the nonreservation bands had been responsible for the failure of the Allison Commission, the Government decided they must control these Indians. They were to return to the reservation, peacefully if possible, by force if necessary.[21] Thus, the stage was set for the Great Sioux War of 1876–77. When the army issued an ultimatum to all the Sioux and Northern Cheyenne to appear at the various agencies on the reservation by January 31, 1876, or suffer the consequences, few were surprised when only a few groups responded.

First into the field was Gen. George Crook, commander of the Department of the Platte, and a fighting force of 883 soldiers, guides, and
packers.[22] In the forthcoming battles, a part of what is probably the best-
known of all the Indian campaigns in the 19th century, Mills had an important role to play. Yet, in his book, he mistakenly reports its first phase as
happening early in 1875 rather than in the spring of 1876.[23]

On March 17, 1876, Crook's advance column of six companies under
Col. Joseph J. Reynolds attacked an Indian village on the left bank of the
Powder River, approximately thirty-six miles southwest from present-day
Broadus, Montana.[24] A combined Northern Cheyenne and Oglala village
of about 100 lodges (400 to 500 persons), its leaders were Old Bear, Little
Wolf, and Two Moon. While Reynolds's attacking force of two companies
successfully surprised the village, supporting companies under Capt.
Alexander Moore failed to advance. Seeing the problem, Mills and his
company rushed forward to help destroy the camp and its contents. In a
panic, Reynolds ordered the men to abandon the village and reunite with
Crook. The battle had lasted five-hours, resulting in the deaths of four soldiers and two warriors. Although the Battle on Powder River resulted in
the destruction of much Indian property, it did little to break the will of
warriors in unceded Indian territory.[25]

In his book, Mills mentioned the attack proved a failure owing to the
age and feebleness of Colonel Reynolds. He goes on to state that Reynolds
disobeyed Crook's orders to hold the village and that it was "perhaps better
not to go into details here in regard to his humiliating failure, further than
to say that several officers were tried for misconduct."[26] Reynolds's inability to follow up his first successful assault did lead Crook to bring him before a court-martial in January 1877. The court ordered Reynolds
suspended from the service for a year. President Grant remitted the sentence in view of past service, and Reynolds sought retirement. The failure
of Alexander Moore to provide the critical support also brought him before a tribunal. Found guilty of conduct to the prejudice of good order and
military discipline in failing to cooperate fully in the attack, Moore was ordered suspended from command for six months and confined to the limits
of his post. While Grant approved the court's findings, he remitted the
sentence in view of the officer's previous record.[27]

Always the pursuer, Crook prepared for another campaign, and in June
he was back in unceded Indian territory, marching up the Rosebud River.
On June 17, he enjoined Sioux and Cheyenne forces under Crazy Horse in
a full-day's battle, and once again Mills was there to save the day.[28] In this
case, he did provide a detailed account of the engagement, printed as Appendix Three in this volume.

As Mills recounts, the fighting began when Sioux and Cheyenne warriors led by Crazy Horse attacked Crook's Shoshone and Crow Scouts, then swept down upon his soldiers who were having a short rest on the banks of Rosebud Creek. As the battle took shape, Crook had a cavalry battalion on the left, infantry in the middle, and another cavalry battalion under Mills on the right. After some skirmishing, Crook decided to send Mills to find the Indian village, which he believed to be eight to ten miles north. As Mills began his search for the Indian camp, warriors threatened the cavalry battalion on the left, inflicting a number of casualties, and Crook had no choice but to recall his subordinate. Mills's oblique return journey brought him somewhat in the rear of the attacking warriors. The sudden appearance of Mills and his command caused the Sioux and Cheyenne to quit the field and return to their camp on present-day Reno Creek, some twenty miles away. Crook lost ten enlisted men and a Shoshone scout, while the Sioux and Cheyenne left thirteen dead on the field.

After his scouts refused to guide him farther, Crook made an about face to Goose Creek to get much-needed supplies and call for reinforcements. Although the general occupied the field at fighting's end, he did not cause the Sioux and Cheyenne serious harm, and eight days later they defeated George Custer's cavalry in the famed Battle of the Little Bighorn. In his account, Mills refers to Crook as being "humiliatingly defeated" in the Battle of the Rosebud, but he did not understand Crook's method of warfare, which was to keep the pressure on rather than risk everything on one bold stroke. Recognizing the strength and abilities of the allied tribes, Crook returned to his base camp to reorganize and begin a second campaign that would eventually lead to the defeat of his opponents. He planned to wear the Plains warriors down rather than overwhelm them.

As the summer wore on, Crook continued to follow his prey, and on September 7, when the supplies were exhausted and the men were eating mules for sustenance, he sent Mills and 150 cavalrymen to seek provisions in the Black Hills mining camps. On the way, on the evening of the 8th, Mills discovered a Sioux-Cheyenne village of thirty lodges.[29] The next morning, Mills attacked at dawn. In a 1914 interview, he remembered the scene:

> It was fast coming light, and we could see a few of the lodges across the depression. . . . I had told [Lieutenant] Schwatka to be ready to charge on the village the instant the pony herd would stampede, for I knew the minute they smelled us they would start and run into the village, and this is just what they did. I had the rest of the command dismounted except for the horse holders. When the

herd stampeded Schwatka followed them right into the
village, riding through it and firing with pistols into the
lodges.[30]

The troops captured the pony herd and forced fleeing occupants of the
village into nearby hills. Crook and his troops arrived shortly thereafter,
and the combined command focused their efforts on dislodging warriors
and women and children from a deep ravine where they had sought shelter. Most of them surrendered, including a chief, American Horse, who
later died of his wounds. Troops torched the tipis. Warriors soon arrived
from nearby Sioux camps and attempted to recapture the pony herd and
free Indian prisoners, but the men held firm. The next day, skirmishing
continued for several miles as Crook and his command continued their
march to the Black Hills and succor. Significant as the turning point in the
Great Sioux War, the Battle of Slim Buttes was the first decisive army victory since the conflict began six months earlier. After Slim Buttes, the Indians began making their way to the Dakota and Nebraska agencies, the
nontreaty Sioux actually surrendering, others simply returning to their previous way of life. For his role in the fight at Slim Buttes, Mills always believed that he deserved the Medal of Honor.

Mills received a rude shock when he learned that his behavior at Slim
Buttes was being criticized. The critic was Reuben Davenport of the *New
York Herald*, a reporter who had accompanied the troops on campaign. Always critical of Crook, Davenport had added Mills to his list. In a *Herald*
story of October 2, the reporter wrote that "[t]hrough the weakness of an
officer a terrible reverse was at one moment imminent, but the firmness of
a subordinate and the spirit of his troops saved him." He went on to declare that Mills wanted to attack immediately but that Lt. Emmet Crawford "prudently urged the policy of effecting a complete surprise with a
very small force, as the strength of the enemy was unknown." According to
Davenport, Lieutenant Schwatka voiced his support. He also wrote that
when the attack began, Mills seemed cowed by his fright, and when the
firing started, he yelled, "Retreat, men! Retreat!" Crawford, however, drew
his pistol and shouted, "I will shoot any man who tries to retreat." According to Davenport, "This noble insubordination prevented a disaster."[31] The
article so disturbed Crawford and Schwatka that they and the other junior
officer in the group, John Bubb, sent letters to the *Herald* and the *Army
and Navy Journal*. They declared that the story was completely false: they
had fully approved all of Mills's plans and their implementation, and their
"action with him was harmonious in every particular."[32]

Surprisingly, Davenport later apologized. In a letter to Mills dated June 5, 1878, he wrote that he had heard the story from the man who guided the troops, meaning Scout Frank Grouard. He stated that he believed the man in the beginning but subsequently found that he had lied. He explained that at the time he had been very sick and had not been able to check his sources. Mills had the letter prepared in printed form and sent copies to friends and others.[33] The army eventually did recognize Mills for his service. On February 27, 1890, he received a brevet "for gallant services in action against Indians at Slim Buttes, Dakota, September 9, 1876."[34]

During the next fifteen years, Mills continued to receive a variety of assignments. From March 1878 to March 1879, he served as military attaché of the Paris exposition commission.[35] Before reaching Paris, he received a promotion to major in the 10th Cavalry, one of the two black cavalry regiments formed after the Civil War.[36] In the spring of 1879, Mills was back on the frontier, this time in Texas. First at Fort Concho, he moved to Fort Davis in 1882. Spending his off hours in nearby by El Paso, he became involved in a number of projects. With an associate, he built the Grand Central Hotel, then the most commodius in the state. In 1912 he replaced it with a twelve-story concrete structure, which at that time was the largest of its kind in the world. Although no longer the tallest building in El Paso, today the Mills Building remains a major city landmark.[37]

In 1885 the army sent Mills to command Fort Thomas on the Gila River. Leaving in August 1886, he became the commander of Fort Grant, spending much of his time in the field, some of his regiment participating in the Geronimo campaigns. Next, the army detailed Mills to assist officers of the United States Geological Survey near El Paso, as they determined the feasibility of reclaiming lands in the Rio Grande Valley through dams and water storage. Assigned to Fort Bliss, Texas, he was a supervising engineer under Colonel Nettleton of the USGS, a job that prepared him for a significant future assignment. In April 1890, Mills went to the Presidio in San Francisco, which he commanded after he received a promotion on July 13, 1890, as lieutenant colonel of the 4th Cavalry.[38] In 1892-93, he commanded the regiment at Fort Walla Wall, Washington, and on February 27, 1893, he received a promotion to colonel of the 3rd Cavalry, with headquarters at Fort McIntosh, Texas. His final duty in the field was at Fort Reno, Oklahoma, where he served until August 12, 1893.[39]

Mills's experience in the El Paso region, early and late, prepared him well for his next duty. On October 26, 1893, he began work as the sole commissioner of the United States–Mexico boundary commission. Mills's involvement with border problems was twofold: to determine the correct boundary between the United States and Mexico, adapted to the changes in the Rio Grande River, which were often and sudden; and to prove for an equitable distribution of water between the two countries and the settlements therein. During the first years, Mills worked to reestablish the Mexican border on the Rio Grande, the shifting river having created numerous accretions and decrements. He also advocated construction of a major international dam to store water from the Rio Grande above El Paso for use in the dry season. Politics eventually dictated its location at Elephant Butte in New Mexico, 120 miles north of El Paso. He was the principal author of a treaty with Mexico to provide for an equitable distribution of the waters of the Rio Grande, determined to be sixty thousand acre-feet of water per year. In 1905, he authored a treaty for the elimination of all islands in the Rio Grande. In perspective, Mills is best remembered for the boundary dispute with Mexico over the Chamizal tract. Refusing to accept the 1911 arbitration agreement that gave the El Paso Chamizal to Mexico, he received the support of the State Department, which eventually negotiated successfully for the land. Mills retired from the army on June 22, 1897, with the rank of brigadier general but continued with his work on the commission until he resignation in 1914 at the age of seventy.[40]

As a member of the diplomatic corps, Mills moved to Washington in 1894 and bought a home at 2 DuPont Circle, which was his permanent residence until his death. At the corner of Pennsylvania Avenue and 17th Street, he built what was said to be the first steel frame, fireproof building in the city. This was occupied by a branch of the Navy Department and by the Department of Labor for a number of years.[41]

Before his death, Mills amassed a small fortune as the result of an improvement in army equipment. While at Fort Bridger just after the Civil War, he discovered a problem caused by carrying paper and metallic cartridges in the same tin container. The latter rattled loudly in the boxes, even when carried by men on foot. Mills's answer was to devise a leather belt with a loop for fifty cartridges. Worn around the waist, the belts were comfortable and efficient. Judge W. A. Carter, the post sutler at Fort Bridger, suggested that the idea was worth patenting, and on his next trip to Washington he secured one for Mills. But the belts were not universally adopted, the army seeming to have prejudice against innovations in a post–Civil War era glutted by left-over arms and equipment of all kinds.

Mills's next step was to weave the belt and loops together. Experience showed that the acid in the leather acted on the copper of the shell producing verdigris. This sometimes caused the shell to stick in the belt or, after firing, to lodge in the chamber of the weapon. By weaving belt and loops in one piece, cloth replaced leather, and the belts had added strength and longevity. Mills had assisted his mother in weaving clothing for the children and knew what the loom could do. Studying the apparatus with a view of applying it to belt-making, he eventfully succeeded.[42]

When fully developed the belts were quite sophisticated. Woven of 13 6-ply cotton, they varied in width from two to three inches. Loops varied in size to fit the ammunition. In a newspaper article, Mills explained the finishing process. Workmen stretched the belts on a wheel, filling loops with forming shells or empty cartridges of the right size. Boiling came next, the belts with shells in the loops being subjected to a thorough scalding to shape the loops and shrink the material. Then they were hung to dry in a room with high heat to shrink even more. Mills finally made arrangements to have the belt manufactured in Worcester, Massachusetts, by T. C. Orndorf, his brother-in-law. Eventually adopted by both the United States, British, Mexican armies, and a few South American countries, this invention made him wealthy.[43]

Mills was eighty-five years old when his autobiography was published, and it was only fitting that his old commander, Gen. Nelson A. Miles, penned the preface. Mills died in Washington, D.C., on November 5, and was buried with honors in Arlington National Cemetery.

Looking back on his life, we can say that Anson Mills had a great deal of which to be proud. He served with distinction during the Civil War in the nation's most blooded regiment and company. He was the center of things in the Great Sioux War, going to the assistance of his beleaguered comrades in the Indian village on Powder River, protecting Crook's right at the Battle of the Rosebud, and winning a victory at Slim Buttes. He had a great deal to do with the development of West Texas, and he was a pioneer in building construction nationwide. His innovations in military equipment had international applications. Perhaps above all, he should be remembered for his progressive thinking, which included support for the rights of enlisted men, women's suffrage, and organizations for world peace.[44] His autobiography remains one of the best we have of an educated soldier, whose life affected so many disciplines and important events in the last half of the nineteenth century.

NOTES

1. Basic sources for Mills's careers include his Appointments, Commission, and Personnel (ACP) File and his Military Service Record (Civil War), Records of the Office of the Adjutant General, Record Group 94, National Archives, Washington, D.C. L. M. Crist's biographical sketch of Mills found in *History of Boone County Indiana*

(1914) is reproduced at homepages.rootsweb.com/~jaheine/Anson-Mills.html, along with other biographical material. See also Leon C. Metz, *Turning Points in El Paso* (El Paso, Texas: Mangan, 1985); William Wallace Mills, *Forty Years at El Paso* (El Paso, Texas: Hertzog, 1962); and C. L. Sonnichsen, *The North: Four Centuries on the Rio Grande*, 2 vols. (El Paso: Texas Western Press, 1980).

2. *My Story*, 27.

3. "Gen. Anson Mills 85 Today," *The (Washington, D.C.) Evening Star*, August 31, 1919, part 1, 2.

4. "Saved the Capital," *The (Washington, D.C.) Evening Star*, n.d., Mills Scrapbook, 118, Anson Mills Papers, American Heritage Center, Laramie, Wyoming.

5. "Anson Mills," Rootsweb.com, 4.

6. *Record of Living Officers of the United States Army* (Philadelphia: L. R. Hamersley & Co., 1884); Oliver Crane, Carrington (n.p., c. 1898); *Obituary Records of Graduates of Yale University, Deceased from June 1910 to July 1915* (New Haven, Connecticut: Yale University Press, 1915), pp. 348–53

7. "Gen. Anson Mills 85 Today," *Evening Star*, August 31, 1919, part 1, 2.

8. For discussion of the service of the 18th Infantry see "Records of Events and History of the 18th Regiment of Inf., 1861–1865," Records of the Eighteenth Infantry, Records of Regular Army Regiments, Record Group 391, National Archives; Charles H. Cabaniss, Jr., "The Eighteenth Regiment of Infantry," *Journal of the Military Service Institution of the United States* 12 (September, 1891), 1111–20; Arnold J. Hedenheimer, *Vanguard to Victory: History of the 18th Infantry* (New York, 1968), 48–51; A. B. Cushing, "History of the Eighteenth United States Infantry," *Winners of the West* (January, 1938), 1–2; Frederick H. Dyer, *A Compendium of the War of the Rebellion*, Vol. 1 (New York: Thomas Yoseloff, n.d.), 1715.

9. Francis B. Heitman, *Historical Register and Dictionary of the United States Army*, Vol. 1 (Washington, D.C.: Government Printing Office, 1903), 713.

10. John D. McDermott, *A Guide to the Indian Wars of the West* (Lincoln: University of Nebraska Press, 1998), 1–12, 46–65.

11. In his biographical sketch of Mills in his *History of Boone County*, L. M. Crist mentions a second son, William Cassel, deceased. He is not mentioned in *My Story*, probably having died at birth.

12. "Gen. Anson Mills 85 Today," *Evening Star*, 1919, 2.

13. "Big Horn Expedition," unidentified newspaper article, Mills Scrapbook, 100.

14. *My Story*, 155.

15. "Notes From 'INO'," *Evanston (Wyoming) Age*, c. October 12, 1874, Anson Mills Scrapbook, 96.

16. Letter from Capt. Henry M. Lazelle, Near Spotted Tail Agency, March 1874, to Asst. Adj. Gen. W. W. McCannon, Sioux Expedition, and Asst. Surgeon M. W. Woods, "Camp Sheridan, August 31, 1876," in Letters Sent, Camp Sheridan, Records of United States Army Commands, Record Group 393, National Archives; Thomas R. Buecker, "History of Camp Sheridan, Nebraska," *Periodical: Journal of America's Military Past* 22 (1995), 55–60.

17. Letter from Anson Mills, Camp Sheridan, May 23, 1875, to Gen. George P. Ruggles, Letters Sent, Camp Sheridan, Record Group 393; "Personal Liberty," *Omaha Daily Herald*, in General Correspondence, Records of Rosebud Agency, A-35 1, Records of the Bureau of Indian Affairs, Record Group 75, Regional National Archives, Kansas City, Kansas; George W. Kingsbury, *History of Dakota Territory*, ed. by George Martin Smith, Vol. 1 (Chicago: S. J. Clarke Publishing Company, 1915), 918–19.

18. Mills gives the figure as "perhaps 20,000," which appears highly inflated. See *My Story*, 167. For discussion of the treaty council see Rev. Peter Rosen, *Pa-Ha-Sa-Pah, or the Black Hills of South Dakota* (St. Louis: Nixon-Jones Printing Co., 1895), 321–22; Charles Collins, "The Black Hills," *Omaha Weekly Bee*, September 15, 1875, 2; John T. Bell, "The West," *Omaha Daily Herald*, September 11, 1875, 1.

19. The *Chicago Daily Tribune* printed the report of the Allison Commission in its November 18, 1875, issue. See also Charles Collins, "Letter from Red Cloud Agency," *Omaha Weekly Bee*, September 24, September 29, October 6, and October 13, 1875; E. P. Wilson, "The Story of the Oglala and Brule Sioux in the Pine Ridge Country of Northwest Nebraska in the Middle Seventies," *Nebraska History* 21 (October-December, 1940), 269; "The Black Hills," *Chicago Daily Tribune*," November 19, 1875; Reminiscences of eyewitness J. C. Abney, "Big Indian Council," *Chicago Daily Sun*, October 16, 1897.

20. Mari Sandoz, *The Great Council*, ed. by Caroline Sandoz Pifer (Crawford, Nebraska: Cottonwood Press, 1982), 25; Lesta V. Tuchner and James D. McLaird, *The Black Hills Expedition of 1875* (Mitchell, South Dakota: Dakota Wesleyan University Press, 1975), 1; "Report of the Sioux Commission," *Chicago Daily Tribune*, November 19, 1875, 9.

21. John D. McDermott, "The Military Problem and Black Hills," *Gold Rush: The Black Hills Story*, comp. with an intro. by John D. McDermott (Pierre: South Dakota Historical Society Press, 2001), 22–23.

22. For a detailed discussion of Crook's 1876 battles and skirmishes see John D. McDermott, *Gen. George Crook's 1876 Campaigns: A Report Prepared for the American Battlefield Protection Program* (Sheridan, Wyoming: Frontier Heritage Alliance, 2000). This is an electronic book accessed at www.frontierheritage.org.

23. *My Story*, 165.

24. The older standard work is J. W. Vaughn, *Reynolds' Campaign on the Powder River* (Norman, Oklahoma: University of Oklahoma Press, 1961). See also McDermott, *Crook's 1876 Campaigns*, 7–23, 159–68.

25. Mills wrote about this ten years before he finished his book. It is very similar to that which appeared in *My Story*. See Anson Mills, "Memorandum Prepared by General Anson Mills About 1908," MSS Item M-4, Order of the Indian Wars Collection, Military Service Institute, Carlisle, Pennsylvania.

26. *My Story*, 166–67.

27. Zenobia Self, "Court-Martial of J. J. Reynolds," *Military Affairs*, 38 (April, 1973), 52–57. A full transcript of the proceedings of the courts-martial are found in Col. Joseph J. Reynolds, Case QQ #26d and Capt. Alexander Moore, Case QQ #26; the Records of the Judge Advocate General, Record Group 153, National Archives, Washington, D.C.

28. Book-length studies include J. W. Vaughn, *With Crook on the Rosebud* (Harrisburg, Pennsylvania: Stackpole, 1956) and Neil C. Mangum, *The Battle of the Rosebud: Prelude to the Little Bighorn* (El Segundo, California: Upton, 1987). See also McDermott, *Crook's 1876 Campaigns*, 31–57, 176–221.

29. The standard work on the Battle of Slim Buttes is Jerome A. Greene, *Slim Buttes, 1876: An Episode of the Great Sioux War* (Norman: University of Oklahoma Press, 1982). See also McDermott, *Crook's 1876 Campaigns*, 73–90, 247–92. In his appended account of the Rosebud Battle, Mills omits all reference to his victory at Slim Buttes, simply reporting that "the fall campaign ensued" and that he returned to Camp Sheridan. See *My Story*, 411.

30. Walter M. Camp, Interview with Anson Mills, January 24, 1914, Camp Papers, Robert S. Ellison Collection, Denver Public Library. This has been printed in Jerome A. Greene, comp., *Battles and Skirmishes of the Great Sioux War, 1876–1877: The Military View* (Norman: University of Oklahoma Press, 1993), 110–15.

31. Davenport, *New York Herald*, October 2, 1876.

32. "A Munchausen Reporter Corrected," *Army and Navy Journal*, c. 1878, Mills Scrapbook.

33. Letter form Davenport, New York, June 5, 1878, to Anson Mills, Mills Scrapbook.
34. "To Honor Coll. Mills," unidentified newspaper article, Mills Scrapbook, 119.
35. "Gen. Anson Mills 85 Today," *Evening Star*, 2.
36. "One of Sitting Bull's Antagonists in Paterson," unidentified newspaper article, n.d., Mills Scrapbook.
37. *Army and Navy Register*, November 12, 1883, 9.
38. "Retirement and Promotion," unidentified newspaper article, Mills Scrapbook, 117
39. "To Honor Coll. Mills," Mills Scrapbook, 119.
40. Unidentified newspaper article, Mills Scrapbook, 116.
41. "Gen. Anson Mills 85 Today," *Evening Star*, August 31, 1919, 2.
42. "A New Industry," unidentified newspaper article, n.d., Mills Scrapbook, 9
43. "General Anson Mills Indian Fighter," Worcester, Massachusetts, newspaper, c. 1898, Mills Scrapbook, 123.
44. "A Plea for Soldiers and Sailors," *Chicago Citizen*, March 16, 1901; "General Mills's New Army," *Army and Navy Register*, c. 1896, Mills Scrapbook, 115.

CONTENTS

FIRST PERIOD

SECOND PERIOD

THIRD PERIOD

APPENDICES

INDEX TO ILLUSTRATIONS

To General Anson Mills
from his friend
Nelson A. Miles
Lieut-General U.S. army

PREFACE

WASHINGTON, D. C., December 12, 1917.

The record of important events in human affairs as they are placed upon the pages of history and drift into the shadows of the past, should be recorded with sacred fidelity. The historian who places accurate and important knowledge at the disposal of the present and future students and writers is a public benefactor for those not only of his own time, but for the generations that shall follow.

The achievements and failures, the evils and blessings, the benevolence and the injustice, the rights and wrongs, the ambitions, wisdom and intelligence, the happiness and nobility, as well as the distress and sacrifice of a race or people rightly recorded, forms an invaluable guide and chart for the innumerable throng that occupy the field of activities and in their turn pass on to be replaced by others.

Doubly fortunate is the one who takes an important and distinguished part in the important events of his time, and then can write an account of those events for the instruction and benefit of others. It is doubtful if any epoch in history was more important or freighted with more difficult or greater problems to be solved than those presented during the time just preceding, during and subsequent to our great Civil War.

The great Republic formed after seven years of valor and sacrifice from thirteen weak and scattered colonies, had, through several decades of unprecedented development and prosperity, become a most powerful homogeneous nation. In its creation and progress, there was left one element of discord; one vexed question remained unsettled that threatened to dismember the government, destroy the federation and seriously embarrass our advance toward a higher civilization. When reason became dethroned, logic and argument failed, the problem had to be settled by the dread arbitrament of war.

The young men, the very flower of our national manhood,

were required to decide that great problem. For the very important duties of citizenship and soldier, the distinguished author of this volume was well equipped for the important duties of that time and to render important service for his government and the people of our country.

Descending from the best of ancestral stock, born and reared in what was known as the Great Middle West, in an atmosphere of national independence, a region of our country where we find the highest type of our American civilization, he grew to manhood under the most favored auspices. Educated at excellent schools and institutions of learning, his mind became well stored with useful knowledge concerning his own country and the world. He then went to that famous military academy, West Point, where he acquired a thorough military training and those manly attributes for which the institution is noted. His mind naturally sought wider fields of usefulness, and when he resigned, he became identified with that marvelous civil development that has transformed a vast wilderness and mountain waste into productive communities and States.

As a civil engineer, he was most useful and successful. When the great crisis came, he was found true and steadfast in his allegiance to the national welfare amid chaos, doubt and uncertainty. His loyalty was invaluable, his patriotism sublime; among the first to volunteer, his record was most commendable and praiseworthy, ever present in every campaign and battle in which his company or regiment was engaged. Four times breveted for distinguished conduct in battle, he fought for a principle, and had the satisfaction of witnessing its final triumph, and its universal approval by the civilized world.

In that "war for civilization" on our western frontier, he again rendered distinguished service, not only by his conspicuous gallantry in action against Indians, but by his skill and genius as a commander in achieving success and victory where there was little prospect of winning either. In a campaign where success depends entirely upon the ability of the commander, there he succeeded.

During a long life of civil and military achievements, he was blessed by the companionship of one of the most estimable, accomplished and noblest of women, whose gentle influence was refining, whose presence was inspiring, and whose counsel was most encouraging and beneficial.

A successful life, rich with noble designs and good deeds, General Mills has contributed a favor in giving to the readers, the result of his experiences and observations.

These pages are commended to the public with the full knowledge of the fact that they are written for no selfish purpose, but for the highest and best of motives.

Nelson A. Miles

Lieutenant General, U. S. Army.

BAYBERRY LEDGE,
EAST GLOUCESTER, MASS.,
August 31, 1917.

MY DEAR DAUGHTER CONSTANCE:

After retiring from the line of the army, some twenty years ago, I had no further military duty before me save that of Commissioner on the Boundary Commission between the United States and Mexico, which I believed would occupy but a short time. Your mother and I had permanently located in Washington. We believed our lives had been so varied—mingling with so many races during so many vicissitudes and trials—that it would be interesting to you and your children for me, assisted by her, to write of our careers. Of this intention we told you in a letter dated January 1, 1898, that you might help us in such parts of the story as you were old enough to remember, although this was but a small part of our long career, you coming to us when we were middle-aged.

But the duties of the Boundary Commission became so arduous, and my business increased so as to keep me strenuously occupied until two years ago. And now, just as I find time for these reminiscences, the greatest sorrow of my life has come upon you and me—the loss of your mother. This shock has been so appalling that it shook my resolution to attempt the task without her, who had been the inspiration and chief factor in my life. Before giving up the plan, however, I submitted it to friends who had been nearest to us during our married life, and asked their advice. They all think I should not abandon my first intention of writing my life and career, in which my wife took so large a part. I record here my letter to Mrs. Albert S. Burleson and her answer, which is typical of the rest. I have selected her letter for publication because of its womanly sentiment, and because the marital life of General Burleson, my friend for a generation, has been not unlike my own. These letters are as follows:

EASTERN POINT,
GLOUCESTER, MASS.,
May 31, 1917.

MY DEAR MRS. BURLESON:

We, Constance and I, want to thank you and General Burleson for your card of sympathy.

Twenty years ago, after retirement, I had in mind to write a reminiscence of my career, but the boundary duties and my Worcester business so occupied my time that I was unable even to begin it. Now that Nannie has gone, I reflect that she has been the inspiration of whatever success I have had in life for nearly forty-nine years, so that it seems to me that whatever I do in that line should be devoted to her more than to me. I have, therefore, about concluded to write something in memory of her, and I am considering just how to do this. She was so serene, so unassuming, and so devoutly thankful to the Great Creator and her forebears for her rich endowments that she had no incentive to display them, but was always, before all, the same radiantly beautiful, graceful, modest woman, whose sparkling eyes and responsive facial expression foretold her charity for all and malice toward none, that I can not do her too much honor. From my viewpoint, women have as much right to be remembered for their work in this world as men. Certainly she had.

It is difficult to write on such a subject, especially so soon after my great loss, but, as I have but a brief period in which to accomplish what I think I ought to do, I want to ask your judgment as to how I should proceed.

Yours very truly,

ANSON MILLS.

MRS. ALBERT S. BURLESON,
1901 F Street, Washington, D. C.

1901 F Street,
June 5, 1917.

DEAR GENERAL MILLS:

I believe it would grieve your wife—could she know—to have you put aside something you had planned through so many years to do. Doubtless you frequently discussed the undertaking with her—perhaps her interest in it was even greater than yours. And any reminiscence of your life would necessarily include her life—your life together. In the preparation of such a book she would continue to be your inspiration, and that thought alone would give color and strength to all you wrote. From the viewpoint of a devoted, understanding wife myself, I feel deeply that her husband's life history would be the most pleasing of all memorials to her; for surely her memory is perpetuated in your life.

I should be glad to have you write to me again, and if it is not painful to you, to come sometime to see us. You must know that all that concerns you and your wife, whom we too knew as a "radiantly beautiful, graceful and modest woman," concerns us.

With high regard and good wishes that time will bring peace to your wounded heart, believe me,

Faithfully yours,

ADELE S. BURLESON.

I have two objects in undertaking this work:

First. That I may leave to you, your children, and their descendants, some evidence of who and what their forebears were.

Second. To give our collateral relatives something that may interest and possibly encourage them.

As far as practicable, I shall tell the story chronologically, dividing the narrative into three periods: first, my childhood, and up to the time of the Civil War, when I was commissioned in the army; second, the period of the Civil War up to my marriage; and, third—by far the most important—our history as man and wife for nearly forty-nine years.

It may be my narrative runs too much to sentiment—but there is sentiment in our Flag; in the Declaration of Independence; in the Constitution—but we can not make them commercial assets. It was sentiment that caused the armies of the "Blue and the Gray" to amaze the world with the most sanguinary and chivalrous war ever waged during all the tide of time; and it was sentiment that in a few years brought these foes together as one harmonious people. The want of sentiment caused the Goths and Vandals to degenerate into what their name now implies. The same may be said of the Hessians of our War for Independence. The want of sentiment required 300,000 British soldiers, and half as many American mules, three years to overcome 40,000 Boers imbued with sentiment, which brought peace without vainglorious victory.

ANSON MILLS.

* * * *

I am appending at the end of this book three papers which Mrs. Mills assisted me in preparing, as follows:

"Organization and Administration of the Army;" "Address to the Society of the Army of the Cumberland;" "Address to the Order of Indian Wars."

FOREWORD

I am eighty-three years old, having lived two-thirds of the constitutional life of this great Republic, which I believe the greatest institution for self-government ever devised.

Counting service as a cadet, in the line of the army proper, and as a Boundary Commissioner, I have served fifty-four years, nine months and four days in the United States Army; longer, I believe, than any other officer.

Mrs. Mills and I often congratulated ourselves that we lived in this nation and generation. In no other could we have seen and enjoyed so much, conducive to the belief that mankind was rapidly advancing to the greatest possible perfection.

Of the four greatest scourges, war, pestilence, famine and flood, we have seen the three latter almost entirely eradicated.

Only the scourge of war, the most cruel, barbarous and destructive of all, is left uncontrolled and unhampered, although there is hope this may soon be so restrained that it will be no longer a menace.

We have seen the nation develop from twenty millions to over one hundred millions of the most civilized, righteous and just people. We have seen it become foremost in the sciences, arts and industries. We have seen sixty per cent of hand labor transferred to machinery; we have watched railroad and steamboat transportation develop from their infancy; we watched the birth of electric light and power; we have seen the bicycle, motorcycle, automobile, sewing machine, knitting machine, typewriter, telegraph and its wireless associate, telephone, dirigible balloon, aeroplane, undersea boat, washing machine, power printing press, linotype, and hundreds of other inventions developed to their present perfection.

We have had a part in the pride that most of these betterments were brought about by the study, energy and ability of Americans, who, by reason of their superior inventive genius, excelled the rest of the world in manufacture.

We, too, tried to invent and discover. If we constantly

combated what we believed to be error, ignorance, inertia, and non-progressiveness, it was because we tried to lead those believing, as we did, that their souls should lend the best in them to pave the way for those coming after.

As the spirit, impulse and efforts of the two characters portrayed in these reminiscences have been those of reformers striving for the advancement of their fellow men, it is probable that a free criticism of errors and wrongs will incite a suspicion that they are relating grievances. Therefore, I ask the reader to distinguish between vindictiveness and vindication. What I here record is not a relation of grievances, but an endeavor to explain to those who have the courage to follow our line of life, the antagonisms we met. For those who are willing to live a commonplace life, it is perhaps better to observe the opinions and customs of neighbors and those in authority, but for others it is sometimes wise courageously to defy and disobey injurious and useless commands. Such actions often injure the reputation of the reformer for a time, but eventually they will distinguish him above the large number of his fellows:

> ". . . *who yearly creep*
> *Into the world to eat and sleep,*
> *And know no reason why they are born,*
> *Save to consume the wine and corn,*
> *Devour the cattle, fowl and fish,*
> *And leave behind an empty dish.*"

FIRST PERIOD

FIRST PERIOD

My Ancestors

I was born near Thorntown, Indiana, August 21, 1834.

My father, James P. Mills, third child of James Mills 2nd and Marian Mills, was born in York, Pennsylvania, August 22, 1808. His father, James Mills 2nd, was born October 1, 1770, and died December 3, 1808.

My father's mother died in 1816, leaving him an orphan at the age of eight. He lived with his Aunt Margery Mills Hayes for about two years, when he was "bound out" as an apprentice to a tanner by the name of Greenwalt, at Harrisburg, Pennsylvania. Here he was to serve until twenty-one, when he was to receive one hundred dollars and a suit of clothes. All the knowledge that he had of books was derived from night school, Greenwalt not permitting him to attend during the day. His apprenticeship was so hard he ran away when twenty, forfeiting the hundred dollars and the clothes.

His only patrimony was from his grandfather, James Mills I, who, as father told me, sent for him on his deathbed and, patting him on the head, said: "I want Jimmy to have fifty pounds."

After running away, my father went to Geneva, New York, and served as a journeyman until twenty-two. With his inheritance of $250, he and his brother Frank started West in a Dearborn wagon, crossing the Alleghenies. He traveled to Crawfordsville, Indiana, and here, about 1830, entered eighty acres of the farm on which I was born. The land was covered with walnut, oak and ash, many of the trees being one hundred feet high and three or four feet in diameter. Felling and burning the trees, he built his house with his own hands, neighbors aiding in raising the walls.

My father had little knowledge of his ancestors, other than that they were Quakers, but, by correspondence with officials of counties where his ancestors lived, I have learned that the first of his family came over with William Penn and settled in Philadelphia.

My father married Sarah Kenworthy, on November 22, 1832. My mother was born December 30, 1810, at Coshocton, Coshocton County, Ohio, and died on the farm September 4, 1849 (before the daguerreotype, hence I have no picture of her). The Kenworthy family had only recently emerged from Quakerdom, and were known as "Hickory Quakers," so I am of Quaker descent through both my parents. My mother's father, William Kenworthy, born January 22, 1780 (presumably in Guilford County, North Carolina), lived about a mile and a half from our place, and died at Thorntown, August 31, 1854. In North Carolina he married Lucretia, the third child of my great grandmother, whose maiden name was Lydia Stroud, and who was born in 1765, near Guilford Court House, Guilford County, N. C. She married Jacob Skeen, and had eight children: Abraham, Mary, Lucretia, Jacob, Clarissa, John, Sarah and Lydia.

Her second child, my mother's Aunt Mary (Polly), married Benjamin Hopkins, whose death left her with four children in indigent circumstances. With her two daughters, Betty and Lydia, she lived in a small cabin almost in sight of my mother's house. Later these two girls came to live with my mother, picking, carding, spinning and weaving wool into Kentucky jeans and linsey-woolsey, which they made into garments for the family.

My first useful labor, when I was perhaps seven or eight years old, was to "hand in" the warp, thread by thread, to these girls as they passed it through the reed and harness of the loom. The knowledge I thus acquired of warp and woof laid the foundation of my future financial success.

About 1844 my great grandmother Stroud came to live with us. I remember well the stories she told me of the outrages of Lord Rawdon's troops when he invaded North Carolina with the Hessians and destroyed her father's property. Her father was once arrested for secreting a neighbor rebel in a sack of wool under the bed, discovered by the Hessians sticking their bayonets into the wool and wounding the rebel.

They placed a rope around her father's neck and were taking him out to hang him, when he was rescued by the sudden arrival of some of Generals Lee and Sumter's soldiers. She described, too, her visit to the battle-field of the Cowpens near her father's plantation, to care for the wounded, and told of her three brothers who served in the Revolutionary Army, one of them being killed. She was so vehement in her denunciation of the English and Hessian soldiers that, all my life, I have been intensely prejudiced against the English.

Later she left our house to live with her youngest daughter, Lydia (Mrs. John Frazier), and died there in 1847, aged eighty-two.

Like my father, my mother had small patrimony, only two hundred dollars, which her father gave her in lieu of the one hundred and sixty acres he gave each of her brothers. Like him, she never attended school. In Coshocton, Ohio, by an unwritten law, no girls were permitted to enter the school house during sessions, so her knowledge of letters was gained through instruction by her parents and brothers. But, if lacking in schooling, both my parents had the greatest of all endowments—strong hands, clear heads and brave hearts, with which to enter their life struggle for existence.

They had nine children: Anson, William W., Marietta, Eliza Jane, Emmett, Allen, John, Caroline and Thomas Edwin, seven of whom grew to maturity. (Cuts, 28, 29.)

Thorntown had been a partially civilized Pottawottomi village under French Jesuit control, the seat of their reservation, where corn and other products were cultivated. When their reservation was opened to settlement, the Indians moved to Kansas. The birds carried the hawthorn seed and deposited it on the freshly plowed furrows of the farm land the Indians abandoned, which resulted in a beautiful orchard of hawthorn. Hence the name, Thorntown.

Grandfather Kenworthy purchased a good portion of these fields, including the old Indian burying-ground. He built a store and employed two six-mule teams to carry supplies from

ANSON MILLS.

W. W. MILLS.

EMMETT MILLS.

ALLEN MILLS.

MYSELF WITH BROTHERS.   (TEXT, 27.)

JAMES P. MILLS.

MARIETTA BURCKHALTER.

ELIZA JANE SMILEY.

CAROLINE MILLS MARTIN.

MY FATHER AND HIS DAUGHTERS. (TEXT, 27.)

Cincinnati. One day, when Grandfather was plowing near this graveyard, a number of chiefs in war-paint came to his house.

After the Indians had smoked awhile, one of them drew a long knife, faced Grandfather and, pointing toward the grave-yard, said:

"Kinwot, bimeby you gee-haw; gee-haw cut my brudder!"

Grandfather replied: "No, I will never plow the land under which your dead are buried," and it is today preserved as a graveyard.

Subsequent experiences with Indians led me to realize more than before the seriousness of this interview.

PRIVATIONS OF THE EARLY PIONEERS

My early life was primitive. For instance, there were no machine-made nails in this country. All nails were made by the village blacksmith from nail rods, and I often watched him while he wrought those I was sent to buy. All pins and needles were imported from England, and none of the pins had solid heads. They had wire-wound heads brazed upon the stems.

There were no shoe factories in the country, and no shoe stores in the villages. We were shod by itinerant cobblers, who made their lasts and pegs from maple wood from our wood pile. There were no rights or lefts, but each child had his own last. We children were so curious to handle the cobbler's tools that father authorized him to draw a chalk line around the corner where he worked, and use the knee strap, with which he held the shoe while pegging, to chastise us if we crossed it!

Farmers made their own brooms and axe helves from young hickory trees. We raised the wool and flax required for our clothing, all of which my mother spun, wove and fashioned, as did all other housewives. Stockings and mittens were all knit by hand; there were no knitting machines, sewing machines or cooking stoves. Practically everything necessary for existence was raised or made on the farms, save coffee, spices, tableware, hardware, glass and cutlery, which came from abroad and up the Mississippi by boat. Our nearest market was Cincinnati—two hundred miles away over rough and at times impassable roads.

There was then no Federal currency. Commerce was carried on with Spanish coin, and legal contracts were liquidated in "Spanish milled dollars." There were no postage stamps. Postmasters collected from writer or recipient ten cents for letters east of the Rocky Mountains and twenty-five cents for letters sent elsewhere. There were no envelopes. Letter paper had the fourth page unruled and was folded into an envelope, leaving the unruled page for the address. They were sealed with wax wafers.

There were no matches in general use. A Kentucky flint-lock rifle hung over the mantel, and this, with powder in the pan, was used to start fires by flashing the powder against tow or fine shavings. All farmers' boys became experts with these Kentucky rifles. Squirrels were so numerous that when the corn was maturing they would ruin three or four rows of corn next the fence. Partly to procure fresh meat and partly to protect the corn, it was our business to destroy these squirrels. I remember one Saturday I killed over sixty squirrels.

Carpenters learned their trade by five years' unpaid apprenticeship. A carpenter's chest of tools cost one hundred and twenty-five dollars, and contained approximately one hundred implements.

My father provided me with a carpenter's bench and tools and, without serving an apprenticeship, I became an expert carpenter, repairing farm tools and making furniture, as well as toys for the children. I was put to work "dropping corn" when not over eight years old and, later, hoeing and cultivating, as were all the children of my time. We were healthy and strong. Few children wore glasses and few had bad teeth.

I first went to school about 1840, when I was six. The school was a log house with a puncheon floor. Benches for the smaller scholars were saw-mill slabs, with four legs, without backs. The older boys had their bench facing the wall, with a broad plank on which to write fastened on pins in the logs.

School teachers, employed by the farmers, "boarded around" for a week or two at a time with the parents. These schoolmasters were almost invariably Irish, and governed entirely by fear, punishing cruelly. Of course, the children became stupid, uninterested, and learned slowly. We were made to sit on the bench eight hours a day, holding a book in our hands, whether studying or not. Hearing of the New England method of "moral suasion," my father interested his neighbors and succeeded in engaging as teacher a young man from New Hampshire.

He, Charlie Naylor, told us that he had come from afar,

where the teachers tried to avoid corporal punishment, and that, unless it was absolutely forced upon him, he would never whip us. He was brilliant, active and industrious, and soon won the love of his sixty scholars.

Many settlers were from Kentucky, where they compelled the teacher to "treat" on Christmas. If he refused, they tied him hand and foot, took him to the river and immersed him under the ice until he consented to supply them with apples, candy and cider. Naylor's predecessor had been treated this way.

When Christmas came nine boys over fifteen years old determined to demand the treat. The day before Christmas these nine boys took the loose benches and barred the double doors. My cousin, Lee Kenworthy, passed a note through the transom to the teacher, demanding the usual Christmas treat.

Naylor read the paper, stamped it under his feet, went to the wood pile and got the axe. Smashing the door panels, he boldly entered, axe in hand, walking to the center of the room ringing his bell violently. Every scholar proceeded to his seat. For some minutes the teacher walked back and forth. Then he asked the larger boys in turn: "Had you any hand in this?"

Each answered clearly that he had. They were brave boys. To each of the nine boys Naylor said: "Take your place out in the middle of the room near the stove." Then he gave his knife to the boy on the right and said: "Go out to that beech tree and cut nine good switches."

Naylor deliberately drew each switch through his hand, laid it on the hot stove, where it began to pop and frizzle, then slowly drew it through his hand again, bending it back and forth. Finally he walked out before the boy on the right and called on him to step forward and give him his left hand. Then, raising the switch with a frightful effort, he brought it down *mildly* on the boy's shoulder, and told the boy to return to his seat. He repeated this with each of the nine, none making any resistance. He then threw the switches in the fire and resumed teaching.

This moderation established Charlie Naylor as the most popular teacher that community had ever known, ended the Christmas treat, and almost entirely ended corporal punishment in our public schools.

My father enlarged his farm. When I was twelve he was raising corn and wheat for shipment, and I remember driving a two-horse wagon loaded with thirty bushels a distance of twenty-five miles to Lafayette. There I saw Perdue's Block, the first brick building I had ever seen. It was celebrated throughout that part of Indiana, yet it was but two stories high and had only three stores!

Father had three permanent farm hands, Matt and John McAleer, refined and fairly educated Irishmen, and Bill Smith, a partially degenerated and cruel American. When the Mexican War broke out, all three wanted to enlist. The nearest recruiting office was Crawfordsville, and I went with them. The recruiting officer had stacked in front of his office many old-fashioned flint-lock muskets, which so excited me that I begged the recruiting officer to take me as a drummer, although I was but thirteen! He replied that he would, provided I could get my parents' consent.

Father met us when we returned and asked the men if they had enlisted. Matt and John said "yes." Then father asked Bill, "did you enlist?" "No, Jim," he replied, "I did not. You should see those big guns. They carry a ball as big as your thumb and three buckshots, and have *spears* on the end of them *that* long, and *just* as *keen* ——!"

Matt and John served through the war, but John died of yellow fever coming home. Matt remained with father many years. All this war experience so inspired me that I persuaded father to apply to our Congressman, Dan Mace, for an appointment to West Point. He replied that he would have given it to me, but that he had already nominated another.

My father was an ardent Democrat of the Jackson type, and when Jackson died he felt for a long time that the country was lost. Although self-educated, he was a great reader, and a very progressive man. Our first corn we shelled by hand, but later my father bought the first corn sheller in the county. He got the first traveling traction threshing machine, which threshed the wheat from the shocks in the field. Formerly we threshed it from the sheafs on the barn floor with a "flail"— two sticks tied together, with which the thresher beat the kernels from the straw. Father also purchased the first reaper in that part of the country. He prospered above his neighbors because he was indefatigable in industry, ambition and economy, but he met with a great sorrow, as I did, in the loss of his wife, my mother, when I was fifteen. Before he was very happy and cheerful, singing and whistling much; but I never heard him do either after my mother's death.

Being the oldest child, I was called on more than the rest to care for the younger ones. Shortly after my mother's death my father asked us to make a great sacrifice to keep the family together. He would not marry again, and it would be impossible to have a woman come to care for us. If I would not assume the duties of a mother with Mary, thirteen, and Jane, eleven, to do the housework, he would be obliged to bind the children out to relatives and neighbors. We promised to make this sacrifice, and while I thought then and for a long time after that it was a great wrong, I now know it was the best thing that ever happened to me. The responsibility, together with the instruction and admonitions that I had received, principally from my mother's knee, prepared me for future responsibilities. My father gave me much advice as to the obligations resting on all to do for those coming after him what those who had gone before had done for him. Once, traveling a good road, well prepared to keep vehicles out of the mud, he said, "Now, Anson, somebody built this road for you; you must build some for those who are to come after you."

In 1851 my father had opened his farm to one hundred and fifty acres. Fertilizing it with the ashes of the consumed forest, he raised a most extraordinary crop, three thousand bushels of wheat and thirty-five hundred bushels of corn. He sold the wheat for one dollar and the corn for sixty cents per bushel, which made him a rich man for those days. Then he told my sister Mary and me that he was going to prepare us to fight the battle of life by giving us an education, which he and our mother had not had.

So in September, 1852, he sent us by rail, a five or six days' journey, to Charlotteville Academy, in Schoharie County, New York.

We made seven changes in the five or six days' journey to Canajoharie, New York. The legal rights of railroads were so involved that the projectors had not devised a means to construct interstate or through-city railroads. In none of the towns was there a joint depot; in most we hired a country wagon to carry our trunks from one depot to the other. At Erie there were two depots, because the road to the east was of a different gauge from the road to the west!

I mention all this in detail that those who are so dissatisfied with the beautiful and efficient methods of railroad transportation in these days may realize what they would be up against if the Rockefellers, Carnegies and other benefactors like them had not made these great improvements possible.

At Canajoharie we took the stage to Charlotteville, thirty miles distant, where we arrived in a snowstorm.

My father had entrusted to me a large amount of Indiana money to deposit with the treasurer of the academy. On presenting it to Mr. Archer, he exclaimed: "Why, what does your father mean by sending us this 'wild cat money!' You could not buy a breakfast anywhere in New York with it! However, since you have come so far, I will send it to New York and see what can be done." He finally exchanged it and put it to my father's credit.

Charlotteville Academy

At the academy were eight hundred students, male and female, occupying separate buildings, the chapel and dining room being between the boys' and girls' buildings, and the only place where they met. In the town, the girls were allowed to walk only on certain streets and the boys on others.

My father equipped me with what he considered suitable clothing for my new environment, but what was fashionable in the West was a matter of ridicule in New York, particularly my hat, a tall, square-crowned beaver. I wore a large moustache, had black hair and rather dark complexion, and I was a curiosity to the students, my dialect and vocabulary being different from the Yankee pupils. I was soon nicknamed the "Russian Ambassador from the Woolly West," and my good nature was somewhat tried by the ridicule. However, I made the best of it, had plenty of company always, and my room was visited perhaps as much as that of any other student.

I had made myself a small box with a lock, in which I kept some personal things, among them some correspondence with a girl cousin of mine in Ohio, whose letters were very sentimental.

One evening, I found the son of the professor of mathematics, Ferguson, about my own age and size, sitting in my room. He began to quote some of the silly expressions of this young lady. I asked him if he had read my letters. When he said he had, I invited him into the hall and blackened both his eyes. He called for help, but the watchman came very slowly! Ferguson was unpopular with the employes and the watchman told me afterward he wished he had let me alone a little longer. The boy reported the incident to his father and the elder Ferguson, the second officer of the academy, sent for me in the absence of President Alonso Flack. He threatened to dismiss me because I should have reported to him, but said instead he would report the case to the president when he returned. I replied, to use a present day expression, that it was a *non-justiciable* case.

Later Mr. Flack sent for me and I told him what had happened. Mr. Flack pondered and then said: "Mr. Mills, I am very sorry that you got into this trouble, but, had I been in your situation I would probably have done as you did. That will do—but don't let it occur again."

At Charlotteville I met two young revolutionary refugees from Cuba, Miguel Castillanos and Juan Govin. Castillanos had been captured and imprisoned in a fortress in Ciuta, Africa, but escaped. By mutual arrangement, we taught each other our respective languages and I thus had an early acquaintance with Spanish.

After a year, during which both my sister and myself got along very well, Father sent me a letter from Mr. Mace, the Congressman, saying that his appointee had failed and that he would nominate me for West Point. The nomination came and Father had me come home until the opening of the academy in June.

Prior to leaving Charlotteville, I obtained from Secretary of State, William L. Marcy, a passport with the view of going to Cuba when I had finished my course, but my appointment to West Point changed that.

My Abandoned Birthplace

West Point Military Academy

I reported at West Point on June 1, 1855. I knew nothing of military discipline or ways and was received, as were others at that time, in a most cruel manner by the older cadets.

I was told to report to two older cadets for examination and assignment to quarters. I expected at least serious treatment, but they asked me the most ingeniously foolish questions. I smiled, but with great sternness they demanded I observe proper respect for the officers of the United States Army.

They questioned me on my political and moral principles, adding that they must observe great caution in assigning room-mates, lest injury might happen. Finally, they assigned me to a room with Cadet Martin (J. P.) from Kentucky, hoping that I would find no difficulty in getting along in peace with him.

After being bedeviled for a week or two, I became despondent and homesick, especially as no cadets would recognize me in any friendly manner or speak to me on any but official subjects, except to jeer and deride me.

One day, I was accosted by an old cadet (whom I afterwards learned to be George H. Crosman), the first friendly salutation I had since my entrance. Learning I was from Indiana, he said he was glad to hear it, as it was his State (which was not true) and began asking me if I knew certain persons from that State, some of whom I did. Crosman seemed glad to make my acquaintance and asked me to call on him.

In camp I was assigned to A Company and Crosman belonged to D. Hoping for some relief from extreme despondency and homesickness by making one friend among the higher class, I proceeded to his tent. I found him lying down in his underclothes smoking a meerschaum pipe.

He greeted me cheerfully, invited me to a seat and asked me if I smoked. He expressed astonishment at my reply and stated I would never graduate, that no man ever had graduated who did not smoke, and that I had better begin at once.

I did not wish to smoke and said so.

"Well, that's all right," he replied, "but examine that pipe. That is a fine pipe—a first class meerschaum pipe."

I took the pipe and began to examine it, when, placing his own pipe on the side of his body opposite the sentry walking his beat outside, he called "Number seven, do you see this plebe smoking?"

Immediately the sentry cried, "Corporal of the guard, number seven."

I said, "Mr. Crosman, you are not going to report me for smoking, are you?"

"Well," said he, "if I should, are you going to deny it? What's the use? Didn't that sentry see you with a pipe in your hand and this tent full of smoke? How could you deny it?"

I moved, my impulse being to return to my tent. "But," said he, "don't be a coward, plebe, face the music. Don't run away."

So I sat still waiting results. Shortly I saw a corporal with two men armed with muskets approaching. They marched up facing me, one on each side. Then the corporal sternly ordered me to take my place between them.

When I refused to move each member of the patrol placed an arm under mine, lifting me from my seat. They dragged me along, the corporal placing his bayonet against my back. I was placed in the prisoners' tent. This was in June and the weather was very warm. The walls of the tent were lowered and a sentinel placed over me and I was ordered to take what was then known as the Shanghai step. The tactics had just been changed from Scott's to Hardie's, Hardie's step being quicker and longer than the step formerly used. The exercise I was ordered to take was marking time by raising the feet as high as possible, bringing the knee up against the stomach.

I did this until wet with perspiration and so exhausted

that I almost fell. Presently the sentinel called, "Turn out the guard, Officer of the Day," when they hustled me with other prisoners to form on the left of the guard.

The officer of the day was Cadet Lieutenant Porter, whom I had met. My hopes brightened, thinking I would be released as soon as the circumstances became known. When he came to me, he remarked, "Why, plebe, what are you confined for?"

"I don't know," I replied.

"Well," said he, "if you don't know, I think I will keep you in confinement until you find out."

I remained a prisoner until late in the evening, exercised frequently, when the guard was again turned out. This time, as the officer of the day said, "Well, plebe, have you found out yet what you are confined for?" I replied, "Yes, sir."

"Well, what is it?"

"For smoking," said I.

"That's not a very serious offense. Will you promise not to let it occur again if I release you?"

"Certainly," I replied, and was released.

I resolved to punish Crosman physically, but at the January examination he was deficient and discharged. Before he left he came to see me. "Plebe," he said cheerfully, "I am going away. Here's a set of text books for your next course. If you will accept them, I will give them to you. My impulse was to refuse and force him from my room, but, on better thought, I accepted the books and thanked him.

He afterwards became a captain in the Tenth Infantry.

This was an extreme case of hazing of the kind that eventually brought it into disrepute. I believe hazing held within bounds is of benefit to the academy, in teaching the bumptious and presumptuous how little they are prepared to enter a life of absolute discipline, and how little imaginary personal, social, or political superiority has to do with their future training.

Long experience as a commanding officer has borne out my

belief that the graduate (by reason of the cadet being placed upon honor in all communications with his superiors) is generally superior to other commissioned officers. But I am willing to admit that Crosman's apparent cruelties and other similar vicissitudes better qualified me to fight successfully my long battle of life.

One of the things that impressed me most during my stay at the academy was the painting above the chancel, "Peace and War" by Professor Robert Wier. Underneath it was written, *"Righteousness exalteth a nation but sin is a reproach to any people."* The painting was so beautiful and the sentiments so inspiring that it impressed me all my life.

Among the two hundred and fifty cadets was more diversity in dialect, pronunciation, and ways of thought than there had been at Charlotteville. One could soon tell, after a brief conversation, what part of the country one's companion was from. There was so little traveling from State to State that almost every State had its own dialect, as well as peculiar theories of morals, politics and government. The Kansas troubles were then at their height and there were many encounters between the extremists of the North and the extremists of the South, but, after a year or two at the academy, each became reconciled to the other's ways so that the corps, as a body, was more homogeneous than the people at large.

Cadet life then was much simpler than now. Our dining table was without covering, our tableware heavy Delft, and the diet very simple. Years afterward my classmate Samuel Cushing and I were guests in the barracks at the centennial commencement. To our astonishment the adjutant read an order: "Cadets of the first class (graduating) will turn in their napkin rings immediately after guard mount." Cushing jokingly drew his sleeve across his mouth indicative of the absence of napkins in our day.

My experience with the Kentucky rifle had made me one of the best shots in the corps. After marching off guard, it was the custom for each member to go to the target range and fire at a target, the man making the best shot being excused from his next tour of guard duty. I frequently got excused for this excellence.

In camp, I drew a beautiful musket, new, clean, undented, with a curled walnut stock, and my mechanical experience enabled me to make it the handsomest gun in the corps. At guard mount it was the adjutant's duty to select three cadets having the cleanest uniforms and rifles for the "color guard." When the corps stacked muskets at dress parade in the morning, these three color guards walked post in front of these rifles for two hours only, after which they were given freedom for the day. I frequently was detailed on this guard.

We were not allowed to go off the reservation without permission, but on one occasion I was seized with a desire to "run it." Getting a ferryman to take me across the Hudson to Cold Springs, I procured a bottle of brandy. As it was contraband, I placed it under my tent floor.

We were required to keep our brasses and other trimmings bright, but were prohibited from using oxalic acid. Nevertheless, many of the cadets used acid for cleaning brasses, keeping the bottle well hidden.

Unfortunately, I placed my brandy near my oxalic acid bottle. At my suggestion my tentmate, Andrews, drew out what he supposed was the brandy, pouring out a drink. It burned his mouth, so he spit it out, saying," That's not brandy."

"Of course it is. Give it to me," I said, impetuously taking a big swallow. Immediately it began to burn. Lighting a candle, Andrews cried, "Mills, you have taken acid." Someone called out I was poisoned, and older cadets begged me to run to the hospital. I ran through the sentinel's post without permission or my cap to the surgeon's office. The German steward produced a ball of chalk about the size of a small orange and told me to eat! It was an unsavory meal, but I swallowed it; and the steward told me I would be all right, which I was.

The story spread through the whole corps, even to the instructing officers, and I never heard the last of it.

It was then the custom for cadets to settle private quarrels by personal combat. Cadet Wesley Merritt, of my company and class, and I, each weighed about one hundred and sixty pounds, were five feet ten and a half inches in height, as near physically equal as any two men could be. A question of veracity arising between us, our friends decided we should go down by Dade's monument and settle the matter. Merritt selected his tentmate, Alfred T. Smith, and I mine, John N. Andrews, to act as seconds.

Although our hearts were not in it, and we were always the best of friends afterward, we had one of the hardest fights that took place while I was at the academy. We were finally separated by our seconds, covered with blood, and started back to camp, when, like Roderick's Clan Alpines in the Lady of the Lake, nearly a hundred cadets, secretly assembled as spectators, arose from the surrounding foliage.

General Scott was a great friend of the academy and of the cadets, and often visited us. Once when a plebe in camp, I was on post No. 1 at the guard house. As was his habit when walking out, General Scott wore all the gaudy uniform to which he was entitled. The corporal of the guard called out to me: "Be careful; General Scott is approaching."

As he arrived at the proper distance, I called out, "Turn out the guard; Commander-in-Chief of the United States forces."

General Scott halted, faced me, threw his right hand to his military chapeau with its flaming plume, raised it high in his hand, and called out in a very stern military manner: "Never mind the guard, sir."

He was the most formidable, handsome, and finest-looking man I have ever seen, and carried himself with all the pomp of his high position. Every military man admired him.

Congress had passed a law making the course at West Point five, instead of four years, which necessitated dividing the class ahead of mine in two parts, so that our class was more than twice as large as either of the two classes preceding it.

It may be that there was more or less disposition to equalize the classes. However that may be, in the February examination, I was found deficient in mathematics and resigned. Although realizing that I had no just complaint, I was so greatly humiliated, I was ashamed to go home.

I therefore wrote my father that, as he had favored me above the rest of his children, I wished him to leave me out of any consideration in the distribution of his property, but to give it exclusively to my brothers and sisters, and that I would show the world I could make a living for myself.

Although not a graduate, I have always had the greatest respect for the teachings and discipline of the academy. I believe the U. S. Military Academy has turned out the best officers known to the world's history. Schaff says, in "The Spirit of old West Point," that my class was not only the largest, but the most distinguished during that period. Of this class nine became general officers, and nine were killed in battle.

Early Days in Texas

I went to Texas, then a small State, *via* the Ohio and Mississippi rivers from Cincinnati to New Orleans, thence up the Red River to Shreveport, and from there to McKinney, Colin County, on foot, arriving in April, 1857.

Here I made the acquaintance of Judge R. L. Waddell, the judge of that district, formerly a member of Congress from Kentucky. He offered to get me a school, stating that he had five children who ought to be taught, and gave me the privilege of studying law with him. As I had nothing else to do, I commenced teaching a class of sixty scholars, studying and reciting law to him meanwhile.

Judge Waddell had a plantation near the town and, in his absence on the circuit, placed me in charge of his affairs, including the management of the plantation and his thirty slaves. A strong Union man and earnestly opposed to slavery, Judge Waddell often told me that if his slaves could make a living for themselves he would freely manumit them. But they could not, and he was justified in holding them for their own sakes as long as he could. It was here that I became acquainted with the negro character, its childish simplicity and numerous admirable traits.

The judge was a remarkable man and a most worthy character, unselfish and law abiding. I have often heard him refuse cases because he could not defend clients believing them guilty. He treated me as a son, giving me much good advice. He never entered a saloon and advised me not to, which advice I practically have followed all my life.

At McKinney I met Sam Houston, a personal friend of Judge Waddell. Although then an old man and I a very young one, he took quite an interest in me, and we took many walks together in Trinity Bottom, where, one day, he cut a stick of osage orange (bois d'arc) which he fashioned into a cane and presented to me, and which I have to this day.

In teaching school at McKinney, I adopted Charlie Naylor's methods of avoiding corporal punishment, but there was a surly rowdy about eighteen years old, as large as I was, who often made trouble with the other scholars, even after I threatened to punish him if he did not change. One afternoon, a little boy ran up to me, saying: "Master, you better look out for Tom Shane; he's got a pistol, and he's going to shoot you."

Tom, as usual, was late. When I saw him coming, I placed myself just inside the door. As he entered I seized him by the collar, saying, "Tom, give me that pistol!" He was so overcome by surprise that he handed it to me without a word.

I took it to Tom's father, a blacksmith. Young Shane probably received a more severe punishment that night than I could have given him. After that, I had no more trouble.

At this time there was great excitement between North and South, caused principally by the troubles resulting from the settlement of Kansas and the many conflicts between those who were taking slaves there and those who were determined it should be a free State. The negroes became so excited the legislature passed a law making it a felony for any person to teach a negro how to read or write. The new statute also prohibited free negroes from living in the State, and set a date on which all free negroes who had failed to choose a master would be sold into slavery.

One Sunday, a large free negro blacksmith about twenty-eight or thirty years old came into Judge Waddell's office and asked me if it were true that he would have to choose a master or be sold into slavery. I told him it was. He then asked me to be his master, that he might avoid being sold to another. For many reasons I declined, though I could have sold him for a thousand dollars. As he had means, I advised him to go where he would not be sold. I never knew what became of him.

During the winter there were four or five times as many fires in adjacent counties as there had ever been before. It was generally believed that Northern abolition influence had been communicated to the negroes, and that they were trying to terrorize their masters. Consequently, a law was passed forbidding negroes to remain out at night, and authorizing anyone to arrest and take to jail more than two negroes found together.

I remained in McKinney about a year, when the Butterfield Overland Mail was chartered from St. Louis to San Francisco, an eighteen-day journey, with daily service each way. El Paso was a promising Mexican settlement, and would probably be the half-way house, and eventually a place of some importance. I therefore bid Judge Waddell good-bye and started for El Paso. Before going, however, I visited my father, going with a Mr. Ditto of Kentucky through the Cherokee Nation, where we bought a small drove of very beautiful little Indian ponies, and drove them to St. Louis and sold them. I remained a month or so with my father and, upon returning to Texas, on my father's advice, took my brother Will to McKinney, and he took up school teaching where I left off.

El Paso Experiences

The journey to El Paso, where I arrived on the eighth of May, 1858, was through the most desolate country, with Indians on all sides, some hostile and some friendly. Coyotes and other wild animals abounded, but most interesting were the numerous buffalo east of the Pecos. There were literally millions. I have seen the plains black with them and, when moving, which they did at a kind of lope or gallop, I have felt the earth tremble under the impress of their heavy shoulders. When we encountered one of these moving herds, so impetuous in its advance no obstacle could resist it, we would turn the coach horses in the direction of its flight and the passengers would dismount and fire their guns to scare the buffalo away.

At a station, near the Pecos River, that had been robbed by the Indians, we had to remain two or three days, until we received fresh horses. The Indians had carried off all the eatables, except some corn and sugar, and we parched and ground the corn into meal with the coffee mill and boiled it with sugar to keep us alive until relief came.

Save for this one delay, we made this distressing journey without stopping night or day except for meals. If I gave up my seat at a station there was no certainty that I would get a place in the next coach, so we all stuck to our seats, although passengers sometimes became crazed for want of sleep, and one or two had dashed into the desert and been lost.

After seven days' and nights' travel, when I arrived at the bluffs overlooking the valley of the Rio Grande, I thought it was the most pleasant sight I had ever seen. When we drove into the town, which consisted of a ranch of some hundred and fifty acres in cultivation in beautiful grape, apple, apricot, pear, and peach orchards, watermelons, grain, wheat and corn, it seemed still more beautiful, especially when, under the shade of the large cottonwood trees along the acequias (canals for irrigation), we saw Mexican girls selling fruits of all kinds grown on the opposite side of the river at what was known as Paso del Norte, a city of thirteen thousand people, controlled by well-to-do and educated Spaniards.

The town on the American side was simply a ranch owned by "Uncle Billy" Smith, an illiterate Kentuckian. One Franklin Coontz asked to be made postmaster, and when the Post Office Department informed him he would first have to name the office, he named it after himself, "Franklin."

Mr. Smith was generous, but unbusiness-like. He had given or sold small parcels of land to many who built without any survey having been made. Two or three hundred people lived here, mostly Mexicans and their families, engaged in cultivating the ranch. There were three wholesale stores which sold goods brought up by mule trains from Kansas City via Santa Fe to supply the needs of Paso del Norte, Chihuahua City and other towns in Chihuahua. The Butterfield Overland Mail established a headquarters with many employes and made Franklin somewhat of a money center. The Mexican disposition to gamble and the wild and lawless character of the times brought perhaps twenty professional gamblers to Franklin.

The Texan war with Mexico for independence, in 1836, and the war between the United States and Mexico, in 1847, together with the hostile Indians on the north of the Rio Grande during the early Spanish settlement, forced most of the population and wealth to the Mexican side of the Rio Grande. Few towns on the American side were of any importance. The county seat of El Paso County was then San Elisario, twenty miles below Franklin, with about twelve hundred inhabitants. When I arrived in El Paso it was dangerous to go far from the village. Mesquite root gatherers were attacked, the men killed and the animals driven off within a half-mile from the village.

But on the Mexican side were large, wealthy towns, with good society and well ordered governments. After the Doniphan expedition to Chihuahua, our government had established Fort Bliss, a mile and a half below El Paso, with seven companies of infantry and mounted rifles. I made the acquaintance of the officers, finding several who had been cadets with me at the academy, among them a classmate, Will Jones, the adjutant. Through them I got an earlier standing among the people than would otherwise have been possible for me to do.

The act of annexation of Texas to the United States provided that Texas retain her public lands. The El Paso and Presidio land district included all territory west of the Pecos River (El Paso and Presidio Counties), an area larger than New Jersey.

With the recommendation of the army officers and Judge Crosby of that judicial district, I was appointed surveyor for that district by the State government. Immediately I had plenty of work on pending locations for two hundred miles below Franklin, many tracts embracing five thousand acres each, and also the reservations leased by the War Department for the posts of Quitman, Davis, Stockton, and Fort Bliss. All of them I surveyed within the next year.

The Overland Mail Company also employed me to build a station covering almost an entire block.

At my suggestion, Judge J. F. Crosby, J. S. and H. S. Gillett, W. J. Morton, and V. St. Vrain formed a company with Mr. Smith, the owner of the Ponce grant, on which Franklin was located, employing me to lay out a town, as Freemont's projected Memphis, El Paso & Pacific Railroad, the advent of the Overland Mail and westward immigration made it necessary to enlarge the village.

I made a survey and a plat of the town. As the houses had been built at random, without a survey, on plots given by Mr. Smith, the few streets were neither parallel nor at right angles. I had difficulty in making a plan agreeable to the then owners. I made several different sketches before I produced one that all six proprietors adopted and signed.

All these original sketches, together with a copy of the first map, are still preserved in the El Paso Public Library. (Cut, 56, 57.)

The work, which I was glad to get, occupied me two months. My pay was one hundred dollars and four lots—Nos. 116, 117, 134 and 137—valued at fifty dollars each.

Franklin Coontz turned out an undesirable citizen, and it was suggested that I rename the city. As this was not only the north and south pass of the Rio Grande through the Rocky Mountains but also the only feasible route from east to west crossing that river, for hundreds of miles, I suggested that El Paso would indicate the importance of the location. It was decided to so name it.

According to an act of Congress, approved June 5, 1858, a commission to establish the boundary between Texas and the Territory of New Mexico was organized. John H. Clark was appointed United States Commissioner and Major William R. Scurry, Texas Commissioner. After they established the initial point near what is now called Anthony, there was a disagreement, and the Texas Commission surveyor resigned. Major Scurry appointed me in his place.

The commission, with its escort of two companies of the Seventh Infantry, Lieutenant Lazelle commanding, was a very pleasant organization aside from the quarrel between the commissioners. Major Scurry was a most genial companion. Mr. Clark was ambitious in his assumption of highly scientific attainments and overbearing to those he deemed not his equal in such acquirements.

Major Scurry, like Judge Waddell, took quite an interest in me. The three army officers and one or two members of the commission often played poker for stakes. The bets were not large, but Major Scurry, observing that I generally lost, said to me one day: "Mr. Mills, you ought never to play poker. You are not qualified for it. A poker player has to be a cold-blooded man. I can look into your face every time you draw a hand and tell just about what you have drawn. I advise you never to play another game, for you will never succeed in it." And I never did.

The disagreements between the United States and Texas commissioners became acute. As I thought Mr. Clark was mostly to blame, when Major Scurry finally resigned, I did also.

I never saw Major Scurry again, but learned that he raised a Confederate regiment and was killed at the head of his troops in a battle with Banks' Expedition on the upper Red River.

On returning to El Paso, I wrote to my brother, W. W., whose school term had expired, that I had secured him a position as clerk in the sutler's store at Fort Fillmore. He held this position a year, and then joined me in El Paso. He had enough money to buy a lot, on which I built him a house, costing about a thousand dollars.

W. W. and I then sent for our brother Emmett, and we three built a ranch eighteen miles above El Paso, called "Los Tres Hermanos." Emmett occupied this ranch, which was made into a Santa Fe mail station.

Previously I lived on lot No. 116 in a tent, doing my own cooking. I built myself a nice adobe house, doing much of the work myself. Mexican peons made the bricks from a mixture of adobe soil and straw. They were two feet by one foot, four inches thick, and dried in the sun. These were very substantial, withstood the rain and made a house cool in the daytime and warm at night. The house was on the bank of a ditch supplying running water to the farm and under many cottonwood trees. In summer I often slept on the adobe earth roof. Strange to say, even in the hardest rains the water would seldom go through the roof, which was about eight inches thick.

At the same time I built my house, I superintended building houses for many others.

I early learned the ways of the roaming Indians, and in my surveying expeditions took only a burro for my pack and two

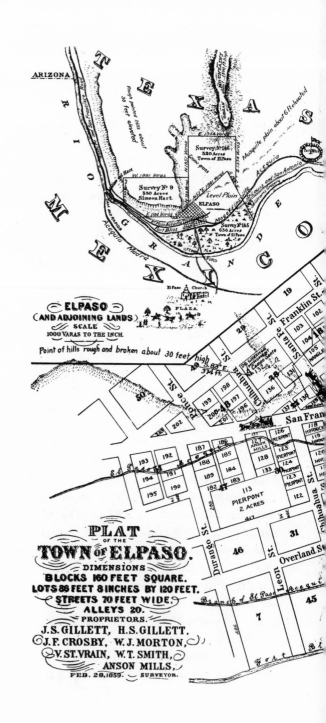

ARIZONA

TEXAS

MEXICO

RIO GRANDE

ELPASO
(AND ADJOINING LANDS)
SCALE
1000 VARAS TO THE INCH.

Point of hills rough and broken about 30 feet high

PLAT
OF THE
TOWN OF ELPASO.
DIMENSIONS
BLOCKS 160 FEET SQUARE.
LOTS 86 FEET 8 INCHES BY 120 FEET.
STREETS 70 FEET WIDE.
ALLEYS 20.
PROPRIETORS.
J. S. GILLETT, H. S. GILLETT.
J. F. CROSBY, W. J. MORTON,
V. ST. VRAIN, W. T. SMITH,
ANSON MILLS,
FEB. 28, 1859. SURVEYOR.

Mexicans for chain carriers. I wore a buckskin suit made by myself, and carried a single change of underclothing. We moved from tract to tract, camping without a tent under the mesquite trees, our provisions consisting only of coffee, hard bread and bacon, and occasionally some fresh meat we could kill. Although Indians undoubtedly saw us, they never attacked us during the three years in which I did surveying. The risk of being killed to secure only one animal and a small amount of provisions was not worth while.

My principal employer was Mr. Samuel A. Maverick, of San Antonio, formerly from South Carolina. A run-away boy, he had joined an expedition of about twenty men, which invaded Mexico at the town of Mier prior to the Mexican war. The party was captured. The Mexicans put ten white beans in a bag with ten black ones, ordering them to draw a bean each. Those who got the black beans were immediately shot. Maverick began locating land soon after the war and became the largest land-holder in Texas, if not in the United States.

He owned more cattle on the free public range than any other man in Texas. In 1861 nearly all the people went into the war. Maverick's cattle ran wild on the range, and, when the war closed there were tens of thousands of cattle bred during the four years. Maverick was the greatest claimant to these wild cattle, and marked them with his brand wherever caught. Other owners, and even men who had never owned cattle, would brand with their own marks such cattle as they caught unbranded. It thus became the custom among cattle owners using the free range to stamp as their own any un-branded cattle they found during the "round up," and to this day these stray cattle are known as "Mavericks."

Maverick accompanied me on every surveying expedition I made, following my tracings and examining my notes. He expressed the greatest patriotism as a Unionist, was bitterly opposed to the then proposed secession, as were most Texans, including Governor Houston.

When placer and quartz gold was discovered in the Penos

Altos range of mountains in Arizona, near the present Silver City, Maverick requested me to find how valuable these mines were. With a gambler (Conklin) I bought a good two-horse team and traveled the hundred and fifty miles to reach these mines.

At Penos Altos I met James R. Sipes, a clerk for Postmaster Dowell. I said, "Hello, Sipes, how is it; is there plenty of gold here?"

He laughed and answered, "Mills, there is the greatest quantity of gold here, but there is too damned much dirt mixed with it!" which I found to be true.

Locating a claim, I worked a month, 8,000 feet above sea level, where in the day it was scorching hot and at night freezing cold, and discovered that by hard work I could make about three dollars a day. Fortunately, I had brought my surveying instruments, so I abandoned mining and laid out the town of Penos Altos. I also surveyed many claims, about which there were constant disputes. But I soon returned to El Paso, reporting to Maverick that the mines were not of sufficient importance to interest him.

At this time slavery agitation became very violent, creating unrest in Texas, especially among the New England emigrants, who became the most rabid secessionists of all. Some of my friends in the North wrote me what would today be called treasonable literature, sending me the New York Tribune with the most violent abolition articles marked. Postmaster Ben Dowell was induced to open my mail, and later refused to deliver any to me, forming a committee to burn it publicly!

When my term as district surveyor expired, I was the only candidate for election, being the only person in the county competent to survey land. But several political enemies publicly stated that I was an abolitionist, and that it would be unpatriotic to vote for me. As I had always been a Democrat, voting for Sam Houston and Stephen A. Douglas, and never sympathized at all with the abolition movement, I posted the following notice on a tree:

Notice

I have just been informed that J. S. Gillett, W. J. Morton, and J. R. Sipes stated last night to R. Doane and F. Remy that I was an abolitionist, for the purpose of injuring my character. As I never cast any other than a Democratic vote or expressed other than Democratic sentiments, I denounce these three above-named persons as wilful and malicious lying scoundrels. Sipes and Morton owe me borrowed money for the last two years. I would like to have a settlement. I never asked any one to vote for me as surveyor and I now withdraw my name as a candidate, and will not serve if elected.

A. MILLS.

EL PASO, TEXAS.
2 O'Clock, P.M., August 6, 1860.

The men I denounced tacked their reply on the same tree, as follows:

Notice

A certain contemptible "pup," signing himself A. Mills, having publicly published the undersigned as scoundrels, we have only to say that he is so notoriously known throughout the entire county as a damned black Republican scoundrel, we deem him unworthy of further notice.

However, we hereby notify this fellow that his insignificance shall not protect him in future.

W. J. MORTON,
J. R. SIPES,
JOHN S. GILLETT.

Then, I received this letter:

EL PASO, TEXAS,
August 7, 1860.

MR. MILLS:

SIR: I have noticed my name in connection with two others denouncing us publicly as malicious, lying scoundrels.

For my part, I now ask of you an immediate retraction of the same, and as publicly as your accusation.

JOHN S. GILLETT.

Gillett, a wealthy wholesale merchant, had fought a duel with an army officer. As I paid no attention to his implied challenge, he sent word he would attack me on sight. I always went armed, and though we often met, he never carried out his threat. After the war he became a common drunkard, very poor, living with a Mexican woman. I often met him, and he frequently asked me for a quarter (which I gave him), stating that he was hungry. What horrible miseries war brings about. He wanted to be an honorable man.

In my address before the Society of the Army of the Cumberland (Appendix 390) will be found a statement of some of the reasons which led to political unrest in Texas, and particularly why vigilance committees were formed in many counties. Many people were lynched; principally Germans— especially at New Braunfels and vicinity—who voted against secession or denounced the principle.

I was ordered before the vigilance committee of El Paso County by the sheriff, John Watts. I told him no one man could take me, and I knew that he was not coward enough to bring a posse. He said: "Mills, I'll never come for you." And he never did.

I was notified by this same committee that the vote of the county must be unanimous for secession, and that I would imperil my life if I voted against it.

Phil Herbert, a violent secessionist and a personal friend of mine, came to my house on election day and said, "Mills, are you going to vote?" I said that I was. "Well," he said, "I know how you are going to vote. I am going to vote for secession, but I would like to go with you. If there is trouble, I will defend you." He had a pistol and advised me to carry one, and we went together to the polling place. This was in a large gambling house, in which was Ben Dowell's postoffice.

The judge of the election was Judge Gillock, recently from Connecticut, a violent secessionist.

Herbert and I entered, arm in arm, and Herbert first presented his ballot, which Gillock received and cast into the ballot box near the door. I drew from my pocket a sheet of foolscap paper on which was written, "No separation—Anson Mills," in large letters, and, unfolding it, I held it up to the sight of half a dozen army officers and others playing billiards, faro and other gambling games, saying, "Gentlemen, some of you may be curious to know how I am going to vote. This is my ballot." Gillock refused to receive it, but Herbert said, peremptorily, "That is a legal vote. Place it in the box." And Gillock did so. We left the room unmolested.

My vote was one of the two cast against secession in El Paso County, when there were over nine hundred cast for secession. Some were legal, but the majority, cast by Mexican citizens from the other side of the river, were not.

My friends, particularly Herbert, felt it would be foolhardy to remain longer. Herbert went to Richmond, joined the Confederacy, and was killed in the Battle of Mansfield, La., at the head of his regiment.

I decided to go to Washington and join the Federal forces. The evening before I left, Colonel Reeve, commanding Fort Bliss, invited me to dinner with his adjutant, my classmate, Will Jones. During the dinner, Colonel Reeve remarked that he did not want to obey Twiggs' order to surrender to the Texans (text, 71) because he had large government stores, which would be of great value in case of war to either the government or the Confederates. Therefore, he wanted me to see the Secretary of War, and explain the circumstances, and get him verbal or written authority to take his command and this property into New Mexico.

When I finally arrived in Washington, I explained the situation to Judge Watts, who went with me to Secretary Cameron and delivered Reeves's message. I agreed to take back to El Paso any verbal message that the Secretary would entrust to me, but Mr. Cameron was so uncertain as to what might happen that he refused, saying that Colonel Reeve must act on his own judgment.

I had been prosperous and was well-to-do. But now men who owed me refused to pay, and all I owed demanded immediate payment. It was all I could do to raise money enough to take me to Washington. The baggage allowance was but forty pounds, so I left everything I had to the mercy of my political enemies. I did not dream that it would be twenty years before I again saw El Paso.

In Washington

We left in the coach on the 9th of March, 1861. I was one of eight passengers. Some were going to Richmond and some to Washington, but we agreed, as this was expected to be the last coach to go through, to stand by each other and declare we were all going on business.

The secessionists had organized several companies of State troops commanded by the McCullough brothers and others, with instructions from the bogus legislature commission to take over the military posts and property according to General Twiggs' treaty (text, 71). We met part of this force, under the younger McCullough, near Fort Chadbourne, and we were all excitement to know what they would do, as it was rumored they would seize the mail company horses for cavalry. Marching in columns of two, they separated, one column to the right and the other to the left of the stage coach.

We told the driver to drive fast and to say he was carrying United States mail. The soldiers laughed at this, and four of them, taking hold of the right-hand wheels and four of the left, the driver could not, with the greatest whipping, induce the horses to proceed. They laughed again, and called out: "Is Horace Greeley aboard?"

Horace Greeley had been lecturing in California, and had announced his return by the Butterfield route. The soldiers were familiar with his picture and, after examining us, allowed us to proceed.

When we reached Denton, the county seat of Denton County, my old friend Judge Waddell was holding court, and while the rest of the party ate breakfast, I went to the courthouse. Judge Waddell recognized me, adjourned the court and, taking my arm, walked out in the courtyard. We were in full sympathy. He was a thorough Union man and knew I would be glad to know the flag was still flying over the McKinney courthouse. This was about the 13th of March. He was proud that I was to join the Union Army, and said that if he was without a family he would also go.

We arrived at the town of California, terminus of the Missouri & Pacific Railroad, in a snowstorm. We had had but little sleep and little to eat for several days. While waiting for the train for St. Louis, I went to sleep in a chair so soundly my companions could not waken me in time to catch the train. The hotel proprietor had me put to bed. I did not waken until the next morning. I arrived at St. Louis Sunday, found that there was no train out and, having a classmate stationed at the arsenal, Lieutenant Borland, I decided to visit him.

I did not know that General Lyon had just captured General Frost and the Missouri troops forming for the Confederacy in a camp outside the city. There was a great crowd standing around the arsenal with a sentinel outside the gate. I pressed my way through the crowd and told the sentinel I desired to visit Lieutenant Borland. The sentinel would not let me pass, but called the sergeant. The sergeant asked me where I was from. When I answered, "From Texas," he said I could not enter. Just then Captain Lyon, later General Lyon, came out. In a rough manner he asked me where I was from and what I wanted. When I told him I was simply passing through the city, he said, "Well, you had better go back to your hotel, or I will put you in the guard house." I took his advice.

Monday, I left for Washington *via* Thorntown and Cincinnati. Telling my father of my purpose, he called a neighbor, Harvey G. Hazelrigg. "Well, Anson," said Hazelrigg, "my brother-in-law, Caleb B. Smith, is Secretary of the Interior. I will give you a letter to him."

At Cincinnati I saw Lieutenant Jones' father and mother and gave them the messages he did not want to pass through the mail; in effect, that he would be loyal to his country, and that if ordered to fire on Cincinnati by the Federal Government, under his oath he would execute the order.

In Washington I found two captains in the Adjutant General's office, Fry and Baird, one of whom had been adjutant

at the military academy, and the other my instructor when I
was a cadet. I told them of my desire for a commission, and
asked them from what State I should apply. They advised
me not to apply from Texas, nor from Pennsylvania, which
would have several times its quota, as the Secretary of War
was from that State. Eventually, I applied from New Mexico.

Charlie Hazlett, of my class, from Zanesville, Ohio,
later killed while commanding a battery at Gettysburg,
had been turned back to the class below. I wrote him, asking
if he could help me. Calling a meeting of the class, he read
my letter, and every member signed the following recommendation, except four, who were to join the Confederacy,
and who sent an apology to me, stating that they did not think
it would be proper for them to sign:

UNITED STATES MILITARY ACADEMY,
WEST POINT, N. Y.,
April 30, 1861.

LORENZO THOMAS, Adjutant General,
Washington, D. C.

DEAR SIR: We, the undersigned, members of the First
Class at the United States Military Academy, respectfully
recommend to your favorable consideration the claims of
Mr. Anson Mills, an applicant for a commission as Second
Lieutenant in the United States Army.

Mr. Mills was formerly a member, for nearly two years,
of the class preceding ours, when he resigned.

During that time his habits and character conformed to
the strictest military propriety and discipline, and we feel
assured that he would be an honor to the service and that
its interests would be promoted by his appointment.

Respectfully submitted.

Hazlett suggested I see General Scott and prevent the four
cadets above mentioned from getting their diplomas. Captain
Townsend introduced me to the General. When he read Haz-

CAPTAIN CHARLES E. HAZLETT.

lett's letter, he said those four cadets should not receive their diplomas until they had taken the oath.　They never did graduate, and all four joined the rebellion.

A few days afterward, this class was prematurely graduated and ordered to report to General Scott.　They started in their cadet uniforms, wearing their swords.　In New York the police took them for Confederates, and in Philadelphia the whole class was arrested and detained all night, until the police got authority from Washington to let them proceed.

Upon arrival at Washington, they reported to General Scott, who asked them if they had all recently taken the oath.　They replied that they had and he, in the vernacular of the bibulous, said, "Well, gentlemen, it is a good thing to take.　I don't mind taking it every morning before breakfast."　He invited one of them to administer it to him, and then, asking them in a body to raise their right hands, he administered the oath to the whole class.

My Brothers in Texas

One of my first acts in Washington was to call on Secretary of the Interior Smith. There were three or four gentlemen present, two being members of the Cabinet, one of whom was Montgomery Blair, a graduate of the academy.

I presented my letter. Mr. Smith read it, and in a violent rage, said: "Well, so you are from Texas? Do you know what I wish? I wish the Indians would come down on the people of Texas and murder the men, women and children. They have received more consideration from this government than any other State in the Union, and now they have betrayed it."

I left the room, indignant, after addressing some plain remarks to Mr. Smith.

The next day I met Mr. Blair, while walking.

"Mr. Mills," he said, "for heaven's sake don't repeat what happened at Mr. Smith's last night, lest it get into the papers. Don't be discouraged. Your experience at West Point will doubtless enable you to get into the army."

I had heard nothing from my brothers, W. W. in El Paso, and Emmett on the ranch, but some time after I received my commission and had left Washington I saw in a New Orleans paper that W. W. had been taken prisoner at Lynde's surrender, and that Emmett, in trying to escape to California, had been murdered by the Indians, July 21st, at Cook Springs, Arizona. All the passengers and the stage driver were killed after a two days' siege in the rocks above the springs, and their bodies had been found by the California column of troops going to El Paso. Immediately I wrote to Mr. Smith, as follows:

TOLEDO, OHIO,
Oct. 7, 1861.

CALEB B. SMITH,
    Secretary Interior.

SIR: I am sorry to acknowledge that your "hope and prayer," as expressed to me at your residence in April last—"that the Mexicans and Indians would come down on the Texans and murder the men and children and ravish the women," has been partially heard. One of my two brothers (whom I left in Texas last March and who, not being able to procure means to carry them to the States, were compelled to go to Southern New Mexico for Union sentiments, where they joined the 1st Regt. N. M. Vols.), was brutally murdered by the Apache Indians, on the 21st of July at Cook Springs. The other was taken prisoner at Lynde's surrender. I think too much of our cause to speak publicly of these matters at present, and only write you this note to remind you that I shall one day hold you personally responsible for the above language.   Very respectfully,

ANSON MILLS, 1st Lt., 18th Inf.

To this I received the following answer:

WASHINGTON, D. C.,
October 14, 1861.

LT. ANSON MILLS,
    SIR: I am in receipt of your letter of the 7th inst., referring to a conversation which you allege occurred at my house in April last. I have no distinct recollection of the conversation to which you refer, but I know that I felt much indignation toward the rebels and traitors of Texas, who not only repudiated the authority of the Federal Government, but expelled from the State the friends of the Union. I thought there was less excuse for them than the rebels of the other States, because they were indebted to the Federal Government for protection against

the Mexicans and Indians. In expressing my indignation against their conduct I may have expressed the hope that the Mexicans and Indians would attack them. I intended to express only the wish that they might be made to feel the value of the protection they had forfeited. I certainly did not suppose that my language could be construed to imply a wish that the Union men who had been expelled from their homes by these rebels should suffer from such agencies.

I regret very much to hear of the misfortunes which have befallen your brothers and which add to the long catalogue of evils which have resulted from this most unnatural rebellion. For the last five months I have been urging the War Department to send troops to New Mexico to protect the loyal people of that territory and keep the Indians in proper subjugation. If my urgent request upon this subject had been complied with, the disaster which has befallen your brothers would not have occurred.

Very respectfully,

CALEB B. SMITH.

I learned later that the newspaper was incorrect and that my brother W. W. was unlawfully seized by the Texans in Mexico as a spy.

Smith soon afterward left the Cabinet.

I learned later of the events which led to my brother's death. The Texan Rangers, under the McCulloughs and Colonel Baylor, were rapidly receiving the surrenders stipulated in the treaty between Twiggs and the Texas commissioners. My brother, W. W., much persecuted and threatened, wrote to Judge Watts of the disloyalty of Captain Lane and several other officers at Forts Bliss and Fillmore. Then he went to Santa Fe to confer with Colonel Canby, in command of the Department of New Mexico, to explain the large quantities of government stores at Fort Bliss, and the danger that they might fall into the hands of the rebels. Colonel Canby had already sent Major Lynde with reinforcements aggregating seven hundred and fifty men to Fort Fillmore, directing Lynde to relieve Lane. Canby sent my brother to Fort Fillmore to report to Major Lynde with dispatches.

Lynde was reluctant to believe many of his officers either disloyal or in sympathy with those who were. My brother found that his letter addressed to Judge Watts had been made public and both the loyal and disloyal officers were angry, and treated him with much discourtesy.

Baylor had arrived in El Paso and received the surrender of Colonel Reeve's command, with all his stores and property, and Reeve and his troops had started on their march to San Antonio as prisoners. My brother urged Lynde to retake Fort Bliss and the government property with his seven hundred and fifty men, as Baylor was reported to have only three hundred men, poorly armed and equipped. Lynde hesitated, fearing Baylor's force was too large, but promised my brother if he would go down to Paso del Norte on the Mexican side of the river and ascertain positively that the strength of Baylor's command was no larger than three hundred men, he would retake the place.

My brother traveled forty miles to Paso del Norte in Mexico at night, where a mounted force from Baylor's command arrested him in this neutral territory. Charged with being a spy, he was placed in irons in the Bliss guard house and a court was being organized for his trial and execution. Hearing of his arrest, Canby arrested General Pelham, U. S. Surveyor General of New Mexico, who had resigned and was proceeding to join the rebels. Canby then sent a flag of truce to Baylor, stating that he would execute Pelham on the execution of my brother. Baylor removed the irons from my brother, gave him the liberty of the post, and he finally escaped and joined Canby, who was marching with troops from New Mexico toward El Paso. He was made lieutenant in the New Mexican Volunteers, and appointed on Colonel Roberts' staff.

Meanwhile, Baylor, with less than three hundred poorly equipped Texans, had moved on Lynde's seven hundred and fifty regulars, but such was their demoralization that these Texans captured bodily every man and all the supplies during Lynde's attempt to escape into New Mexico.

General Sibley organized a force of about thirty-five hundred Texans, to take the Territory of New Mexico, and reinforced Baylor, to march on Fort Craig. Canby organized two New Mexican regiments, one under Kit Carson, and moved to support Colonel Roberts, arriving just before the Confederates. Canby had one thousand regulars and about twenty-five hundred New Mexican volunteers, so the commands were nearly equal. Crossing the almost impassible mountains, Sibley appeared at Val Verde, six miles above Fort Craig, to engage in what was, perhaps, the bloodiest battle for the numbers engaged, in the whole war. Neither side was victorious, but Canby was compelled to retire to Fort Craig, and Sibley passed on and overran the whole Territory of New Mexico, even taking Santa Fe, but he was cut off from any Confederate supplies.

Colorado raised two regiments of volunteers, which moved on Sibley and drove him south, where Canby met him. Of the four thousand Confederate troops that had entered New Mexico, only about fifteen hundred reached Texas. El Paso was reoccupied, and my brother made collector of customs. Another brother, Allen, eighteen years old, anxious to participate in the allurements of the Western country, asked me to send him to my brother, W. W., who had promised to make him deputy collector, which I did by a supply train from Kansas City for Santa Fe.

Meanwhile, my brother Emmett, hearing of W. W.'s arrest and proposed trial as a spy, endeavored to escape to California by taking passage on the Overland Mail, where he met his death.

On February 8, 1869, while in Austin as a member of the constitutional convention for reconstruction from El Paso,

W. W. married Mary, daughter of Governor A. J. Hamilton. In his El Paso home she shared as loyally as any wife ever did in all his misfortunes and successes, his joys and sorrows.

In 1897 W. W. was appointed United States Consul at Chihuahua, Mexico, where we often visited. He worked there ten years, relieving unfortunate Americans who, by reason of ignorance of conditions in Mexico, got themselves into difficulties. The City of Chihuahua was unfortunately the rendezvous and refuge for felonious, law-breaking Americans, who could no longer live in their native land, and sought Mexico, believing they could defy the laws of that country. Popular report stamped Mexicans as lawless, with a government not stable enough to punish them. Such conditions made my brother's position a difficult one, as the following will show:

Three New Yorkers, including a physician and an insurance agent, entered into a conspiracy to establish themselves in Chihuahua to insure unsuspecting Americans for $20,000 each, murder them and collect the money. The plan, which was practically carried out, was this: The insurance agent approached eligible Americans residing in Chihuahua, solicited insurance, offering very low terms, and stating that the proposed victim, living in a lawless country where he was likely to be killed and where whatever he had would be absorbed by Mexican officials, should insure for the benefit of those dependent upon him. Having written the insurance, he would tell his victim, "Now my company is interested in your life. They direct me to admonish you not to patronize Mexican physicians, as they are unskilled. They authorized me to recommend to you Dr. ————." The doctor then recommended the victim to appoint an American administrator to see that his estate would be kept out of the hands of Mexican officials. He would recommend the third member of the gang.

In three cases the victim took the whole of the advice, appointed the gang member his administrator, and called upon the criminal doctor when ill. The doctor promptly killed him with poison, the administrator took possession of his body, collected the money from the company, and divided it among the three conspirators.

They had collected $20,000 each, for two victims, when the insurance company sent a detective to investigate. He fixed the murder on the doctor and discovered the other criminals. They were arrested by the Mexican authorities, fairly tried— W. W. being present at the trial—and sentenced to be shot.

A great clamor was raised in the American newspapers about the cruel and barbarous conviction of innocent men by Mexican law. A member of Congress, the lawyer employed by the men, and the relatives of each of the condemned came to my brother with tears and pleadings, demanding that he intercede with the State Department for their relief. W. W. also received instructions from the State Department to make a thorough examination and report. He was unable to find any palliating circumstances, and reported through Ambassador Clayton his belief that the Mexican judgment was just. The Secretary of State sustained my brother, but the member of Congress, the lawyer, friends and relatives of the condemned, besieged the great President Diaz with pathetic appeals and tears, and, in the goodness of his heart, Diaz commuted the sentence to imprisonment for life.

When General Villa captured Chihuahua, the convicts were released from the penitentiary. The murderers were among the number, and Villa appointed the doctor as a commissioned medical officer on his staff.

W. W. filled his position honorably and well for ten years, when ill health compelled him to retire. In accepting his resignation, the State Department gave him a very complimentary letter. He returned to Austin, where his wife still lives, and, after a lingering illness, died there on February 10, 1913.

W. W. lived in El Paso two score of years, and in 1901 published a book entitled "Forty Years in El Paso."

AFTERTHOUGHT:—Last page in W. W.'s book.

"ENEMIES AND PHILOSOPHY

"In the summer of 1900 my brother, General Mills, and a sister paid Mrs. Mills and myself a visit at the United States Consulate at Chihuahua. One evening he, being in a reflective mood, said, 'Will, you and I have had many difficulties, and quarrels and fights with our personal enemies, and it is very gratifying to know, as I am growing old, that these are all over with me. My enemies are all reconciled to me, and I wish you could say as much.'

"I replied: 'I do not know that my enemies are all reconciled to me, but they are all *dead,* and that is better, or at least *safer.'* And it is the literal truth. All my bitterest foes have been taken hence, most of them by violence, and I neither rejoice at nor regret their taking off. I do not claim that I was always right and they always wrong, for I tried to return blow for blow, but it is certain that they often resorted to means which I would, under no circumstances, employ. Alas, most of my friends are gone also. Why I have been spared through it all is a mystery which I do not attempt to explain.

ADIOS."

SECOND PERIOD

SECOND PERIOD

Four Years of Civil War

Before any Federal troops arrived in Washington, Cassius M. Clay, of Kentucky, organized the "Clay Guards," composed of 150 Southern Union men who, like myself, were in Washington awaiting appointments. I joined this organization, became a sergeant, and was discharged as such. The government furnished us an armory, arms and ammunition, in Willard's Hall, where the New Willard Hotel now stands. Detachments slept at the Navy Yard, where attacks were expected from Alexandria, Virginia, and in the White House, as it was feared the President might be assassinated.

My commission was dated May 14, 1861, but confusion in the War Department prevented early delivery of all appointments. I had little money and, although I lived in a cheap room in a mechanics' boarding house in the poorer part of the city, and economized in every way, my clothing was shabby and I was indebted to the landlord. Every morning I went to the War Department, hoping for my appointment, but without success.

One morning, in the Assistant Adjutant General's office, I saw my appointment lying with hundreds of others on a big table. I pointed it out to Captain Garesche, and asked him for it. He said the Secretary had ordered all appointments to be sent to the appointee's postoffice address, and added that he had been severely reprimanded because he had delivered to one man an appointment intended for another of the same name. As I knew I would never receive the appointment if it was mailed to El Paso, I was discouraged. But when I told Public Printer Sol Meredith, who was from Indiana and knew my father, the situation, he explained the circumstances to Mr. Cameron, and on June 22 I received my appointment as first lieutenant of the 18th Infantry, one of the nine new regiments of twenty-four companies each then being formed.

I was directed to report to its Colonel, Henry B. Carrington, at headquarters, Columbus, Ohio.

Still without money, I went to the paymaster, hoping to receive the money necessary to pay traveling expenses and get a uniform. The paymaster refused to pay me until the end of the month and, finally, in my dilemma, I went to a friend and borrowed enough to carry me to Columbus and buy a uniform.

Before leaving, Judge John S. Watts, delegate from New Mexico, and I recommended my brother W. W. to the Secretary of the Treasury for collector of customs at El Paso, and to the Adjutant General my brother Emmett for the appointment to West Point from New Mexico.

I reported to Colonel Carrington in Columbus on June 25th. Although adjutant general of Ohio under Governor Chase, he knew less about army matters than I. But he assumed a great deal, and told me he was going to have the best regiment in the army, and that no man who drank could remain in it.

A mile and a half from the city was a camp of instruction, "Camp Thomas." Most officers reporting were instructed under Captain Kellogg, a former artillery officer; but I was detailed on recruiting service at Toledo, Ohio. On July 19th I opened an office there, where I became one of the most successful recruiting officers in the regiment. On August 12th, telegraphic instructions came from Washington to muster in Colonel Gibson's 49th regiment of Ohio Volunteers at Tiffin, Ohio. For perhaps a month, I kept both offices open, traveling back and forth.

I used the fair grounds at Tiffin for the organizing of the regiment. Generally the man who brought the men to camp was made captain, although orders required that men sufficient to form a company be locked in a room to elect their own officers. When elected, I swore in the officers.

When four companies were sworn in they elected a major; eight companies elected a lieutenant colonel; and ten were authorized to elect a colonel, adjutant and quartermaster.

The regiment was formed, equipped with arms, uniforms, tents and other paraphernalia, and aboard trains which started from the fairgrounds in less than thirty days. Twenty thousand relatives and friends watched the regiment depart and heard Colonel Gibson address the multitude. A Democrat, and former treasurer of his State, he was well known as a most eloquent speaker. His audience was in tears before the signal to start, but cheered with excitement and enthusiasm when he threw his hat high in the air over the crowd. His was one of the first regiments to go in the Western army under General Grant, and did able service, Gibson becoming a general.

Of the new regular regiments the 18th Infantry was one of the first organized. It had three battalions of eight companies each under Majors Townsend, Stokes and Caldwell.

President Lincoln had directed the issuance of General Order No. 101, as follows:

"War Department, Adjutant General's Office,
    Washington, November 20, 1861.
General Orders No. 101.
    "The intention of the Government, in reserving the original vacancies of Second Lieutenants for the most deserving among the non-commissioned officers of the new regular regiments, was twofold: to secure the services of brave, intelligent and energetic officers, by appointing only those who had fully proved themselves to be such, after a fair competition with all who chose to enter the lists against them, and to give to the young men of the country—those especially who were poor, unknown, and without any social or political influence—an equal opportunity with the most favored. In General Orders No. 16 of May 4, 1861, this intention was publicly announced. It is now reaffirmed, and commanding officers of the new regiments will see that it is carried out in good faith.
    By order,
                    L. Thomas, Adjutant-General."

This enabled Colonel Carrington, an able recruiting officer, to enlist as privates many college students and other young men of high standing and education. Probably fifty of these were eventually commissioned.

With sixteen companies equipped, Lieutenant Colonel Oliver L. Shepherd reported to Colonel Carrington for duty in the field. Because of my success in securing enlistments, I was kept on recruiting service, but on February 23, 1862, I was ordered to proceed to Louisville, Kentucky, with thirty men, to join the regiment then en route from West Virginia to the Army of the Cumberland at Nashville.

I was too late to join Shepherd's sixteen companies, and was assigned to a river vessel filled with various troops, largely volunteers, including Captain Mack of the regular infantry, temporarily commanding a regular battery. A drunken man reported to me he had been left by Shepherd's command, and asked to join mine. He reported to my sergeant, D'Isay, and asked for food, but boasted that all he wanted was something to eat and that he was going to leave. When he started down the gang plank, one of the men and I caught him, had a fight in which I hurt my hand so I had to wear it in a sling, tore practically all the clothing off the deserter, but we brought him aboard. Soon afterward, the first sergeant of Mack's artillery told me that Captain Mack wished to see me. I reported to Captain Mack, who asked me if I knew who was in command of the vessel. I said I did not, and he said, "No more do I, but, as I am a captain in the regular army and you are a lieutenant, suppose we consider that I am in command. I saw your encounter with that drunken soldier and, as we are probably going to have a great deal of disorder in this mixed command on this trip to Nashville, I think you are a proper person to act as officer of the day for today. There is no time for a regular guard mount, but you assume the duties and, as you are having some considerable trouble with that drunken man, my sergeant will report to you and take care of the disorderly." The sergeant tied his hands, and trussed his knees with a stick, gagged him with a bayonet and sat him in a state room, satisfied he would stop swearing and abusing the officers! The man soon begged for relief, but was tried by court martial and sentenced to be shot for striking an officer, which sentence was later commuted by General Thomas.

Subsequently I carried Captain Mack off the battle-field of

Stone River, desperately wounded. I saw him next at the War Department in Washington in 1870, assistant to the Secretary of War, and he arranged my transfer from infantry to cavalry.

I reported to Colonel Fry, adjutant to Colonel Buell, at Louisville, and was directed to take my thirty men to Major Stokes, commanding the 3d battalion of three companies, 18th Infantry, near Nashville. Major Stokes made me adjutant. He was a military novice, too old to learn, and soon failed of confirmation by the Senate.

The three companies were temporarily consolidated with the other two battalions and Colonel Shepherd made me adjutant of the regiment in the field.

When "Parson" William G. Bronlow, the courageous and persistent leader of the Union men of East Tennessee, arrived at the St. Cloud Hotel, under flag of truce from Knoxville, escorted by an officer of the Confederate army, many of our officers wished to pay their respects. Twenty officers requested me, as adjutant, to introduce them. Admitted to his hotel, I greeted him and introduced my companions. He introduced the young Confederate officer with the remark, "This young man is my nephew, a man with good intentions, but sadly misguided."

Each spoke a few words with the Parson, a nervous, sympathetic and passionate man. Just before we left he exclaimed: "Gentlemen, you are right. Fight 'em, fight 'em, fight 'em till hell freezes over, and then fight 'em on the ice!" A strange speech for a parson, perhaps, but illustrating the intense bitterness the war instilled in all.

Buell's command was ordered to proceed by forced marches to Shiloh to reinforce Grant, about to give battle to the Confederate General Johnson, and on April 6, 1862, my regiment, the 18th U. S. Infantry (two battalions, nineteen companies), as a part of the Third Brigade, First Division, Army of the Ohio, marched all day in the rain toward the sound of the cannon at the battle then raging at Shiloh Church.

We arrived at Savannah late at night, eighteen miles above the battle-ground. The rain made the roads on the left bank of the river almost impassable, and it was decided to send us on by steamer. It was, however, nine or ten o'clock in the morning before a boat could be furnished, so we did not arrive at Pittsburg Landing until about two p.m. of that day, when the battle was almost over.

As we approached the landing, Colonel Shepherd ordered Lieutenant D. W. Benham, the quartermaster, and me, to proceed inland to find someone authorized to place us in proper position. A few hundred yards away we found most of the generals in consultation. General Buell designated our position and we returned to deliver General Buell's instructions.

Here the regiment saw its first horrors of war. Many wounded were carried to the numerous hospital boats tied up at the landing. In a cave under the Bluffs Benham and I saw a large number of ghastly corpses, stained with blood, laid on the leaves. Suddenly Benham exclaimed, "My God, Mills, there's a man who's not dead! See, his face is red, and I can see his chest heave. What a cruel thing to turn him out for dead!"

Feeling his pulse, Benham exclaimed, "This man is alive!" raised his head to help him, when he smelled the fumes of whiskey. Evidently the man had drunk during the battle, been overcome, and, seeing what he supposed were fellow soldiers asleep, had concluded to turn in.

It is needless to say that both Benham and I lost our interest in the "poor fellow" and left him to sleep off his drunk.

In the meantime, Shepherd placed his men in the front line, but we saw little fighting, as the Confederates abandoned the field after Johnson was killed. Later we confronted them at Corinth, and Beauregard, who had succeeded Johnson, retired without giving battle in the direction of Nashville, which the Federals had practically abandoned. It then became a race between Buell and Beauregard as to who should first assemble an army at Nashville.

Iuka, with many public buildings, was selected as the hospital base for the wounded and sick. The 18th Infantry, as the largest regiment of regulars, was ordered to guard the hospital.

Shepherd selected a camp site in a dense forest, which added to our comfort in the heat of May. It was here I became known as the best shot in the regiment. One day, when we were all trying to rest and sleep, somebody called out, "See that squirrel!" pointing to where the little animal was eating buds in the top of an oak tree. He was perhaps one hundred and fifty feet from me, but I was satisfied I could kill him. Many soldiers and officers looking on, I raised my pistol, fired, the squirrel fell to the ground, shot through the head; a better shot than I had intended. This, together with the fact that I was from Texas, gave me a better reputation as a crack shot than I deserved.

We remained in camp several weeks, but as soon as most of the invalids recovered, we were ordered to join the Army of the Cumberland.

En route, we came one day near a little town in Tennessee. As usual, the soldiers were given to pillage, and here they raided a Masonic lodge, which enraged Shepherd, who was a Mason. One soldier brought a letter, written by a doctor, advising the neighbors to poison wells and kill the Yankee invaders. Shepherd ordered me to arrest this doctor and bring him to camp. We readily found his house, and, calling him out, found he had a wooden leg. He admitted writing the letter. Colonel Shepherd ordered him before a sentinel and made him march, in the extreme hot weather, during the sentinel's tour. Shepherd reported the case to General Thomas, but the man was liberated without trial.

Colonel, afterwards General Bob McCook, was in command of our brigade, consisting of the 2d Minnesota, the 9th Ohio, almost exclusively German (McCook's regiment), and our own. McCook was a most excellent officer and, although seriously ill, insisted on retaining command, traveling in an ambulance, and caring for his brigade. On August 4, 1862, he rode forward, as was his custom, with a small guard, to select camps for each of the regiments. Near Decherd, Tennessee, a guerrilla band of thirty or forty men, commanded by Frank B. Gurley, ordered McCook to surrender. Upon his refusal, they shot him in the stomach, and he died in great agony that night. The guerrillas carried off two of his staff officers. He had a father and three brothers killed in battle during the war.

The 9th Ohio became infuriated and burned all the houses in the vicinity and killed many citizens. Gurley, the leader of the guerrilla band, was afterwards arrested, identified by the staff officers who had escaped, tried by court martial, and hanged near Nashville.

After McCook's death, the regiment joined the army under Buell at Nashville, which the Confederates failed to reach before it was too strong to capture. Then began the race between Buell and Bragg, in command of the Confederates, from Nashville to Louisville. I am not writing a history of the war, so I shall say nothing of this extraordinary march which ended with our reaching Louisville twenty-four hours ahead of the enemy, with the exception of a little incident at Franklin, Kentucky.

My regiment was rear guard to this great army, taking care that the sick and exhausted should not fall into the hands of the enemy. Colonel Shepherd was instructed to impress transportation sufficient to care for all helpless men. I was ordered, with Quartermaster Benham, to seize such transportation as was necessary. The Confederate cavalry were harassing us flank and rear and, on arriving at Franklin, we were so hard pressed we feared we would lose a great many of our sick.

A friend reported an excellent ambulance and four mules on the outskirts of the town in possession of the wife of a Confederate. Going with two soldiers to seize it, we found the house doors locked, the blinds down, and got no response to our knocks. We directed the two men to search the barn and, if they found the conveyance, to wheel it out and attach the mules. They found the vehicle, wheeled it into the road, and returned to harness the mules, only to find that someone had cut the traces. While we were deliberating how to get the vehicle away with the ruined harness, the blinds flew open, an infuriated woman thrust her head through the open window and angrily exclaimed, "You miserable Yankees; get out of this! Don't you hear those guns?"

We did hear them, for our rear guard was engaged with the Confederate cavalry. Seeing the hopelessness of the situation, I called to an old colored man chopping wood in the yard, "Boy, throw me your axe!" He tossed the axe over the fence; I took it and smashed the spokes in the rear wheels, and Benham smashed those in front. We then bid good-day to the lady, who was as angry as Petruchio's Kate, and the last we saw of her she was still upbraiding us.

General Buell, although a loyal and efficient commander, was not popular with the volunteer army. Although generally chivalrous, it was disposed to interpret orders to its own liking, and became enraged at Buell's severity. He ordered that the commanding officers should not needlessly destroy private property; that he had noticed a disposition to burn valuable cedar fence rails unnecessarily, and that officers would see that only a sufficient number of rails were used to cook the food. A division commander issued an order in derision directing that thereafter none but the top rail should be taken by his troops. The troops understood this insubordination, and it soon developed that there were no more top rails.

This discontent with Buell made its way to Washington. When we arrived in Louisville, General Thomas sent for Colonel Shepherd, showing him a telegram from Washington announcing that General Buell was relieved and that he, Thomas, should take command of the Army of the Cumberland. Thomas said, "Now, Colonel Shepherd, I don't see how I can in honor obey that order unless it is forced upon me, because

General Buell has consulted me in every movement he has made since we have been serving together, and I approve of everything he has done. In your opinion, should I not, before taking command, communicate these facts to the government?" Shepherd, loyal to Buell, agreed. Thomas telegraphed to Washington, and Buell was retained for some time. Later he was relieved by Rosecrans.

Bragg, failing to get possession of Louisville, and fearing to proceed further north, fell back to Perryville, Kentucky, where the important battle of Perryville took place on October 8th. General Bragg then abandoned further aggressive movements and began his retirement toward Nashville, Buell following him closely and arriving at Nashville in time to hold that city.

When the Civil War broke out, army regulations provided brass mountings for the soldier, retaining many useless and cumbersome impediments for the soldier's person because at one time they were useful. When fighting was done with arrows and spears and short infantry swords, men wore coats of mail, to ward off the strokes of the enemy. When firearms appeared these became ineffective and were gradually but laboriously abandoned. The soldier's "scale" represented the last remnant of the coat of mail, and theoretically was useful in warding off strokes of the saber on the shoulder. While many intelligent men knew its uselessness, no one had the courage to advocate its abandonment.

In November, '63, while my regiment was guarding Belotte's Ford, on the Cumberland River, eight miles from Gallatin, Tennessee, we received midnight orders to proceed within two hours to an expected battle-field. We were to take four days' rations, to be carried by one four-mule team. My company, the largest in the regiment, found it impossible to pack all the necessary articles in one wagon. Coming upon a chest weighing over three hundred pounds, I asked the sergeant what it contained. He replied, "The scales, sir." I told him to throw it into the latrine, which he did, and the box is there now.

Finding no battle-field, we turned out for Sunday morning

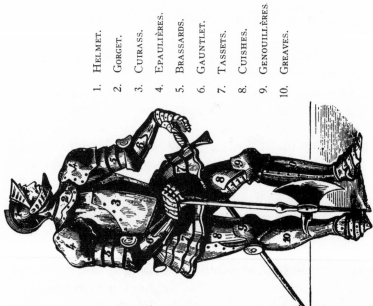

1. Helmet.
2. Gorget.
3. Cuirass.
4. Epaulières.
5. Brassards.
6. Gauntlet.
7. Tassets.
8. Cuishes.
9. Genouillères.
10. Greaves.

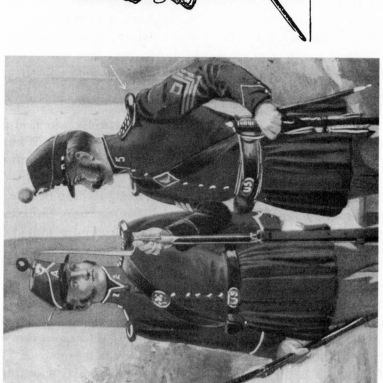

Scales and Armor.

inspection in a beautiful camp in the woods. All the other companies appeared with their shining "scales" and other brass ornaments. My scaleless company presented anything but the so-called military appearance.

Approaching my company, the Major, a martinet, remarked, "Captain, where are your scales?" I replied, "I abandoned them for want of transportation." He said, "You are out of uniform, and I shall have to report you. Have you made requisition for more?" I replied that I had not and did not intend to; that they were a very detrimental incumbrance. Although he ordered me peremptorily to do so, I never did. Whenever my company was inspected by others I was similarly reprimanded, and I dare say the files of the War Department are today full of reports condemning me as a captain for being out of uniform.

Later, out on the plains, where we were less harassed by bureaucracy, one captain after another began to shed, and finally, after ten years' defiance of regulations and orders by courageous and sensible captains, the army shed its scales as a snake sheds its skin. No order was ever issued by any authority for their abandonment. It is the only way in which the army can be redeemed from some of its follies, such as continue to this day in wearing the present swords and sabers, as useless for all military purposes as the scales.

When General W. S. Rosecrans was assigned to the command of the Army of the Cumberland, relieving General Buell, my regiment was detached from Steedman's Brigade of the 35th Ohio, 2d Minnesota and 4th Michigan, and all our officers bade the officers of Steedman's Brigade an affectionate goodbye. On Christmas day we joined the 15th, 16th and 19th regular infantry, with Battery H, 5th Artillery, on the height near Nashville, where we were brigaded with them as the "Regular Brigade, Army of the Cumberland," Col. O. L. Shepherd, commanding.

Bragg's army at Murfreesboro, thirty miles south of Nashville, received reinforcements from Virginia, principally under

Breckinridge. Rosecrans, hastily assembling as large a command as possible, determined to attack. On the last day of December, 1862, and the first and second of January, 1863, these armies fought one of the bloodiest battles of the war about two miles north of Murfreesboro along Stone River.

General Rosecrans issued a confidential order for a general attack by the whole army at eight o'clock, December 31st. Colonel Shepherd, officer of the day for the whole army, rode the lines to see the leading commanders were prepared to make the common assault on time. I rode with Colonel Shepherd all night, and everything seemed to be fairly understood, but General Bragg was informed, massed his troops on the left and assaulted our whole right wing, commanded by General McCook, capturing most of the batteries before the horses were harnessed. Rousseau's reserve division and the regular brigade reserve of his division were the first in our army seriously in action. I was with Colonel Shepherd and General Rousseau when our right was crushed. General Thomas excitedly ordered Rousseau to "put the regulars in the cedars and drive those devils back." We thrust in our battery under the protection of the cedar trees and rocks in time to check the victorious Confederates, giving Rosecrans time to reform his routed right and establish a new line.

That night Doctor Webster Lindsly and I, with the permission of the Confederates, visited the field to care for the wounded, where I carried Captain Mack to the hospital. I found a young man, mortally wounded, a cannon ball having struck his abdomen. He said, "I know I am going to die. Write my mother that you saw me here." I wrote down his name and address, but I lost it. I have regretted it ever since, especially as I could not remember the name.

During the first day our forces were worsted, our supply trains cut off, and, the men carrying no rations, were hungry. Our entire right wing was doubled back on the left, the enemy were in front and rear, and the night was exceedingly cold.

It was midnight before the excitement and confusion abated sufficiently to allow the men a little rest.

When I lay down, I rolled up in my saddle blanket near Captain R. L. Morris, a personal and intimate friend. But I was not to sleep yet. Colonel Shepherd sent me several miles to the rear with orders to seize some unguarded wagons which were filled with hard bread and bacon for the daybreak breakfast.

I folded my blanket, laid it on the ground and carried out the instructions, bringing the wagons back with me. When I returned, my blanket was missing.

The loss was discouraging, and I was cold, but as Morris said he knew nothing of it, there was nothing to do but pass the night as best I could. The next morning I noticed Morris had not only his saddle blanket, but another, tied in a roll behind. I asked where he got it and he retorted it was no concern of mine. I thought the circumstances sufficient to warrant an explanation, and he became angry, exclaiming, "Do you suppose I would steal your blanket, Mills?"

"No," I said, "I don't, but I would like you to untie your blanket and let me examine it."

He untied it, and I showed him my initials worked in one corner with yarn.

Laughing, he said, "Well, Mills, I give it up. That is your blanket. Take it. I stole it, knowing government blankets were as alike as two peas. I wouldn't steal under ordinary circumstances, but such a night as last night would justify a man in doing anything to keep warm."

Bragg assembled half his army on our extreme left during the night, intending to destroy our left as he had our right. General Breckinridge crossed the river opposite our extreme left, expecting to surprise us, but Rosecrans fortunately received notice and concentrated five hundred pieces of artillery on our left, unknown to Breckinridge.

The Confederates were literally cut to pieces with our artillery. On the right we could see nothing, but heard the

roar of cannon for at least an hour, not knowing the result.
Suddenly the firing ceased, we heard a cheer and, crossing a
ridge to our left a sergeant galloped between the lines, carrying an inverted Confederate flag. Although this sergeant was
in easy gunshot of the Confederates, not a single shot was fired
at him.

The third day of the battle resulted decisively. Bragg retired
toward Chattanooga.

On September 19 and 20, Chickamauga, the most sanguinary
battle of the war, was fought. Here the regular brigade (one
battalion each of the 15th, 16th and 19th, and two battalions
of the 18th, with Battery H of the 5th Artillery) lost over
thirty-three per cent of their strength in killed, wounded and
missing, and during the fight, the battery was taken by the
Confederates, all the horses killed, but the guns recaptured
later on.

At the close of this battle, my company, the largest in the
brigade, was selected for picket duty to cover the brigade
front. Lieutenant Freeman, the adjutant, posted me close to
the rebel lines. He rode out a couple of hundred yards and
was taken prisoner by rebel pickets springing from behind
trees, and sent to Libby Prison, from which he escaped
through a tunnel in time to join Sherman's army near the sea.
During the entire night our picket line was compelled to listen
to the shrieks and cries for water and help from the wounded
and dying, who lay immediately in front, but whom we were
unable to assist, although they were only a few hundred yards
from us. Some time after midnight an order came for a
change in the position of the army, which moved our brigade
a mile and a half to another position. As Freeman was absent,
the regimental commander was unaware of the exact location
of my company; and, in the morning, hearing no noise from
the location of the regiment, I sent a sergeant to find out the
cause. The sergeant returned, reporting that the regiment
and the troops adjoining had abandoned the field, so I relieved
my company and marched, following the trails of the different

regiments, and finally arrived at their line of battle. I did not see Freeman again until on recruiting duty at St. Louis.

Rosecrans was practically defeated at Chickamauga and retired to Chattanooga, where Thomas concentrated his army for defense. Bragg besieged the city with so large an army it was found necessary to reinforce the Army of the Cumberland by the Army of the Tennessee, under Grant and Sherman, and two divisions of the Army of the Potomac, under Hooker.

General Thomas, who succeeded Rosecrans, was besieged and on half rations for months, the Confederate cavalry cutting off supplies. Finally there came the wonderful battle of Missionary Ridge, with Grant commanding the whole army; Hooker, the right (Lookout Mountain); Thomas, the center; and Sherman, the left. Hooker took Lookout during the night, but neither army knew it until daylight. As the sun rose, a bugle was sounded and a sergeant and three men presented to the breeze a large American flag from the point of Lookout Mountain, announcing the defeat of the Confederate Army. The whole Federal Army took up the cheer that swept from right to left.

By ten o'clock, Thomas' army, numbering perhaps twenty thousand men, was in battle line at the foot of Missionary Ridge, five hundred feet high, well designed for defense. Three guns from Thomas' headquarters was the signal for the whole line to charge.

Thomas' army stood for hours, with fixed bayonets, reflecting dazzling sun rays to the Ridge.

At last we heard the signal and cheered as we charged. The Confederates reserved their fire until we had passed up one-third of the ridge, when they opened fire. Their guns were so depressed, however, that the recoil destroyed their accuracy, and the shells went over our heads. Finally my company arrived so close I heard one of their gunners call out, "Half-second fuse," which meant that the shell would explode one-half second after it left the gun. It seemed difficult to believe that we could mount that rough mountain ridge and drive the

Confederates away from their five hundred pieces of cannon, but no part of the line was ever halted. In half an hour the whole Confederate line was in our possession.

After this defeat, Bragg retired towards Atlanta, to which we also went.

At the battle of Jonesboro, near Atlanta, Captain Andy Burt and I had many men wounded. Visiting these men in a large tent containing perhaps seventy-five men, we found that certain Union Christian Societies had pinned upon its white walls large placards reading, "Are you prepared to die?" "Prepare to meet your God." As soon as Burt saw these senseless signs, he tore them down, stamping them under his feet, crying out, "Never say die, men! Never say die!" A badly wounded sergeant of my regiment answered, "If more officers like this visited us, there wouldn't be so many of us die!"

One of the most distinguished field batteries in the army was raised by the Chicago Board of Trade. Commanded by a fine-looking young German, Captain Dilger, this battery was given carte blanche to proceed where it pleased to do the most destruction, and his men seemed to be inspired with his own spirit and ambition. In his buckskin suit he would ride about, seeking a place to set up his battery to advantage. Dashing even beyond the skirmish lines, he would go into action and do all the destruction he could before the enemy could get his range, and as suddenly disappear.

At New Hope Church, Lieutenant Bisbee (now Brigadier General, retired) and I, with our two companies, were on picket duty when Dilger's battery passed through our lines and into action. Knowing the Confederates would soon get his range, our men protected themselves behind rocks and trees. Bisbee and I were behind a pine tree twenty inches in diameter, when a solid shot cut the tree in two, throwing us to the ground with splinters in our bodies. Neither of us was seriously wounded, and we returned to duty in a few days.

The regular brigade was so depleted with losses, discharges and failure to enlist that it was determined to send it while waiting recruits to camp on Lookout Mountain, overlooking Chattanooga. As the senior officer of the 18th Infantry, I marched it to the mountain for indefinite encampment.

At this time General Steedman, with ten thousand men, was ordered to defend Chattanooga in the apprehended march of Hood to Nashville. Learning I was out of active service while my regiment recuperated, Steedman called me to his staff as inspector general of his provisional corps. When Hood avoided Chattanooga, we moved the whole ten thousand men, reaching Nashville and joining Thomas just in time to escape being cut off by Hood's army.

Hood, relieving Bragg, invested Nashville and, on December 16, 1864, the Battle of Nashville took place. Hood's retreat toward the Cumberland River was disastrous, but floods saved his army. We were unable to cross streams over which he had destroyed the bridges. Thomas ordered Steedman to Murfreesboro to entrain ten thousand men for Decatur, Alabama, to prevent Hood's crossing.

We halted Sunday morning at Huntsville to repair some small bridges. While waiting, a bell began to ring for church services, and the General suggested that we all attend. A dignified, gray-haired old man mounted the pulpit, and began the services, bringing in with more than necessary vehemence the prayer for Jeff Davis and all those in authority. General Steedman, a man of intense passion combined with the tenderest affection, was bitterly insulted, but he remained until the services were completed. Retiring from the church, he arrested the preacher and placed him under guard. He was the Reverend Dr. Ross of Knoxville, Tennessee, who some years before had canvassed the Northern States with Parson Bronlow in a political-religious discussion of slavery. In that canvass Parson Bronlow took the side of slavery and Dr. Ross the opposite. They had now each honestly changed their views completely.

When the Doctor was brought in, the General exclaimed, passionately, "Dr. Ross, have you no more respect for the authorities of the Federal Government than to pray for Jeff Davis in their presence? If you have no more respect, have you no more sense?"

The Doctor stood calmly and said, "I have more respect for my conscientious convictions as a minister, my creed in religion, and my God than I have for the authorities of the United States Government. If I have committed any crime in your eyes, you have the power to punish me; but I shall cheerfully accept any punishment you choose to give me, even to death."

The General made no reply for some time, but finally said, "Very well, sir; I will carry you along with the command as a prisoner." The Doctor replied, "General, I am perfectly willing to go with your command, but I am too old to march. I will do the best I can." He appeared to be about sixty-five or seventy years old, quite gray and rather feeble.

The General replied, "Very well, sir, I will give you transportation—I will give you an ambulance, and" with some oaths, "I will give you an escort of your own color." We had three brigades of colored troops in the command, and the Doctor was of so dark a complexion as almost to suggest a mixture of blood.

Dr. Ross was carried on the cars and, later, on an ambulance with a colored escort. But General Steedman realized he had made a mistake. When General Roddy (commanding the Confederates on our front) requested an exchange of prisoners, General Steedman gave me instructions to give Dr. Ross any military rank that would secure his exchange. We had no difficulty in making the exchange, together with many others.

When my regiment was withdrawn from active service to Lookout Mountain, Tennessee, for reorganization, Lieutenant William H. Bisbee was my adjutant.

The beauty and symmetry of his reports was marked, but some apparently irrelevant figures excited my curiosity. Written in rather large figures in bright red ink was, "S-T-1860-X."

Asked why he had made use of these particular letters and figures, he said he had copied them from a manufacturer's trade-mark for "Hostetter's Bitters," which, translated, read, "Started trade in 1860 with $10.00." He had noticed papers from Washington with red ink figures which he could not understand, and so interspersed the notations throughout his own reports, knowing that no one would understand them, but believing it would be assumed to be the result of much study and care!

Sure enough, in due time Bisbee received a personal letter from the Adjutant General of the Army, complimenting him on the most perfect monthly returns ever submitted by any regular regiment.

The Confederates had a fort at Decatur, and we had some gunboats on the river. General Steedman sent me at night to get such information as the naval commander could give about Decatur and the Confederate supplies supposed to be there. Employing a boatman to carry me to the gunboat Burnsides, commanded by Lieutenant Moneau Forrest, I reported myself staff officer from General Steedman, and asked the commander whether he could assist us in crossing the river with the Federal transports to take Decatur and its supplies. Learning he could protect Steedman's crossing and could assemble enough transports to carry the ten thousand men across in a short time, and would assault Decatur with his gunboats, I reported to Steedman. He and his staff officers crossed with his army in the early part of the day, leaving me on the gunboat. He assaulted Decatur from the rear, while the gunboats assaulted from the river.

This was my only naval engagement. Several men were lost, and the missiles from the Confederate guns tore up the planks of the deck. Decatur surrendered, and we had the supplies which Hood was unable to take.

We pursued Hood's straggling army, the rear guard of which was commanded by General Roddy, and on the 21st day of December, 1864, after a lively chase in a drenching

rain, arrived at "Swope's House," a plantation six miles from
Courtland.

The general camped midway between the road and the
house. We were wet, and the General sent me to ask if the
occupants of Swope's residence, a large, typical Southern
home, would permit us to enter.

When I knocked at the door a lady appeared, but she
slammed the door in my face! Reporting to the General, he
excitedly called his staff to follow, and rapped violently at
the door. The same lady appearing, he said to her, very
sternly, "Madam, is there a man in this house?" She replied
quietly, "Yes."

"Tell him General Steedman wants to see him." In a few
minutes a gray-haired man, about seventy, asked us what was
desired.

The General replied, "I sent one of my staff officers here
to request a simple courtesy, usually accorded foe as well as
friend—simply to warm by your fire. This officer was insulted
by one of the ladies in your house. You can prepare the fire
yourself or I will have it prepared for us."

Mr. Swope replied he would have it prepared as quickly
as possible.

We visited some of the camps, and on our return found a
cheerful fire in the parlor. The room was bare of everything
but chairs, everything in the way of ornaments that could be
stolen having been removed. But the fire was comfortable,
and we stayed until the orderly announced our camp supper
was ready.

A young man on our staff, Davis by name, was something of
a ladies' man. While we enjoyed the fire, he encountered a
young lady in the hall. Strange to say, the lady greeted him
cordially—an unaccountable thing to those men who approach
the feminine sex with difficulty. They laughed and joked,
another lady appeared, and there was quite a gay scene.

One of the ladies was Captain Swope's daughter, and the
other a cousin from Nashville. We had been there for some

time, and as she had heard nothing since the battle she was anxious for news from Nashville.

Returning to the house after supper, all the ornaments had been returned to the parlor, curtains were hung, rugs and carpets down, the center table had regained its cover, and was piled with books. Davis introduced the ladies to the whole party.

Picking up an autograph album, I saw the signatures of Jeff Davis, Beauregard, Bragg, and many prominent officers of the Confederacy. Between the leaves was an order reading as follows:

"Headquarters, District of the Etowah, In the Field, Swope's House, Northern Alabama, December 21, 1864. Special Order No. ————.
"Immediately upon receipt of this order, Doctor ————, in charge of Post Hospital at Courtland, will deliver to Captain Swope the basket of champagne seized in the express office by him on yesterday. By order of General P. D. Roddy.

. . . .
"Adjutant General."

The Generals of both armies commanded districts of the same name, "Etowah." I turned the sheet over and wrote as follows:

"Headquarters, District of the Etowah, In the Field, Swope's House, Northern Alabama, December 22, 1864. Special Order No. ————.
"Immediately upon receipt of this order, Captain Swope, Quartermaster in the Confederate Army, will turn over to Major General Steedman and staff the basket of champagne recovered from Doctor ————, in charge of the Post Hospital at Courtland, and mentioned on the opposite side of this paper.
"By order of Major General Steedman.

ANSON MILLS,
"Captain, 18th Infantry, Inspector General,
District of the Etowah."

Both the ladies eyed me intently. I laid the book on the table, and one of the ladies picked it up and read the paper. She passed it to her cousin, who also read it, and, after a short conference, they went upstairs. Soon Mr. Swope entered, asking, "Can I speak with Captain Mills?"

I announced myself and he said, "My dear sir: your order is good. I would obey it with pleasure were it possible, but, unfortunately, I was unable to recover the champagne. It was used in the hospital before this order was presented to the doctor. I regret exceedingly that I am unable to do so, for I realize the propriety, in case it were possible."

By this time we were well established in good relations with the family. Our evening passed as pleasantly there as anywhere during the war, and we flattered ourselves the family was as reluctant to part with us as we with them.

On the 23d of December we established headquarters at Courtland, abandoning a vigorous pursuit of Hood. The next day in Steedman's office, Oakly Bynam came in and greeted him as a fellow Mason, and asked for help. He had bought several thousand bales of cotton, which the Federal troops were destroying. He wanted a permit to ship it to Louisville by the government vessels then in the river. Steedman angrily told him that neither former friendship nor Masonic brotherhood should influence him to aid one willing to play "Good Lord, good devil" to either the Confederates or the Federals who might be in control.

That night Mr. Bynam told me he had several thousand bales of cotton worth a dollar and a half a pound in Louisville; and that, if the soldiers burned it, it would ruin him; but that if I had sufficient influence with General Thomas to allow it to be shipped north, he would make a fortune and would divide it equally with me! Of course, I declined, and most of the cotton was burned by Steedman's army.

MAJOR GENERAL JAMES B. STEEDMAN.

BRIGADIER GENERAL O. L. SHEPHERD.

BRIGADIER GENERAL H. B. FREEMAN.

BRIGADIER GENERAL WM. H. BISBEE.

AFTER THE WAR

In February, 1865, the War Department detailed three officers from each of the new regiments for recruiting service, selecting those who had served longest during the war. I headed the list of my regiment, and was sent successively to Toledo, Zanesville and St. Louis, where I again met the former adjutant, Freeman. (He died recently, a brigadier general.) He was also on recruiting duty, and we were both ordered to Jefferson Barracks to reorganize our companies from the men we had enlisted. Almost all of these were volunteers discharged in St. Louis.

I was ordered with my own and Company A, commanded by Lieutenant Carpenter, to Fort Aubrey, Kansas, *via* Leavenworth, to relieve two companies of one-year Ohio volunteers, whose time had expired, and who were near mutiny. I left St. Louis December 5, 1865. The weather was so cold, and the supply train furnished me at Fort Leavenworth so inadequate, that I seized and exchanged wagons and teams with a quartermaster's train returning from Santa Fe. One of my men froze to death on the journey, and several were severely frost-bitten.

I found the Walnut Fork of the Arkansas River impassable from floods, and traveled without a trail from Fort Larned for three days, until I could cross, thence moving south toward Fort Aubrey, as I supposed.

During the march a hostile band of Cheyenne Indians (called "dog soldiers") under young Bent, a half-breed, attempted to surprise us. Frustrated, they followed us into the Arkansas River, four miles above Fort Dodge. The Indians asked for parley, during which I discovered a captive American girl, who attempted to talk to me, but was silenced by the chief. I was later instrumental, through the Indian agent, Major Wyncoop, in securing the ransom of this girl, Mary Fletcher.

Leaving A Company at Fort Dodge, I took my own to Aubrey, where I relieved the Ohio volunteers. I remained until April, relieving the monotony by killing some of the buffalo which covered the whole country, riding a spirited horse which could overtake any buffalo.

My company clerk was Henry Garrells, an excellent penman and accountant, but so near-sighted I had to get special permission to enlist him. He was not only the most unprepossessing man I ever saw, but one of the most troublesome drunkards in the army. He got drunk periodically, generally selecting a time when urgency in the preparation of company papers was most desired. When under the influence of liquor, he was absolutely uncontrollable, requiring two or three men to keep him from violence. When sober, he was one of the mildest mannered men I ever saw.

Our post near the river was composed of rude huts and dug-outs. It was far from any settlement, and we had no liquor, so Garrells got along very well until, one Sunday morning, he obtained two bottles of bay rum from the post trader, with which he got gloriously drunk, smashing things right and left in the quarters. The sergeant detailed several men to restrain him (there being no guard house), reported the damage and asked what to do with him. I told him to get a cavalry lariat, about one hundred feet long, and with two strong men carry Garrells to the river bank. They were to divest him of clothing and throw him into the stream until the chill (it was January) should sober him.

I followed Garrells and his party on the opposite side of the stream. Arrived at the bank, about ten feet high, Garrells exclaimed, "Sergeant, here's a river! 'Twill require some engineering skill to pass this river!"

"Never mind," said the sergeant, "we'll cross it, Garrells." The men took off his hat and coat, and one of them reached into his pocket for his money, when Garrells became alarmed and began to shout, "Murder! Robbers! Help!"

By this time they had the rope around his body, and one

man seizing his head, another his heels, they tossed him far
out into the stream.

When Garrells rose he spouted like a whale, and swam for
the opposite shore.   Every few yards of progress he was
checked by the rope, which threw his head under water.   When
he came near the bank on which I stood, he exclaimed, "Major,
damn you, do you think I'm a goldfish or a dolphin?"

I signaled to the sergeant to pull him back, and by the time
he returned he was thoroughly sobered.

I had heard very little from my brother.   The stage line was
irregular on account of hostile Indians.   One evening when it
drove up, it brought my brother, W. W., and Judge Watts,
neither of whom I had seen for four years.   They could only
remain the night with me, but shortly after I procured leave
and joined them in Washington.

Judge Watts and my brother had an interview with President Johnson in regard to Federal appointments in New
Mexico and Texas.   The President had a Texas vacancy on
the board of visitors to West Point, and proposed to appoint
W. W.   Both Judge Watts and my brother preferred I be
given the place, as I was a military man; and I was appointed.

Adjutant General Townsend protested to the President that
my appointment was illegal because the regulations of the
academy provided that no one who had failed at West Point
should be made a member of the board for ten years after
such failure.

Learning this failure was nine years past, the President sent
for Colonel Townsend and asked if there was any other objection to me except my failure at the academy, and what my
standing was.   Townsend had no other objection, and said
my standing was good, when the President said, "Well, if the
faculty discharged a man who nine years after has become a
captain in good standing in the regular army, I think it best
that Captain Mills should be sent there to see what's the matter
with the academy!"

General Grant was anxious to have the superintendency of

the military academy (by law confined to officers of the engineer corps) opened to the line of the army, and Senator Nesmith, a member of the board, promised to try to secure a recommendation from the board to this effect. I felt the engineer corps conducted the academy too much as a purely scientific institution. While they made every effort to produce high-grade engineers, less attention was given the absolute requirements of officers of the line, so I was glad to promise General Grant my assistance. At his suggestion, I made the acquaintance of Senator Nesmith, who set about the accomplishment of his task immediately upon the organization of the board of sixteen members. An animated and somewhat bitter discussion continued during our whole session, finally resulting in a vote of eight to eight, so the resolution was lost. General Grant later submitted the matter to Congress, which changed the law so that any line officer could be made superintendent.

While the board was at the academy, General Scott died there, and the board as a body were his pall-bearers.

At the expiration of my leave, I was ordered to the command of Fort Bridger, Utah, where my company had arrived in my absence.

The volunteers, under General P. Edward Connor, were being relieved. The posts and the territory were both in a chaotic condition, the soldiers harassing the Mormons and encouraging the Gentiles in unlawful persecutions.

Among the volunteers at Fort Bridger was Patrick Tully, who had come over from Ireland with General Connor. These friends served their first enlistment together. Connor took up the study of law, became prominent, and, when the war broke out, was colonel of a volunteer regiment from California, afterwards brigadier general of volunteers, and assigned to the command of the District of Salt Lake.

Tully left the regular service and joined a volunteer regiment. He was one of those soldiers who, either by misfortune or bad conduct, was constantly in the guard house. At inspections, the general generally found Tully confined, and Tully never failed to plead the ground of their former friendship for release, Connor as constantly granting it.

Somewhat ostentatious, General Connor, when leaving one post for another, invariably telegraphed, "I leave for your post today. Have quarters prepared for me on my arrival," being always careful to sign himself "P. Edward Connor," leaving out the Pat or Patrick, by which both he and Tully were known.

All the volunteers at Bridger were ordered to Salt Lake to be mustered out—Tully among the rest.

When Tully was ordered to make preparations for the march, he sent a request from the guard house asking to send a telegram. Arrived at the telegraph office, he dictated the following:

"To General P. Edward Connor, Commanding District of Salt Lake:
"Sir: I leave here for your post today. Have quarters prepared for me on my arrival.   P. EDWARD TULLY."

It is needless to say that Connor honored the requisition and had secure (if not ample) quarters, prepared for "P. Edward Tully."

I was prejudiced against the Mormons, but found they were the best people in the country, and the only ones who would fill contracts fairly. The Gentiles practiced every device to beat the government, but the word of a Mormon was his bond. With Major Lewis commanding Fort Douglas at Salt Lake, I called upon Brigham Young. He looked like General Grant, and was an earnest and, I believe, a sincere and conscientious man. He said he was glad to meet a regular officer, because the regular army always treated them well, but that the volunteers under Connor had been demoralizing to those of the Mormon faith. Discussing my prejudice against his people, about which he asked and I answered frankly, he said, "You have doubtless heard we are disloyal to the Union." Pointing to the flag flying over his Tabernacle, he said it had waved every day since the war began. Upon his invitation I attended his church and heard him preach the next Sunday. I visited the Tabernacle in company with his son-in-law and saw open on the pulpit the inspired volumes from which they preached —the Old Testament, the New Testament, and the Book of Mormon. He presented a copy of the latter to me, inscribed with his name, which I still have. My experiences changed my mind regarding the Mormon people. I believe their church the equal of any in the inculcation of those qualities which make the Mormons law-abiding, industrious, economical and faithful to all their agreements.

Christmas Eve, Judge Carter, the sutler, gave a dancing party. While the officers and ladies were dancing, I received a dispatch announcing the massacre of Fetterman and his command, part of my regiment, at Fort Philip Kearny. We were all of the same regiment. I stopped the band and read the despatch, which cast the garrison into gloom, and presaged a general war with the Sioux.

Jim Bridger, a well-known frontiersman, who had been with the Indians since he was fourteen years old, was the post guide. He was reticent and hard to know, but a genius in many ways.

One day the Overland stage from Omaha arrived, and an English-looking gentleman stepped out and inquired in the "sutler's store" for both the post trader and for me. He delivered letters of introduction from General Sheridan, stating that he was a captain in the British Army on a journey around the world for the purpose of writing a book, and that he wished to see Jim Bridger. (Cut, 154.)

We took him to call on Bridger, who lived alone in one of the officers' quarters. We found the old man looking grave and solemn. Our English friend plied him with questions, stating he had been told by General Sheridan that he, of all others on the Western plains, could give him the most thrilling reminiscences regarding the exciting scenes of the settlement of the frontier.

Bridger made no advances, appearing like a child, reluctant

to "show off." The captain continued his conversation in his most winning way and earnestly requested the old scout to tell them something interesting. Finally, Bridger told the following story:

"Well, I think the most thrilling adventure I ever had on the frontier was in the winter of 1855, when Jack Robinson and I went trapping, about two hundred miles down the Green River in the Ute country. We knew the Utes were unfriendly, but we did not think they were war-like, so we got two horses and a pack outfit, and in December went into camp on the Green River. We had spent two months trapping, and were about ready to return, when early one morning we saw a large party of warriors coming up the stream. We had only time to saddle our horses, gather our rifles and ammunition and mount. We estimated their party at about one hundred, and started up the river at full speed, abandoning everything we had in camp.

"As we became hard pressed, one of us would dismount and fire, then mount and pass the other, and he would dismount and fire, and so continuing, checking our pursuers until we gained some ground. Their horses were not only fresh, but they had lead horses with them, which gave them great advantage over us, who had but one horse each.

"We continued this method of defense all day, and by night had killed thirty of the Indians. But our horses were so tired we feared the enemy would take us.

"At the foot of a mountain, where there was dense timber, we took shelter about dusk, knowing the Indians would not follow in the dark. We spent the night in great fear as to what would become of us the next day. Knowing that at dawn they would be after us, we started to lead our horses out of the valley, but had no sooner started than we heard the Indians behind us.

"We continued our defense until about two o'clock, when we had killed thirty more of the Indians. This left only about forty to continue the pursuit, but they did not seem at all discouraged. If anything, they were more active than ever.

"By this time, our broken horses began to give way at the knees. Observing a narrow canyon, we concluded to follow it as it gave us a better chance of defense than the open. This canyon was narrow, with a swift stream running down it, and we made our way as fast as we could for two or three miles, when, looking around, we saw immediately in our rear the whole force of Indians.

"Matters were desperate. The canyon walls were perpendicular, three hundred feet high, and growing narrower every mile. Suddenly, around a bend in the canyon, we saw a waterfall, two hundred feet high, completely blocking our exit."

Here Mr. Bridger paused. The captain, all aglow with interest, cried anxiously, "Go on, Mr. Bridger; go on! How *did* you get out?"

"Oh, bless your soul, Captain," answered Bridger, "we never did get out. The Indians killed us right there."

This closed the interview. Though I have never heard of his book, I dare say the captain did not include this story in it.

While I was at Fort Bridger, the regular army was increased from thirty to sixty thousand men, making each of the three battalions of the nine new regiments a full regiment. The vacancies thus created were filled by meritorious volunteers, so that many regular officers were set back many years in prospective promotions. The first battalion of my regiment remained the 18th, the second battalion the 27th, and the third battalion the 36th, which resulted in many changes of stations and locations, but I retained my company, H, of the 18th.

In my administration and discipline of the garrison at Fort Bridger I adopted as far as I could the moral suasion ideas of Charlie Naylor. Instead of punishing the men by confining them in the guard house for trial, I had the post carpenter construct a very unprepossessing wooden horse and a wooden sword about six feet long, with its business end painted a bloody red. Any man reported for any disorderly conduct

MORAL SUASION HORSE AT FORT BRIDGER.

SIOUX TEPEE CAPTURED AT SLIM BUTTES,
WITH KEOGH'S GUIDON AND CAPTURING OFFICERS.
(Text, 171.)

had to ride this horse for a certain period, dismounting occasionally to curry and water it with currycomb and water
bucket. This method of punishment proved most efficient, as
the men soon came to dread "riding the horse" a great deal
more than they did spending a month in the guard house.

While at Fort Bridger, about a thousand Shoshone Indians
came in, camping near the post for a couple of months.
Having a telegraph line and a military operator, I sent for the
most intelligent of the Indians, and told them we would talk
over the wire. They were much mystified, and could not
understand when I told them I sent the words over the wire.
Finally I gave one the wire to hold so he could feel the message going through him. While the Indians are stoics and
their outdoor life prevented the shock from affecting them as
it would a white man, they threw their hands up when the
current passed through, understanding for the first time there
really was something that went over the wire. Later they
used this knowledge in cutting down and burning the poles
and destroying the wire to keep the whites from telling where
they had been in mischief, and to prevent the soldiers from
following.

When I first arrived at Fort Bridger, the volunteer garrison
was equipped with Spencer breech-loading carbines. I turned
in my muzzle-loading Springfields and equipped my two companies with the Spencers which, of course, had heavy metallic
cartridges, Cal. .50. Our equipment consisted of the regular
old-fashioned cartridge box for paper cartridges to be carried
in tin cases inside the leather boxes, and were wholly unsuited
for metallic cartridges. I furnished mounted guards and
patrols to the daily Overland Mail, and the metallic ammunition carried in these tin boxes rattled loudly, and were even
noisy when carried by men afoot.

So I devised a belt, which the post saddler manufactured out
of leather, with a loop for each of the fifty cartridges. The
men wore these belts around their waists, and they proved

much more comfortable and efficient than any other method of carrying cartridges.

W. A. Carter, the sutler, was going to Washington, and suggested that he procure me a patent. This patent was the foundation of my various subsequent patents, which enabled me to change the method of carrying cartridges, not only in our own army, but in the armies throughout the world, and by which I eventually made an independent fortune.

I remained in command of Bridger until the spring of 1867, when I was ordered to escort Gen. G. M. Dodge, chief engineer of the Union Pacific Railroad, on a recognizance to find a route from the vicinity of Salt Lake, *via* the Snake River, to some point in Oregon or Washington State for a branch road to the Pacific. We were two months going west of the Rocky Mountain Range *via* Snake River, and returning through the south pass at the head waters of the North Platte River. We finally abandoned the expedition when we reached Fort Sanders, Wyoming.

General John A. Rawlins accompanied the expedition, on the advice of his physician, he being afflicted with tuberculosis, and was a very interesting companion.

From Sanders I reported to Fort Fetterman, where my regiment established headquarters, after the return of Colonel Carrington's expedition, abandoning the posts of Reno, Philip Kearny, and F. C. Smith. The regular route to Fort Fetterman *via* Fort Laramie was twice the distance across the mountains, so I took no wagon transportation, but only the men carrying rations. We had a very difficult march, but succeeded in arriving long before the wagons carrying our baggage *via* Laramie.

I remained at Fetterman during the winter of '67, but in the spring went to Fort Sedgwick, where Colonel Carrington had a large post of seven companies, most of them of his own regiment. These isolated posts were thoroughly cut off from civilization.

I remember a humorous incident that occurred there one

day. There being no chaplain or civil authorities for hundreds of miles in any direction, their functions were necessarily sometimes performed by the adjutants of the military posts. One day the adjutant, Lieutenant Carroll Potter, invited Captain Morris and me to go with him across the Platte River to Julesburg, where he said he was going to perform a marriage.

When the ambulance drove up to Potter's porch, Morris and I heard him call "Lizzie, Lizzie, bring me the prayer book." His wife brought the prayer book, and he put it in his coat, asking, "Have you turned down a leaf?"

"Yes, Carroll, I have."

Arriving at the town, we were escorted to a small building where we found about twenty persons congregated to witness the ceremony. Drawing the prayer book from his pocket and opening it at a turned-down page, Potter started out on the service in a vigorous, solemn and authoritative tone, as follows:

"I am the resurrection and the life, saith the Lord. He that believeth in me though he were dead, yet shall he live, and whosoever liveth and believeth in me shall never die."

By this time his voice began to fall, and he said: "Hold on. I think I've got the wrong place!" Remembering his wife had turned down a leaf for him to read the burial service a short time before, he turned quickly to the proper service and finished the ceremony, with many apologies.

MARRIAGE

Up to this date I had had no thought of marriage and, consequently, had made nothing of what little opportunity there was to associate with female society. Now, realizing that I was to settle down in a quiet way as a captain of infantry, I began to think that it was time to marry, if I ever intended to do so. I resolved to take a leave for the purpose of looking for a "household mate."

Recruiting at Zanesville, I had made the acquaintance of the best men, but paid little attention to young ladies, though, from my office window on Main Street, I had observed a quartet known as the "Cassel girls." Their father was the handsomest man in the city, and one of the most respected, and the girls were in a class by themselves. They knew everybody, were accosted by everybody, and were respected and admired by all. They were all fine musicians, and sang in the church choir. They were carefully reared, but their position was such that they felt free to do many things other girls would hesitate to do for fear of criticism.

Everywhere I sought the acquaintance of girls I thought might fill my requisition for a wife. I have always believed that women should have as many rights as men, and that a man and his wife should be equal partners in all that relates to human affairs. From my first recollection, I have been a "Woman's Rights" man, although at that time there were very few, even women, who believed in such rights. There were a few women at this time who dared advocate such things as equal rights in schools and colleges, but they were usually maltreated, insulted, and even made the target for rotten eggs. But that did not change my opinion as to the kind of woman I wished for a partner in life.

I had not been long on leave when I visited Zanesville and sought the acquaintance of the Cassel girls. A friend, Charlie Converse, took me to call, and I met all four. I was greatly attracted by the brilliancy of conversation, beauty of features and bright expression of the second daughter, and asked Miss Hannah Cassel's permission to call again. I have since learned that while discussing my visit with her sisters that night, she remarked, "I am going to have some fun with that fellow."

Although deeply impressed with her beauty and charms, I felt it only fair to explain my views to her and find out whether she possessed the qualities I hoped to secure in a wife before asking her to marry me.

We took many rides and walks together, during which I gradually told her my sole purpose in securing leave of absence was to select a household mate; I told her my story fully, that I was thirty-four, born and raised on a poor man's farm until eighteen, and about my failing at West Point and, ashamed to return to my father, making a living for myself. I described the subsequent sixteen years of struggles and the experience which made me a captain in good standing in the army. I was plain about having no prospective patrimony or no expectations, save the patent cartridge equipment which, with persistent work and improvement, I hoped would finally be adopted by the army to my ultimate profit. I told her, too, of my only other source of financial expectation, my lots and a house in the town of El Paso. Although the town had been practically destroyed by the war and the Mexican War against Maximilian, I believed even then it would some day become a city and my property become valuable.

It was easy to tell her she had impressed me beyond all others by her beauty, vivacity, and her apparent courage to fight the battle of life. In these sixteen years I had satisfied myself I had been endowed with sufficient physical and moral strength and ambition to acquire an independence and the respect of the world, provided I could find a woman endowed with the courage to assist me as an equal partner in life. I had always believed that women should possess the same rights as men; that their needs were equal to those of men; that their aspirations should be in the same direction as those of men; but I knew that imperious custom had forced woman into an inferior position in life, so that the best hopes of many mothers were for their daughters to marry someone who could support them, without other exertion on their part than to adorn themselves. In spite of this prevailing idea I was looking for a woman who would disregard the tyranny of society and undertake to do whatever was necessary in mental and physical labor to acquire such means and reputation as would enable us to leave the world better than we found it; all of this I discussed with her fully and plainly.

She was at this time twenty-two years old. She had had a private school education, including a year at the Catholic convent in the city, but, beyond that, she had improved her mind by books and reading far beyond what was taught at the schools. More, she was liberal minded, had few prejudices and, like myself, was ambitious to play some part in the world. She had many suitors, but, luckily for me, she was heart whole and fancy free. Her parents were in good circumstances, and she and her sisters had always been provided with more luxuries than most, so she realized that if she married, she would have to sacrifice much to become a successful homemaker. Her views of life came not only from her parents, but from her great aunt, Hannah Martin, a cultured English woman, for whom she was named, and with whom she had been associated since childhood. She had the reverence for her aunt that I had for my great grandmother.

I was wedded to my profession, and my salary was a hundred and fifty dollars a month. It would, of course, increase by promotions and length of service pay, but as my stations would probably be among the Indians in the far West, where there was no desirable civilian society, and perhaps but a half dozen ladies at the post, the woman who was willing to become my mate would have to sacrifice all the allurements of Eastern society and content herself with the drumly incidents of military life on the plains. Be sure I showed her I had sufficient sentiment to make a good lover, and so I told her she was the one I wanted for a lifelong partner, asking her to deliberate on it for some days before answering. Shortly she told me she was given to rebel against many of

ANSON MILLS AND NANNIE CASSEL, DAY BEFORE MARRIAGE.

ANSON MILLS, DAY BEFORE MARRIAGE, WITH "BIG FOUR" CASSEL GIRLS.

the conventionalities of society, that she believed she could make all the sacrifices necessary, and was willing to undertake it.

During one of our picnics where there were some half-dozen girls and boys (among the girls I remember best were Lucy and Mame Abbott and Julia Blandy), we took our refreshments to a stream in the woods near the town. After eating, the girls sought the water to wash their fingers, soiled with cakes and jellies. I induced Miss Cassel to come a little way from the rest up the stream, to show her a good place to wash her hands. Then, not knowing others were within hearing, I said, "Miss Cassel, how tall are you?"

She replied, "Five feet, three."

"Just tall enough to enter the army," I answered.

Immediately the girls below began to giggle, and during the rest of the day and the journey home one would occasionally cry out, "Just tall enough to enter the army." I did not hear the last of the incident for some time.

Shortly after, our engagement was announced, and the date of the ceremony set for October 13th.

My leave being about to expire, I returned to Fort Sedgwick, but applied for another leave the first of October, expressing my purpose of getting married.

I had accumulated three thousand dollars in the bank, which I took with me. Miss Cassel and I spent this money together in the stores for such household equipment as we concluded would be necessary. We had our photographs taken the day before we were married.

On the 13th of October we were duly united. We had a very simple wedding, with only relatives and close personal friends of the family present. I remember the venerable Mr. Cushing, a friend of the family, who was then in his eighties. When he came to bid the bride good-bye, he remarked, "Hannah, I am going to kiss you, for this is perhaps the last time I shall ever see you," and it was.

As Miss Cassel in her family and among her intimate friends was always "Nannie," and as I always spoke of her and addressed her by that name after we were married, I shall hereafter refer to her so, thinking it unsuitable in so intimate a reminiscence as this to be too formal.

Earlier I have referred at length to my forebears and the history of my family. Nannie's family is equally as well rooted in American history as mine.

Her father, William Culbertson Cassel, was born in Franklin County, Pennsylvania, in 1817, and was the son of Jacob Cassel, who was born in Lancaster County, Pennsylvania, in 1775. His father was born off the coast of Ireland on a vessel which was wrecked there, and on which his parents (Nannie's great-great-grandparents) were coming from Germany to this country.

Mr. Cassel's mother was Elizabeth Culbertson, born in Franklin County, Pennsylvania, in 1779, and married there to Jacob Cassel, in 1796. The Culbertsons were a Scotch-Irish family, who settled in Pennsylvania before the Revolution, in which many of them took an active part. This family is very completely described in "The Culbertson Genealogy," by Lewis R. Culbertson.

Nannie's mother was Lydia Martin, born in Morgan County, Ohio, in 1822, and married there in 1840. Her family were English and, as one old record states, were largely composed of "jolly, fox-hunting parsons." Her father, Samuel Martin, one of nine children, was born in Trowbridge, England, in 1796. He received an excellent education, studying medicine in London. In 1819 Dr. Martin, after his father's death, started to Liverpool with his older brother, Alfred, to come to America. They were overtaken by a message telling them of their mother's death. They waited over one vessel, so their sisters could join them, and all come together to the new country. One of these sisters was Hannah Hippisly Martin, Nannie's great aunt, who lived with Nannie's parents for many years, and who was affectionately called "Auntie" by all. Nannie received a great part of her training from her, as did the other Cassel children—Elizabeth, Leila, Kate, and the one son Samuel, who died in 1865 at the age of 22.

120

W. C. Cassel.   "Auntie."   Mrs. W. C. Cassel.

THIRD PERIOD

THIRD PERIOD

TRAVELS WEST AND EAST

We arrived at Fort Sedgwick on October 16th.

My quarters were half a knock-down double house, made in Chicago, the other half occupied by the adjutant, Lieutenant Potter.

When Nannie first heard the drums beat for guard mount, she called, "Anson, where in the world did all these officers come from?" referring to the gaily decked soldiers assembling for guard, showing how little she knew of the army. There were only half a dozen officers in the post.

The day we arrived, Mr. and Mrs. Potter asked us to luncheon. Potter sat at the head of the table facing a door opening into the yard.

While we were seating ourselves, a large yellow cat came in, jumped on a chair, and looked over the table. Potter excitedly raised his hands above his head, exclaiming, "Lizzie! Lizzie! Look at that cat. I hate a cat, but damn a yellow cat!"

Nannie as yet knew nothing of the army or the West, and I could see that she was about ready to run, impressed with the idea that Potter had gone stark mad. But my former classmate, though eccentric, was an excellent man and officer, and Nannie grew to like him as her acquaintance with him and the army progressed.

Potter's five-year-old boy often came to our dining room and invited himself to meals. He asked numberless unanswerable questions, one of which—while helping himself to the sugar, was "Why does a sugar bowl have two handles?"

The South Platte country around Fort Sedgwick is supposed to be that visited by Coronado in his far northward explorations from Mexico (see my address to the Society of Indian Wars).

It is also claimed by the Book of Mormon that here were the final battles between the descendants of the two lost tribes of Israel, supposed to have made their way to North America.

Legend has it that one of the tribes developed into a highly civilized white race, the other into a dark-skinned race of roving habits, ancestors of our Indians. The two became enemies and the white race was exterminated; more than a million men, women and children being killed. The book claims this contest between the Indians and the civilized whites, who had built cities and made great advancement in civilization, continued for many hundreds of years throughout the continent with varying defeats and victories, but the final disappearance of the white race occurred in this part of the West.

We purchased a one-horse buggy, with which Nannie and I explored many miles in every direction through the roadless prairie country. The only road followed the North Platte toward Denver. The Indians were comparatively peaceable, and we went where we would, with an escort of two or three cavalrymen.

For household help, Nannie had a woman cook, and her soldier husband, Lenon, did many chores about the house, but otherwise Nannie managed the household; made my shirts, underwear and stockings, doing all the mending and keeping me neat. We apportioned certain allowances from my salary for necessities, cutting everything to the lowest possible cost. Table supplies purchased from the commissary were to cost no more than thirty dollars per month. It was Nannie's work to keep within the allowances, so that we might lay by money each month for a rainy day. She kept this rule throughout our equal partnership.

Although her education in household economy and management was incomplete, she was quick to learn. But her time was not all spent in housekeeping. The garrison of five companies of the 18th Infantry and two of the 2d Cavalry had an occasional dance or ball, which she greatly enjoyed and became prominent as a dancer and in the social life of the post.

There were no settlements for a hundred miles in any direction. Julesburg, three miles across the river, was one of the largest stations because of its proximity to the post. The river was a torrential stream, half a mile wide, and its quicksands made it almost impassable. In the winter, when ice crowded the channels, it was difficult to cross with any kind of vehicle. The nearest posts were Fort Omaha, Nebraska, three hundred and fifty miles east, and Fort D. A. Russell, at Cheyenne, two hundred and fifty miles west. These distant points were the only ones with a sufficient degree of civilization to entice visits. The Union Pacific, just completed to these points, with the capable assistance of the army, adopted the generous policy of giving passes to officers and their families desiring to visit these remote posts, so that during our six months' stay at Sedgwick we attended a regimental ball of the 9th Infantry at Omaha, and a regimental ball of the 30th Infantry at Fort D. A. Russell. These were about the only diversions we had from the monotonous life of the garrison at Sedgwick.

Nannie knew the expense of visiting home would be so great she probably would not see her family again for two years, and she did not; but she was sometimes homesick, and more than once I saw her with dampened eyes.

Feeling the necessity for a large army obviated by the nearly accomplished reconstruction, Congress passed a law decreasing the army from sixty to thirty thousand, in 1870. The law stopped promotions pending that event to absorb as many surplus officers as possible. In April, 1869, my regiment was ordered to Atlanta, Georgia, with five others, to be consolidated into three regiments of infantry. Half the officers of these regiments were on sick leave or detached service, but when it was announced that the officers retained would be those best suited for service, nearly every ill officer in each regiment immediately recovered! No one wanted to be ordered home for discharge, with even a year's pay and allowances.

We left by rail to Omaha, took steamboat to Memphis, and finished the journey to Atlanta by rail.

The influx of these six regiments, with almost a full complement of officers, rendered even the quarters of a complete regimental post insufficient. The unmarried officers lived in tents, the married ones crowding the houses. It often happened that eight captains with their wives would be quartered in eight rooms. This discomfort, added to summer heat, rendered life almost unbearable, but deciding who was to remain and who to be sent on waiting orders occupied time. Meanwhile, concentration of too many people caused various contagious diseases, especially typhoid, to become epidemic.

However, the consolidation was finally accomplished, the 16th merging with the 18th, retaining that designation, and I retaining my captaincy in Company H.

General Ruger was mustered out as General of Volunteers and assigned to the colonelcy of the 18th. A most excellent executive officer, he soon had us organized and assigned to comfortable quarters with nearly all the officers present. General Upton was assigned as lieutenant colonel. He was then developing his tactics and selected Captain Christopher and myself to review with him every Saturday the progress he had made, and to apply during the week his new principles of tactics in drilling our companies, and occasionally a battalion.

Nannie and I had now lived long enough together to discover our appraisement of each other was correct. We each had sufficient sentiment to make us permanent lovers and, better still, we each had such perfect digestions and such an intense sense of the humorous as to make us content with our surroundings wherever and whatever they might be. Best of all, we were each blessed with enough courage, self-denial and ambition.

I purchased foot-power lathes, drills, etc., to develop models of my various patents in belts and equipment. I installed them in one of her best rooms in each succeeding one of perhaps twenty posts, soiling the carpets with grease, filings and shavings, which would have driven most wives mad. Nannie not only endured patiently, but encouraged and assisted in the work. She was also my amanuensis for sixteen years, until I became proficient on the typewriter, I believe the first army officer to do so.

The Secretary of War ordered that any officers of the newly organized regiments of infantry and artillery who so desired could apply for transfer to the cavalry, to fill the vacancies caused by the stoppage of promotions. I was so restive and likely to be contentious that duty in the infantry, where I would have little to do, I feared might lead me into controversies. I thought the better opening for success would be in the cavalry, but as I knew the cavalry would be among the hostile Indians and farthest away from civilization, I left it to Nannie to decide whether our mutual success would be enhanced by the transfer and whether she was willing to make it. She decided that my prospects would be bettered by participation in the hazardous and more serious duties of the cavalry, so I applied for transfer.

After recovering from a severe case of typhoid that summer, Nannie, by her lively character and natural accomplishments, assumed a prominent place in the regiment, and was one of the chief organizers of the many dances, balls, and other social gatherings which we had during our stay at this post.

A large regimental ball was scheduled for December 29th, and Nannie invited her sisters, Lulie and Katie, to visit her in time for this event. In those days it was unusual for young ladies to travel long distances alone, and their parents were uneasy about the journey. They should have arrived at Christmas, but floods intervened, and they reached Atlanta on the 28th at four o'clock in the morning.

I wrote my parents-in-law immediately, handing the letter to Captain Ogden, who promised to mail it. Some days after, I received a telegram inquiring what had become of the two girls. On questioning Captain Ogden, I found he still had the letter in his pocket!

Lulie and Katie were beautiful, and in the prime of their

girlhood, and were much sought after at dances and other social gatherings.

Among their admirers was Captain Kline of the regiment, an efficient but reserved young officer, who took a fancy to Lulie, and early asked if I would permit his attentions to my sister-in-law, to which, of course, I found no objection. On account of his reserve, he had more difficulty in speaking than I had in similar circumstances, and another embarrassment intervened when he was ordered with his company to Barnett, South Carolina, a full day's journey away. However, a court martial was being organized, and knowing how agreeable duty at Atlanta would be for him, friends procured his assignment to the court.

Still he was not entirely happy. We had only four rooms and a kitchen, and were therefore pretty crowded; and the hall was our dining room. Nannie, Katie, Lulie and I occupied the sitting room in the evenings, so his chances alone with Lulie were few.

The court, of which I was president, often had officers absent for a few days at a time. Regulations prescribed that a returning absentee retire until the case being tried was finished; the formula of the presiding officer being, "Those members of the court who have not participated in previous proceedings will please retire." One evening, when Captain Kline appeared rather early, and we were engaged in conversation in which Lulie and the Captain did not appear to be interested, I called out, "The members of this court who have not participated in previous proceedings will please now retire," whereupon Nannie, Katie and I sprang to our feet and retired to our room upstairs.

In one of her letters to her mother, Nannie wrote, "Doesn't the mother of Pauline say, in the 'Lady of Lyons,' something about 'losing a daughter, but gaining a prince.' Well, if being a mighty good, honest fellow is any claim to royalty, you will gain a prince surely when Major Kline becomes a son-in-law."

No two girls ever had a gayer time for the four months they

were with us. They had a large mirror with a dressing table under it, and when they left we discovered they had worn out the carpet for a space of five feet in diameter in front of it, primping before the glass.

They left us reluctantly the first of May, much to the disappointment of the numerous unmarried youngsters. Lulie shortly after married Captain Kline. Katie married Mr. George H. Stewart, of Zanesville, where they still live.

Next autumn, with two months' leave, we went to visit my wife's parents, whom she had not seen for two years. Nannie was delighted when a passenger, surmising from our conduct that we were bride and groom, asked if we were on our honeymoon.

Mr. and Mrs. Cassel were happy to have us with them again. In these two months I made a most intimate acquaintance with my father-in-law. He took me everywhere, to his office in the daytime and to his clubs at night. An expert driver and an admirer of horses and horse racing, he often drove me behind fast trotting animals, sometimes to the races. Neither he nor Mrs. Cassel, like my own parents, attended church. All four greatly respected all religious denominations, but saw none they honestly believed was the only true church.

Mrs. Cassel was very affectionate, and her children were very near to her, so she was much distressed at Nannie's long absence. Mr. Cassel asked me if it would not be better for me to resign, offering to start me in his occupation, the milling business. He proposed to give me sufficient means and go with me to Kansas to establish the enterprise. I had seen enough of the world to understand the uncertainty and vicissitudes of business life compared to a commission in the regular army. So I thanked him, but said that, notwithstanding I knew it would be a great gratification to Mrs. Cassel, I was certain of my present calling for life, and although my compensation was slight, Nannie was satisfied, and loved the profession as much as I did. In this point of view he finally concurred, and Mrs. Cassel also became reconciled.

Returning to my regiment at Atlanta, I found my company with E Company had been ordered to Laurens Court House, South Carolina, because South Carolina was then in the throes of reconstruction, with carpetbaggers and Ku Klux Klan in full swing.

We had rail transportation to Newberry, but from Newberry the railroad had been denuded of rolling stock, so that our journey to Laurens was made on a handcar, propelled by two soldiers.

The two companies were quartered in abandoned Confederate residences. Nannie and I stayed at Mr. George F. Mosely's hotel. He was a kind and generous host, who took particular care to meet our wants. During the few weeks Nannie remained we made many acquaintances, being invited out to dine by the best people in the town.

One dinner was given by Col. Wm. D. Simpson (later Governor and still later Chief Justice of his State), previously in affluent circumstances, but now poor. In the dining room he remarked that as his servants had all left him he had devised a round center table which turned on its support to take their place. All the courses were arranged so, as a guest wanted anything, he could turn this table until the contents arrived opposite his plate!

We had been guests at the hotel for several weeks when a young man in the uniform of a captain of cavalry arrived at the hotel to see me privately. In my room he told me he was not an army officer, but a United States marshal, direct from the Secretary of War, with warrants for the arrest of about sixty prominent persons of Laurens County. He did not wish to arrest all for whom he had warrants, but only those most guilty of participation in the riots and murders. Under instructions from the Secretary he read me the names on the warrants and asked suggestions as to whom he should eliminate. Among these names was that of my host. As I had heard nothing to lead me to think him guilty, I suggested that his name be stricken from the list, which was done.

I immediately sent Nannie to Newberry on the handcar. At one place on the way the Ku Klux obstructed the rails with ties presumably to rescue prisoners that we might attempt to spirit away. At another place, where the highway was near the rails, she met General Carlin at the head of the 16th Infantry marching toward Laurens with the band playing martial airs. More than a thousand hilarious and frenzied negroes of all kinds, from the aged to babes in arms, followed the band. Nannie stopped the car to enjoy the amusing spectacle, and finally burst out in a laugh, when her servant, Maria, who had gone with her, exclaimed, in disgust, "Mrs. Mills, niggers ain't got no sense nohow!"

That night I arranged a room in the abandoned railroad depot for the prisoners, disposing my men behind cotton bales piled upon the platform to resist any efforts at rescue by the Ku Klux organizations. The marshal informed me that Lieutenant Colonel Carlin would arrive at about twelve o'clock with sixteen companies of infantry, and convey the prisoners to Columbia.

Two small detachments, under the command of Lieutenants Adams and Bates, made the arrests, while Lieutenant Hinton, officer of the day, took charge of the prisoners as they arrived. The marshal went first with one, then with another, detachment. Colonel Jones, the sheriff, was one of the first arrested, and by ten o'clock we had some fifteen of the sixty mentioned. My host, Mr. Mosely, appeared and said excitedly, "Why, Colonel, what does all this mean? Is it true that you have arrested Colonel Jones?"

"Yes," I said, "he is in the building."

"Well, Colonel, I want to see him."

Fearing some complication, I said, "Mr. Mosely, if you will take my advice you will go back to your hotel and remain quiet."

"But, Colonel, Jones is my brother-in-law. We are in business together. Are you going to take him away? I must see him if you take him away—no one will be here to attend to his business. I must see him. Does his family know he has been arrested?"

I replied, "I don't know," and advised him to go quietly to the hotel and remain there until the excitement subsided.

He became offended and said, "Colonel Mills, after all the kindness I have shown you and Mrs. Mills, I think it is as little as you can do in return to allow me the poor privilege of seeing my friend in his distress."

"Very well," said I, "you can see him," and calling the officer of the day, Lieutenant Hinton, I gave the necessary instructions. Upon Mosely's entrance, Colonel Jones called his name and proclaimed his pleasure in seeing him. The marshal pulled out his list and said, "Excuse me, is your name George F. Mosely?" Informed that it was, the marshal served the warrant and made him a prisoner. When I entered he burst into tears, declaring he was the biggest fool in South Carolina; that I had given him the best advice he had ever had, and he had not known enough to take it. He begged me to tell his family his condition, which I did.

Later, a Mr. A. Kruse, a United States commissioner, served a writ of *habeas corpus* upon me, demanding the body of prisoner S. D. Garlington. I had no experience with writs of *habeas corpus,* and was at a loss what answer to make. To delay him until Carlin's arrival, I questioned his authority as such commissioner. Courteously he informed me that he had a commission at home with President Johnson's signature. He left, and soon returned with the document. I invited him to my room, from which I had a view of the Newberry highway, over which Carlin's command would approach, and kept him there until I saw Carlin's command. Then I told him it was an army regulation that an officer, not in a permanent station, only commanded within a radius of one mile, and that I had a senior in the person of Lieutenant Colonel Carlin of the 16th Infantry, then approaching, the proper person on whom to serve the writ. Kruse accepted the situation, and I introduced him to Colonel Carlin, who, however, directed me to endorse upon the writ "refused, by order of the Secretary of War."

A Mr. Hugh Farley (brother of Farley of the U. S. Ordnance Corps), reputed to be at the head of the Ku Klux which gathered in numbers, approached Colonel Carlin frequently with requests to see different prisoners. As he gave no good reason, his requests were refused. He followed Carlin's command to camp that night, strenuously insisting upon another request; whereupon the marshal arrested him, his name on one of the warrants having been omitted at my suggestion.

Sixteen were carried to Columbia, South Carolina, and imprisoned in the State penitentiary, but I understood none of them were convicted.

Order being restored in Laurens, I was directed to take station with my two companies at Columbia. There being no public quarters, the quartermaster's agent took us to an old-fashioned southern building. It was comfortable and commodious, with outside quarters for the colored servants. This house had belonged to the late Dr. Gibbs, father of a classmate of mine, Wade Hampton Gibbs, who went South, joined the Confederates, and became a Colonel on the staff of General Lee.

Major Van Voast, 18th Infantry, with his wife, arrived two days later, assumed command of the post, and took quarters with us in the Gibbs House.

Carpetbagging was in its prime about this period. The governor, Chamberlain, had been appointed by the Federal authorities. Both senate and house elected under Federal laws were almost entirely colored. The president of the senate and the speaker of the house (Moses) extended the privileges of the floors of those chambers to Major Van Voast, myself, and our wives, and, partly to acquaint ourselves with governmental affairs and partly through curiosity, we often attended, the Major and I dressed in uniform.

The trouble at Laurens originated by the Ku Klux arming themselves and arresting and murdering the county officers.

Carpetbaggers and negro supporters proposed a large army to protect them against the Ku Klux. While we were at a session of the house, a bill to create a State force of some thirty negro regiments and money to buy thirty thousand Remington arms was introduced. Seeing the folly of placing so much power in the hands of the colored people, some white man introduced an amendment that the colonels of these regiments should be selected from the regular army. A colored member denounced the amendment, protesting that the two army officers were present to promote this bill, and should be ejected from the floor. This placed us in a very embarrassing position. To leave the hall in indignation would betray weakness, so we sat it out for an hour, hearing many bitter and insulting references.

Knowing I wished to transfer to the cavalry, Colonel Carlin, who was going to Washington, offered me seven days' leave and to introduce me to the Secretary of War. But, Captain Mack had already arranged my transfer, and on January 1, 1871, I was transferred to the 3d Cavalry and ordered to the headquarters of the regiment at Fort Halleck, Nevada, and to proceed thence *via* San Francisco and San Pedro to Fort Whipple, Arizona.

Nannie's Impressions of the West

In a letter to her parents from Washington, January 17th, Nannie describes our good-bye to our company, as follows:

I can not tell you how sorry I was to leave Columbia. I really had become very much attached to the place, and I believe like it better than any city I was ever in. I suppose one never knows how much one is thought of 'til they take their departure. The day before we left, Anson received a note requesting his presence at his company quarters. He went over, and saw a table nicely covered with a red cloth, and on it *something* which was covered up. The first sergeant then made him a little speech in behalf of the company and then, with a majestic wave of his hand, uncovered the article and presented him with a splendid pair of epaulets and a case containing two very handsome pistols, the whole costing nearly eighty dollars. On a paper inside was written "The compliments of Company H, 18th Infantry, to their beloved Captain, Anson Mills, 3d Cavalry." I went with Anson when he bade his old company good-bye, and it really was very sad. I cried, and Anson almost did. He went along shaking hands with each one. It is something to be *very* proud of when sixty men without one exception like their commander, and one of them told Anson that there was not a man in the company but regretted his going away. I do not believe there are many company commanders who have won the affections of their men so completely.

We could take but little baggage, so in Washington I asked a delay of thirty days to leave our belongings with Nannie's parents in Zanesville. General Sherman had, a few days before, ordered that there should be no more delays. When I applied, he said, "Well, Captain Mills, I can not revoke my order; but in your case I don't object to your taking a 'French,' and I don't think your colonel will make any trouble with you if you arrive thirty days late. Should he do so, refer him to me and I'll see that you get into no trouble in the matter."

The headquarters and band at Halleck were ordered to Fort Whipple *via* San Francisco, where I purchased an ambulance for the land journey.

We sailed February 2d on the Government transport Orizaba. We had never been to sea, and as it was a beautiful day and the waters of the bay were smooth as glass, we congratulated ourselves that we could hardly have a bad time. But when we struck the bar outside, the ship seemed to rise at least fifty feet, and otherwise moved and rolled in every possible manner. Nannie proved to be a poor sailor, which affliction she retained through life. I fared better, but was not immune and never have been.

Among the many military passengers was Captain I. M. Hoag, who occupied a stateroom next ours. As we passed down the smooth bay he claimed never to be seasick. I soon recovered sufficiently to take lunch, after which I took a chair by our stateroom to be near Nannie. The stewardess, passing, asked if she could not bring Nannie some "nice jelly cake," when Hoag's coarse voice broke out, "Jelly cake! jelly cake! Oh, my God, why does that woman want to come around talking about jelly cake! Give me my bucket. Give me my bucket!"

We arrived at San Pedro (Drum Barracks) near Wilmington, March 4th.

Nannie described the eventful march from San Pedro to Whipple Barracks in letters to her parents, better than I could describe it now, as follows:

March 5th.

My Dear Mother:

As you may imagine, we are very busy making arrangements for our wagon trip. Anson is having our vehicle fixed up 'til a queen might be proud to ride in it. He is having it covered with white canvas, and he bought an elegant green blanket to line the top to keep off the heat and protect the eyes.   It has curtains all 'round to roll up to let the air in, and at night we can take out the seats, make up a bed in the bottom, and there is a large front curtain which shuts everything in and keeps out the damp.   He is going to have pockets inside to put little articles in, and altogether it is as convenient and elegant a thing as one could imagine, and I am very proud of it, especially as he got it on purpose for me.   We expect to have a very nice time on the route.   There are quite a number of officers going, but no other ladies.   I am very glad we are going with this party, as we would not have had as good a chance probably for a long time, and very likely would have had to go by stage, which would have been very unpleasant.

Anson is ordered on a court martial at Date Creek, which is on our road, so we will have to stop there.   We received a letter from Lieut. Ebstein (you remember his picture in the group), who is at Date Creek, asking us to stop there.

I do not expect to get really settled this year, for there does seem to be some truth in the old saying about the first of January determining the rest of the year.

If possible I will write to you while we are on the march, but if I do not you need not be surprised, although I think I shall, but you know it is very hard to write after riding so far and getting so tired, but I shall try to write to you if it is only a few lines, so as to keep you from being anxious.

This place (Drum Barracks) is on the coast and twenty-five miles from Los Angeles, which latter place is said to be the paradise of the whole United States.   A woman came here today from there, and she was carrying in her hand a branch broken from an orange tree, just *full* of large oranges, just as we at home might have a branch full of apples.

March 9th.

We actually did leave this morning, and made twenty-five miles, which is a pretty long trip for a first day's march.   The day was lovely, and the road a nice, level one, nothing particularly interesting, however, 'til we neared Los Angeles, which has been called the garden of the United States, and then we came to the orange groves with the ripe fruit hanging on the boughs, peach trees in bloom, lemon trees, and we saw in one place some men harvesting barley. Rank green weeds grew all along the roadside, in some cases as high as your head, while pretty little red and yellow wild flowers covered the meadows, and the meadow larks sang so gaily that it inspired Anson to repeat a piece of poetry on the lark, not that I mean to say that my hubby dear mounted the little songster to spout forth the flow of poetic words, but the subject of the piece was "The Lark." My first day's experience in this line has been very pleasant. We are camped in a beautiful spot before getting to which we had to cross one of my much dreaded streams, which was nothing at all and wouldn't scare a chippy. Los Angeles is quite a town, and if any angels take a notion to visit this mundane sphere and namesake, I advise them to put up at the Pico House, where we went in to dinner. The house is a clean, nice place, Brussels carpet, lace curtains, mirrors, piano, etc., in the parlor, and a very nice dinner— fresh peas, cauliflower, etc.; but that which struck my fancy most was an open court in the center of the building in which a fountain was playing, and in a gallery running all 'round the second story, looking down on this fountain, were fastened numerous plants in pots and bird cages. As we left the house three Mexicans were playing on a harp, violin and flageolet, which completed a very romantic picture.

We invested eighteen dollars in apples, lemons and oranges, and Anson also found some fresh *tomatoes,* all, of course, grown in the open air, for it never frosts here. It looks strange to see the tropical fruit growing while snow-capped mountains look down on them.

Our tent is pitched, our bed made down, and everything is very easy; our only regret is that dear Lizzie did not come with us. Anson repeatedly expresses his regret that she did not.

Our carriage is perfectly splendid; in fact I *don't* see how people can possibly *exist* without a carriage.

I was made very happy last night by receiving a letter from home, the first one since we left. It was addressed to Drum Barracks. We have not as yet received those directed to Halleck, but they will be forwarded to us. We also got two newspapers, and one the day before, which were devoured.

March 12th.

We are camped in the loveliest spot you ever saw. A little mountain stream runs rapidly down on one side of us, the mountains on another, the wagon road on another, and on the other the valley stretches miles and miles away in the direction where lies our road. The ground (Cocomonga Ranch) belongs to a Mexican who owns a tract of land nine miles square, over fifty thousand acres. One hundred and seventy of it is planted in a vineyard. All of this work is done by Indians, civilized, of course. Anson brought one boy down to see me, or rather for me to see him. They jabbered away in Mexican together at a great rate. Anson can speak a good deal of Spanish, carried on a conversation very well, and is fast relearning what he had forgotten of it.

I forgot to tell you that we saw flying fish and porpoises while we were coming down on the steamship.

Last night Anson and I climbed a mountain, and a mighty steep one it was, but we were rewarded when we reached the summit by a most lovely view on all sides. I think the mountain is probably an extinct volcano, as something like lava was all over it. It also had quantities of wild flowers on it.

The nearer you get to the Indians the less you hear of them. There are no wild Indians this side of the Colorado River, and very few tame ones. It is perfectly safe to travel alone as far as the Colorado River, which is almost half of our journey; after that, an escort is necessary, although the mail coach travels almost all the way with no escort at all. You need have no fears for us, as even if they do not furnish a regular escort in the Indian country, there are enough of us to do without, as there are thirty men in the party. By the time you get this we will probably be at Date Creek, where we stop for a while on that court.

March 21.

When I last wrote to you we had gone ten miles on the desert; we have now gone one hundred and twenty-three miles over the same desert, only some was worse, and I suppose it is the same thing until we reach the Rio Colorado, which is now only forty-nine miles. To fully describe the trip since my letter would be impossible, for one can have but a faint idea of it unless they were to go over the same country. I had no idea that such a forlorn district was comprised within the limits of the United States. To begin at the beginning, after leaving the Sulphur Springs of which I told you, we traveled eighteen miles through deep sand, which is the hardest thing imaginable on the poor mules, for their feet being very small sink deep in, the last few miles being through choking dust. We reached Indian Wells, a large station consisting of one house, or, more properly speaking, hovel, where they *sell* water. There are some poor Indians here whom one can not help but pity. They had heard that the government intended moving them away onto a reservation, and when they found our train was coming said they wanted to see an officer. The chief and the interpreter (who spoke Indian and Spanish) came down, and Anson went over to talk to them. The poor old chief said he did not want to harm any one, but he was born in that place, and he wanted to die there, which assertion you would wonder at, could you but see the place and know that they have not even tents or huts to live in, but lie down in the sand. Anson brought them over to our tent to give them something to eat. The old chief was, I suppose, gotten up for the occasion, and was attired in a clean white shirt and a hat, that's all, which was at the same time unique and cool. They both shook hands with Anson on leaving, and trudged off, barefooted, through the sand and cactus to their home (?). It made me feel badly to see them, the descendants of Montezuma, reduced to such a state of humiliation. They have a strange custom in regard to their dead. They burn the body, and then break over the ashes all the oyas or earthen jars which once belonged to him. The next day we went eighteen miles through a dreadful sand-storm, which blinded and choked men and mules. After reaching Martinez, however, the sand stopped blowing over us, or we might have been compelled to eat for dinner the same kind of pies which we used to make when we were children—mud pies.

The next day we traveled 26 miles to "Dos Palmas," which means two palms; but someone burnt up one of them, so the name is hardly proper now. Anson told me to be sure to tell you that we have seen a real palm tree, and he went bathing under its foliage. It was indeed an oasis in the desert to see this beautiful tree standing alone in its glory. I wish you could have seen it, for it was most lovely. Something else there was not quite so lovely; we had some rolls baked by the man who keeps the station house, and for ten large rolls he charged three dollars in coin. The next day at half past five we were on our way again, traveled sixteen miles, where they rested and watered the mules, and then on again to a dry camp, which explains itself, there being no water for the mules. We could carry with us enough to drink, but in the morning we rubbed off our faces with a wet towel, for we could not spare water for a greater ablution. We were off very early next morning, for the mules could get no water 'til we had traveled twenty-four miles. There is a stretch here of thirty-five miles where they always have to make a dry camp. Three more days and we reach the river, where we rest a few days, and then only six more days. At Martinez, one of the mules had a great big piece taken out of its breast by a bull dog, and Anson actually turned Vet. and sewed it up, and did it well, too. A horse died at this place last night, and today the Indians are making merry over its carcass, eating it. I was interrupted while writing this letter by the tent blowing down.

March 28.

We camped at Ehrenberg four days, during that time had two dreadful wind-storms. Anson had great big stones piled on all the tent pins, as the ground was not very hard, but the tent shook and flapped until it would have been almost a relief to have had it go over. We went to bed, however, and in about fifteen minutes after, a terrific gust brought the whole thing down with a crash. The worst feature of it was that it tore a piece out of the tent so that it could not be put up again, so we very coolly slept under the ruins all night. This is Tuesday, and we expect to be at Date Creek on Saturday. They say they are making great preparations there, and are going to have a dance, and expect some ladies down from Fort Whipple.

March 29th.

We came twenty-eight miles today. Wind-storm part of the way, which is heavy enough to make us fear another blow-down, so we are going to sleep in the ambulance. Anson has taken out the seats and we will have the bed right on the floor, which is large enough to be very comfortable. I am in it now and feel perfectly satisfied, as I have none of that nervous, uncomfortable feeling, which the flapping of a tent in the wind is sure to give one.

DATE CREEK, April 1st.

Although this is All Fools' Day, what I am going to tell you is no joke, but sober reality. Yesterday found us forty-five miles from the creek, and as Captain Meinhold, Mr. Kimball, one of the wagons and four mounted men were going to make it in one day while the rest of the party would have to be two days, we concluded to go on with the small escort, as everyone assured us there was not the least bit of danger. We rode gaily along, and were within eleven miles of the post, when Anson saw one of the horsemen ride up to something, stop and, taking out his carbine, cock it. He looked again, saw a lot of wagons, and said, "there is a train." We rode a few yards farther and found that a train of five wagons and forty-

eight mules had been attacked by Indians (as we afterwards
learned only a few hours before we got there). Three miles
before we reached there I forgot to tell you that we heard a
wailing sort of sound and saw a stray mule. This sound was
undoubtedly a signal from an Indian sentinel to the party
robbing the train, giving them warning that another party was
coming, and for them to get off. The Indians were no doubt
at work on the train when we heard this noise. Imagine the
feelings of all. We did not know but that Indians were lurk-
ing behind every bush. They had cut the harness from all the
mules and captured all of them excepting three. They had
emptied out sack after sack of flour and carried off the sacks
to make clothes, leaving the flour piled all around. Boxes
were broken open, and it really was a dreadful sight, when the
position of affairs which we were in was thought of, and my
being there was the first thing that they all thought of. They
concluded to turn 'round and go to meet the rest of the train
to give them warning, as well as for the safety of ourselves.
For one moment I wanted to cry, the next I laughed actually a
little bit, and after that I was not in the least afraid. Anson
directed me not to shoot until they got pretty close, if we came
across them. I laid the pistol on the seat of the ambulance,
and my hand on the pistol, ready to cock it at a moment's
warning, and I feel sure if Mr. Lo had made his appearance I
should have hurt at least one of them. They supposed by not
seeing any bodies lying around that the men had escaped to the
post and sent men out after the Indians. We met our train,
and camped for the night. The next morning (today) we
started for the post. When we came up to where the attack
was made we found that soldiers had been sent and were
guarding the place. I should have been glad that all this scare
happened in order to teach everybody caution, but that it came
too late to teach one poor fellow, and perhaps another, for one
teamster was killed and another badly wounded, and they were
both lying somewhere near when we came up, but the wounded
one must have been unconscious or he would have heard us

and let us know he was there. There were eight men with this captured train, plenty to have defended it had they been prepared, but in an Indian country, they were traveling with but two guns and three rounds of ammunition. It has taught me one good lesson. I shall never go outside of the post without a sufficient escort, and when we get to Whipple I never mean to go even to Prescott, which is only a mile distant, but mean to stay inside of the post 'til we change stations. Everybody has felt so safe all about here, and ladies from this post would ride with only one gentleman for miles and miles over the hills, but they are well scared now. This train was mostly filled with government stores, and I am very much afraid that the papers will make a big talk about it, and as it was so close to ours, you will think it was ours, and worry unnecessarily about it before you receive my letter. You need have no fears about our safety, as there is no danger of their attacking soldiers that travel in such numbers as we will hereafter.

We were very happy in getting a lot of letters today which had been sent down from Whipple. We got three of home written to Halleck, one from Texas, Washington, Kentucky, Columbia, London, Fort Shaw, Fort Laramie. Quite a variety, and as another mail comes in tonight, we expect some more in the morning.

I am sorry to hear of dear mother's being so sick after we left, but glad she is well again.

Mrs. Ebstein has her sister with her. They are very pleasant and very kind to us. They tell us that Whipple is one of the healthiest of places, and also has about the best quarters in the territory.

I forgot to tell you that one of the savages dropped a quiver full of arrows as he was hurrying off with his plunder, and one of the soldiers gave it to me. The quiver is an ugly thing, but I shall bring you one of the arrows when we come home next time as a memento of our first, and I hope last, Indian scare.

April 21.   (Fort Whipple, Ariz.)

We have been here a week, and both of us like the post very well, although it is far from being a handsome post either on the outside or inside, but you know one's content is measured in a great degree by comparison with others that surround you, so we are more than contented with a log house, when we remember that Fort Whipple is one of the few posts in this territory where they have any quarters at all, almost all being quartered in tents, men, women and children. We have fixed up very comfortably, have the carpet on the parlor and gunny sacks on the dining room and bedroom. We have the damask and lace curtains up at the parlor windows, which are arranged so as to hang a good piece from the windows, making a sort of bow window (bowed the wrong way, however), and as it stands a good way into the room it helps fill up, which is a very good thing, as articles of furniture are very scarce at present; the company carpenter is busily at work. He has made us one table and a place to hang clothes. He was fixing the latter, and after he had finished I gave him some newspapers to read and some oranges, when he informed me that he could make anything I wanted, that he hadn't much to do and might as well do that as anything else. I suppose you would like to see how our house is arranged as to rooms, so I will make a plan of the ground floor, and if you can find any other floor you are smarter than I. I wish I could draw, and I would send you a sketch of the view from our window, which is very beautiful, mountains covered with pine. The wind roaring through the pines sounds just like the cars. Anson has laughed a great deal at me because I vowed that never would I leave Fort Whipple 'til we changed stations or went home, and actually I hadn't been in the post twenty-four hours before I was off for town with Mrs. King, and have been down town once since then. There is no danger between here and town, as it is only a short distance, and before one gets out of calling distance of the post the hospital is reached, and before you get out of sound of that the town is reached. There is not

much in Prescott to tempt one, and well it is for our pockets
that this is so, for the price of some things would make your
hair stand on end, although other things are quite reasonable.
Luckily for us we can get anything we want almost in the commissary, as it is excellently supplied. Everything has fallen
in price even in Prescott, and flour there is now only thirty-
six dollars a barrel; it was forty-two a short time ago. We
only pay seven dollars in the commissary. Butter is two dollars, eggs the same. I saw some of the commonest kind of
heavy Delft soup plates marked *fifteen* dollars a dozen. We
bought a lamp in San Francisco for which we paid seventy-five
cents. Mrs. King has two just like it which cost five dollars
each, and a parlor lamp like that which cost us three dollars
in San Francisco was sold here for twenty-five dollars, and
kerosene oil is only five dollars a gallon. Mrs. King tells a
good joke on the chaplain. She went with him to town one
day to assist him in making some purchases. After buying
some things and paying for them he spied some quart cans for
filling lamps, empty, of course. He wanted one, so asked the
price. He was told "seven dollars." The chaplain put down
his bundles and money, raised his hands, heaved a deep groan
and uttered his favorite ejaculation, "tre-men-jious." There
is only one lady here besides myself, and fortunately she is a
very pleasant one, Mrs. King. Tell Gussie Porter I met her
friend Mrs. King at Camp Halleck, not the Mrs. King who is
here, but another one. She met Gussie at Lancaster, and is
now in our regiment. She was very pleasant.

Nannie describes this journey so completely I can add little
to it.

Mr. Lummis, librarian of the Los Angeles Public Library,
asked me, in 1908, as one having something to do with the
development of the country, to write something descriptive
of its wonderful growth, to be placed in an album for stran-
gers visiting the library. I contributed the following:

In 1871, as Captain 3d Cavalry, with the headquarters and band, my wife in an ambulance, I traveled from San Pedro to Whipple Barracks, Prescott, Arizona. The route lay through Los Angeles, then a small adobe village, where we stopped March 9th at the Little Pico House, then by the now beautiful City of Redlands, at that time a waterless cactus desert, and through the Salton Sink.

In all the tide of time I think there has not been a more instructive example of the efforts of man to "replenish the earth" than shown by the brave men of Southern California in the intervening thirty-seven years.

To those who may look over this volume of autographs in the future, I think this simple statement of facts will be more interesting than any literary effort I could possibly render.

The desert over which we traveled, purchasing water at twenty-five cents a bucket, is now productive and beautiful. The Salton Sink, through which we passed, is a depression in the earth one hundred and fifty miles long by seventy-five wide, with its lowest point two hundred and fifty-six feet below sea level. It was formerly the northern end of the Gulf of California, but ages past was cut off by the sand and silt deposited by floods of the Colorado River, the water evaporating in the arid atmosphere and extreme heat. Immense deposits of salt from evaporated sea water were visible, and we saw on the foot of the adjacent mountains the water-mark of the sea level.

We arrived at Fort Whipple on April 14th, only to be ordered to Fort McDowell on the Verde River, one hundred and twenty-five miles distant, over an almost impassable road. Nannie tells the story of that journey:

May 12 (NEW RIVER).

Our first three days' travel was very pleasant, as we had good roads, and it is much better to travel with one's own company. We have four mules in our ambulance, the back seat

of which I occupy alone in my glory as Anson rides his horse.
We have five six-mule wagons, a teamster, of course, to each,
and over seventy men, so you see we have a very large escort.
Our fourth day's travel was a little the worst of anything I
have ever seen.   Anson and Mr. Wessels have traveled a great
deal and over very bad roads, but they both say that this was
the worst one that they have ever seen.   You may judge how
bad it was when we were from seven o'clock in the morning
'til six at night going about fifteen miles, and the wagons were
an hour later.   The first nine miles was over rocks that jolted
the ambulance so that I could hardly sit in the seat, and I was
almost wearied out.   The rest of the road was up hill and down
hill, and the most terrible hills that I ever saw—they were
almost perpendicular.   I walked several miles, because the
hills were so bad I was afraid to ride.   Anyone living in the
States would think it an utter impossibility to take vehicles up
some places where we went.   One wagon was upset, and that
of course caused a delay.   You would have been amused to
see how they brought one wagon up a hill.   The wagons were
all lightly loaded and had six mules; they put an extra pair
of mules in, one man rode one of the wheel mules, another
walked on one side with a whip, and two boys were on the
other with stones, pelting the mules, and with a volley of oaths
and cracking of whips, up they came.   One wagon was eased
down a hill by twenty men taking hold of a rope behind, and
another was helped up with the men's assistance.   It was a
wearisome day for men and mules.   This morning, when we
were about a mile out, the lead bar of our ambulance broke,
which caused another delay to fix.   Mr. Wessels' horse got
lame, and a horse kicked one of the mules so badly that they
couldn't use him.   We have had a chapter of accidents for
two days, and in addition, today we ran across a fresh mocca-
sin track, evidently made today.

May 18th (CAMP McDOWELL).

We reached here on the 15th, being just seven days on the
road.   The day before we got in we rested a day, as one of

the men who had been over the road said there was a thirty-five miles march without water, and the weather being warm the men and animals can do with less water by traveling at night, so we left our last camp at about five o'clock in the evening and traveled 'til midnight, then rested for four hours, spreading our bedding in the sand and with the sky for a covering, then at four in the morning starting again, and got in the post at six, finding that the man had made a mistake in the distance, as it was only twenty-three miles. One of the mules strayed away and was not found again.

We lived very well on the road, as we had quails, fresh fish, and best of all, Anson shot a large deer with his revolver. It was a mighty good shot, as the deer was a hundred yards off. It weighed over a hundred pounds dressed. We had one hind quarter, kept the other one for Major Dudley, who is in command here, and the rest made a meal for all the men, teamsters and laundresses, so you see it was a pretty large one. I told Anson father would have enjoyed it. You know you thought it would be so unpleasant for us to be without vegetables, well today for dinner we had peas, lettuce, and young onions out of the government farm. Anyone can have a garden here if he chooses to take the trouble.

Our quarters are very comfortable; the houses are built of adobe and have three rooms and a kitchen. On first entering the quarters you would say, "It would be folly to put down carpets or attempt in any way to fix up here, for it would only serve to make the rest look worse," but you have no idea how much good a little fixing up does. The floors are mud, which is as hard and as dry as a bone. I have spread the curtains out to hide as much of the wall as possible, and as there is only one window I have arranged the remaining curtains in festoons over and around the front door, which is half of glass. The parlor is only twelve by twelve, so I ripped off one breadth of the carpet and turned it in over a yard on the length. The post is almost destitute of furniture, so we have a large barrel covered with a board, then a red blanket which, with Anson's desk on top, makes a respectable piece of furniture; then a chest with the ambulance cushions on top and covered with the carriage blanket, does duty as a divan, which, with two tables and three chairs furnishes (?) the parlor, the bedroom being luxuriously filled with a bedstead and a washstand, and the dining room being amply furnished with *one table*. The worst of it is there is no lumber in the post to make any of. I have sent by one of the wagons that went back to Whipple for a few articles of furniture I left in the house, as they have plenty of wood up there to make more. I do not know whether I will get it or not, as it is not customary to send furniture from one post to another. They have also sent there for lumber, so we will be able to have things made.

En route we stopped to examine an ancient fort of eight rooms with embrasures on all sides for defense probably for bows and arrows. The walls were twelve feet high, but the roof had been destroyed. Inside one of the rooms was a scrubby cedar tree, perhaps a hundred years old. While walking around on these walls, which were made of thin broad granite rocks, evidently once held in place by mortar, I displaced a stone which rolled down the mound, frightening a large deer, which I killed with my pistol. Tied to my horse's tail after the fashion of the Indians, I dragged it to the train. It is this deer of which Nannie writes.

At Cave Creek, where there were many cougars (Mexican lions), I found in a cave near the spring, which was some distance from our camp, the remains of many deer which had been caught by these lions, dragged into the cave and devoured, some of them being only partly eaten.

McDowell was the most unhappy post at which we ever served. Its commander was of an overbearing, tyrannical disposition, and much addicted to drink. The post traders abetted him and brought about many quarrels between the commander and the officers so that, in the garrison of five companies, there were few friendships.

At this unhappy station Nannie lost about twenty and I thirty pounds in weight.

One day she said to me, "Anson, I am going to Europe some day."

"Whom are you going with?" I asked.   It was a joy for me to see her so much more cheerful than I.

"You," she replied.

I never had any such hope, but, as will be seen later, she actually accomplished it.   (Text, 178.)

Nannie was for about a year the only lady in the post.   On December 1, 1871, to our great relief, we received orders to exchange posts with the 2d Cavalry, at Fort McPherson, Nebraska, the regiments exchanging horses to save transportation.

Western Experiences

Just as we left Arizona a new second lieutenant, Schwatka, joined me. He served with me for eight years, one of the most interesting officers Nannie and I ever met. He afterwards gained a national reputation in his search for the remains of the Franklin Expedition.

Three companies and the band went by wagon train to Fort Yuma, where we sold our ambulance to Captain Taylor, 2d Cavalry. Here we embarked on a river vessel for Puerto Isabel at the mouth of the Colorado, where we took the government steamer Newbern for San Francisco.

So disgusted with our Arizona experience were all the officers that when the boat pulled out from Yuma, we took off our shoes and beat the dust of Arizona over the rail, at the same time cursing the land.

The bore created by the contraction of the north end of the Gulf of California forces tides, sometimes eighteen feet high, along the lower Colorado, and the river is so tortuous that the distance from Yuma is three times what it is in a straight line. On our trip down, there being a very high tide, the captain endeavored to make a cut-off over the sand bars to save twelve miles. But the tide stranded the boat several miles from the main channel, and when morning came we could see no water. We remained until high tide the next night.

After a long but eventful journey we arrived at McPherson January 17, 1872, General Reynolds, who had been serving as general of volunteers in the reconstruction of Texas, assuming command of the regiment.

May, 1872, I was assigned to the sub-post of North Platte, in the fork of the North and South Platte Rivers on the Union Pacific Railroad. Here we met Spotted Tail, chief of the Brulé Tribe. (Appendix, 397.)

In July, 1872, General Sheridan ordered two companies of

my regiment to escort Professor Marsh, of Yale College, with thirty students of that institution, on a paleontological expedition in the Bad Lands along the Niobrara River (one hundred miles north of the North Platte). We spent two months on that very interesting and successful duty, recovering from the washing sands of the steep banks of the Niobrara several wagon loads of prehistoric bones.

On December 2, 1872, Nannie and I spent three months of leave with her parents in Zanesville, during which we purchased an elaborate and very fine ambulance, shipping it to North Platte.

Next year General Sheridan detailed me to escort Lord Dunraven and three friends on a hunting expedition on the Loop River. Accompanied by Buffalo Bill (Cut, 154), the party was very successful in killing many elk, deer and antelope, remaining out about six weeks. One night Lord Dunraven came to my tent and we talked until long after midnight. I have never forgotten his declaration that the possibilities of the development of the American Republic were greater than any ever known in history; adding, "the curse of my country is its nobility."

In 1873 the agent for the Ogallala and Brulé Sioux gave permission for a large party of those sub-tribes to hunt buffalo on the Republican River, southern Nebraska, near the Kansas line. Unfortunately, the agent of the Pawnees gave a large party of that tribe permission to hunt in the same direction. These tribes were traditional enemies. I warned both agents of possible trouble, but without avail. The Pawnees arrived first; placed their women and children in camp and started out for the buffalo. When the Sioux arrived, their scouts discovered the Pawnee families, attacked the camp and killed one hundred and twenty-five, all save one or two children and a squaw, found by Captain Meinhold of the 3d Cavalry, sent out from Fort McPherson the next day. These were so badly wounded that they died.

The Pawnees, inferior to the Sioux, were compelled to

Jack Robertson.

Jim Bridger.
(Text, 107.)

W. F. Cody (Buffalo Bill).
(Text, 153.)

return in sorrow to their reservation; the Sioux continuing their hunt.

In September, 1874, the Sioux entered the parade grounds at Forts Fetterman and Steele, and killed several soldiers (Appendix, 399). General Ord selected me to take five troops of cavalry, and two companies of infantry by rail to Rawlins, Wyoming, thence to Independence Rock, cross the Big Horn Mountains, and destroy a camp of hostiles supposed to be near old Fort Reno. Unfortunately the Indians discovered our movements, and moved north beyond our reach.

April 14, 1875, General Crook ordered me to take command at Camp Sheridan, Nebraska. This march (Nannie accompanying me in her ambulance) was through a roadless, sandy country, with many streams and difficult crossings, practically unexplored.

Relieving Captain Sutorious of the command, I found Spotted Tail, chief of the Brulés, with about five thousand Indians at his agency, some of them Ogallalas. All were much excited at the encroachments of the whites on the reservation, and the scarcity of food. Spotted Tail declared the agent, Mr. Howard, deprived them of their governmental rations. The winter had been very severe and the snow very deep, driving the game out of the country.

Finding his statements true, I complained to the agent, who said he gave them all they were entitled to, and if they starved it wasn't his fault. There was no telegraphic communication, so without authority, I issued them several thousand dollars' worth of bacon and hard bread, telling the agent and reporting it to the War Department. Very shortly Jesse M. Lee, a first lieutenant of infantry, arrived with his appointment as Indian agent, dispossessing Howard.

Beef was issued by driving it in on the hoof, but flour, which was the principal ration, supplied by a contractor in Baltimore, was shipped to Cheyenne by rail, and there loaded onto wagons.

On the plea that so long a wagon journey would break single

bags, and spill the contents, 100 pounds of flour was covered with three sacks. At Cheyenne a Federal inspector marked and weighed the bags.

The Baltimore contractor arranged with this inspector to stamp each sack "100 pounds." This trebled the weight, as the agent emptied the flour into vessels brought by the squaws and kept the sacks as evidence that he had delivered three times the actual weight. Lee, finding that flour was delivered unweighed, looked at the sacks, found they were certified to contain one hundred pounds by the inspector, reported the trick and the contractor was arrested, tried and convicted.

Many of Spotted Tail's young men were getting up war parties to drive back the miners and settlers who were organizing on the Missouri River to enter the Black Hills. It was a violation of our treaties with the Indians, and it was part of the duty of the army to see that the treaties were respected. Captain Fergus Walker, 1st Infantry, wrote me from a point eighty miles east of Wounded Knee, May 15, 1875, that he had captured one such invading party and sent it under guard to Fort Randall, but that his thus greatly weakened force was unable to cope with others, particularly Major Gordon's mining company. He asked me, accordingly, to co-operate with him in this work, and arranged for the Indian scout by whom he sent the letter to intercept him on the Niobrara River with my reply.

General Sheridan's General Order No. 2, of March 17th, directed commanding officers in Indian reservations adjacent to the Black Hills "to burn the wagon trains, destroy the outfits and arrest the leaders, confining them at the nearest military post," of trespassers found on a reservation. Accordingly, with two companies of cavalry and a battery of gatling guns, commanded by Lieutenant Rockefeller, I marched to relieve Captain Walker.

Arriving at Antelope Creek at night, I sent two men in citizens' clothes to Walker's camp to tell him I would at daylight surround Major Gordon's mining company. At daybreak I threw my companies into line, the battery in the center, and when Walker's force appeared, Gordon's men, wakened by the noise, found themselves utterly helpless. Gordon's camp was in a river bend, between precipitous bluffs, with only a few hundred yards' space for entrance or exit.

Seizing Gordon and putting him in a bull pen, I ordered his second in command, Mr. Brockert, to parade his men and surrender their arms. While doing this, one of their guns went off. I called out they might have the first shot, but we would have the last, when they submissively declared they would make no resistance.

The prisoners were sent back to Fort Randall under Captain Walker, except Gordon, whom I took to Sheridan, where he was put in the guard house.

Both the newspapers and the public at Sioux City made complaints about my "arbitrary and unlawful act," and the grand jury found true bills against me, but I never had service.

Gordon was a Mason, as was my post trader at Sheridan. They concocted a scheme for Gordon's release. One Sunday morning the post trader approached and read me his commission as United States Commissioner, serving a writ demanding the delivery of Major Gordon. I told him if he did not tear up his commission I would put him in the guard house with his friend Gordon, as there was not enough room in that post for a commanding officer and post trader who, as U. S. Commissioner, would attempt to dominate the action of the military authorities. He destroyed his commission. Later, Gordon was transferred to the guard house at Fort Omaha, Nebraska, and was there held under indictment for violating the Indian non-intercourse laws. What finally became of him I never knew.

The government contemplated building a permanent post (the one then occupied was temporarily constructed of logs) and furnished a saw mill, lathe, shingle machine, sash and doors, and thirty skilled artisans to take timber from the pine forests, and construct the post as rapidly as possible.

While absent on this expedition, General Crook, who had relieved General Ord, appeared at the post with some of his staff on inspection. He left an order for me to select a new location for a five-company post and construct it after my own plans, which I did.

Having an excellent quartermaster in Lieutenant Rockefeller, we accomplished the most expeditious post construction in the history of the army. Each captain constructed his own barracks and quarters, after plans I prepared, dividing the skilled artisans between them. As the men were anxious to get into their new homes, trees felled in the morning were often part of buildings before sundown, Lieutenant Lemly of the cavalry being particularly active, and all the officers strove hard to complete their quarters as soon as possible. We were comfortably housed before the first of October. All the buildings were constructed as a shell of upright inch boards around a framework, lined with the ordinary sized unburnt bricks, dried in the sun and plastered inside.

Meanwhile, Nannie formed an agreeable acquaintance with Spotted Tail, whom she liked from first sight. He was a fine-looking man, with engaging manners, perfectly loyal to the government, a lover of peace, knowing no good could come to his people from war with the army. He had the highest respect for and confidence in officers.

There was a sub-chief under Spotted Tail named No Flesh, a weakling, not thought much of by the head chiefs. Nannie frequently invited Spotted Tail to dinner, sometimes with other most respected chiefs, and No Flesh tried in every way to establish friendly relations with her. He proffered his services to paint her some pictures of his exploits as a warrior, for which she paid him. In one of these pictures he represents himself engaged in a great battle with U. S. Cavalry, killing a captain. I regret I can not reproduce his detailed description of his heroism.

The shod horse tracks in the picture represent the cavalry, and the unshod pony tracks represent Indian ponies. The

Brulé Chief Spotted Tail.

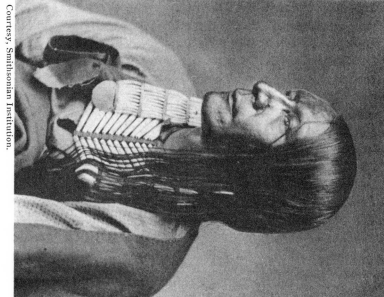

Brulé Chief No Flesh.

No Fles

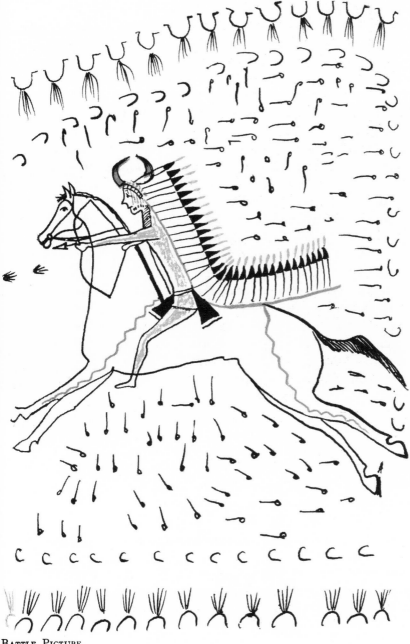

BATTLE PICTURE.

faces on the margin are the attacking cavalry. It will be seen that he killed a soldier before he killed the captain.

Engaged in this work, he would remain at the house for hours, hoping to gain favor with Nannie.

Observing Nannie had great influence with me and with Spotted Tail, and noticing she bought fruits and paid for them herself, he knew of course that she was no squaw, and that she had authority.

One day Captain McDougall and several officers of the 7th Cavalry arrived at the post, with a scouting command to rest for a few days and secure supplies.

Nannie invited the officers to dine with Spotted Tail, Standing Elk, and White Thunder, but, as usual, did not include No Flesh. No Flesh learned the news rather late, but, a few moments after we had taken our seats, announced himself at the door and was seated in the parlor by the orderly.

When dinner was over we returned to the parlor and shook hands with No Flesh. Having held his seat during the dinner in the hope that he might at least be invited to a second table, he was somewhat sullen. After a while he exclaimed, "Well, you must have had a great deal to eat."

"Why do you think so?" I asked.

"Because it took you so long to eat it," he rejoined.

Seeing he was not likely to receive an invitation, and convinced from Nannie's demeanor toward him that the fault lay with her, he shook hands in a very dignified manner with everyone in the room save Nannie. She was sitting near the door, and when he came near he drew himself up in a most scornful manner and passed quickly out.

This amused not only the officers, but the Indians.

Soon after, when strolling together through the Indian encampments, I remarked, "Suppose we call on No Flesh." "Very well," she said, "I would just as soon."

No Flesh appeared much astonished, but he invited us in his tent, asking us to be seated on the ground, which we did.

Two squaws and several children were present. He looked sternly in my face for some moments, and then exclaimed:

"You—no chief!" pointing to me with his forefinger. Then pointing with his left forefinger to Nannie, he held it up vertically, thus, as representing her; and pointing to me with his right forefinger, held it up thus, as representing me.

He then placed them vertically together, thus, as representing our relative standing in authority.

All nomadic Indians have a common sign language and communicate with each other without the use of words.

No Flesh intended the most absolute insult one man could give another. We burst out together in laughter. This greatly puzzled No Flesh, who could not conceive how any man, much less a soldier, could brook such an insult. It was with great effort, stoical as the Indian is, that he preserved his equanimity.

One day while overlooking the construction of the post, Spotted Tail said through his interpreter, "Well, I have been wondering if you were going to stay; now I know you are." I asked him how he knew, and he replied, "I have been among white men long enough to know when they put rocks under their houses they are going to stay."

The old commanding officer's quarters, the best in the old post, was preserved intact, with all its furniture, cooking stove and utensils. When we moved to the new post I formally presented this house to Spotted Tail, in the name of the Great White Father, with General Crook's authority. He and his wives and children were very thankful in their hope for better comforts in the future. A short time thereafter, I saw the house was vacant and found Spotted Tail was again living in tepees under the cottonwood trees in the midst of his village. Asking him why, he replied his squaws found it impossible to

keep the house clean. They threw the bones and refuse on
the floor and could not learn to sweep out or wipe up, so that
flies and maggots became so intolerable they were compelled
to move. They could move tepees in a few minutes to fresh
sward, as had been Indian habit for generations. With all
my knowledge of the Indian habits, this surprised me as I
suppose it will surprise the reader.

One day Spotted Tail brought Lone Horn, a Minneconjou
chief, to my tent, asking me to show him some courtesy. He
had never been in a military post or on an Indian reservation.
The trader supplied a can of lemon sugar and I made some
lemonade. Lone Horn had ridden far, on a very hot July day.
He emptied his glass; then Spotted Tail exclaimed, "Have you
drank all that? You had better lie down and hold on to the
grass, for the whole world will begin to turn over in a few
minutes."

Lone Horn, seeing the rest of us had drank only a portion,
was really alarmed and imagined he felt the influence. I mention this to show Spotted Tail's humor, notwithstanding the
popular opinion that Indians have none.

Efforts to enter the Black Hills had excited the entire Sioux
confederation, and they began to talk of war. The leading
chiefs of all the tribes except the Minneconjous and Ogallalas
tried to restrain them, but it was difficult. In each reservation
the young men organized war bands and went ostensibly to
hunt but really in hope they would find opportunity to attack
and destroy emigrants, prospectors or stock-men unawares,
which they often did.

The great unrest among the Indians and the settlements
adjoining their reservations alarmed the Indian Department.
Before the winter had fairly set in, the President authorized
the War Department to chastise some of the war-like tribes
that were encamped not far from their reservations in the
West, ostensibly for hunting purposes, but really to organize
war parties for depredations in the spring. General Crook was
therefore directed to begin a winter campaign. He organized

a command at Fort D. A. Russell of ten companies of the 3d Cavalry, including mine, several of the 2d Cavalry and four of the 4th Cavalry. I was stationed at Fort D. A. Russell for the winter, Nannie accompanying me.

So many troops made Cheyenne a large and interesting post, Nannie becoming prominent in the garrison. One day she took me to a meeting of the officers and ladies at the post hospital to organize an amateur theatrical company. The call was issued by Major Dubois, who announced the object of the meeting, when, to my surprise, I was called as permanent chairman, the first time, I believe, I ever presided. Three young second lieutenants were appointed to devise a program and name the actors for the monthly meetings. Later a program was sent around in which I, who make no pretensions to theatricals, was designated to act Sir Toby Tittmouse, a leading part.

Nannie and these youngsters had entrapped me. I told her I could not in months commit to memory the long part I was given, but Nannie reminded me I had, as presiding officer, approved the proceedings and that I could not back out! She rehearsed me and taught me to play my part, sitting up many nights, conscious that Sir Toby's loud and turbulent language would impress the help in the kitchen that we were quarreling. Taking an interest in it I found it not so difficult after all, and Nannie rigged me up in a costume that would have surprised Sir Toby himself. She constructed a remarkable wig of angora wool, and made me knee breeches and large buttoned coat, which, with a cane, fitted the character so well that when the play was produced, my own colonel, Reynolds, declared that he did not know who was playing the part. This gave me courage, and I afterward acted a principal part as Mr. Potter in "Still Waters Run Deep."

Early in 1875, the campaign intended to subdue the rising war spirit of the Indians took definite shape, and our command left Fort D. A. Russell and proceeded towards old Fort

Phil Kearny, where it was reported some outlying bands were located on Powder River.

We took thirty days' beef on the hoof, which was issued as rations. Two days from Fort Fetterman, crossing Cheyenne Creek, the command was surprised by some Indians; every head of cattle was driven off, one of the herders killed and one or two soldiers wounded, leaving the troops without any fresh meat. When we reached Phil Kearny, we abandoned every wheel, resorting to pack mules, and struck out for Powder River.

There had been a deep snow some weeks previous, and cold weather succeeding warm created a crust that would sometimes hold a horse. The night after we left Phil Kearny there came another severe snow-storm with high, intensely cold winds. The drifting snow and hard crusts rendered it difficult for our animals to travel.

We followed Otter Creek, which runs into the Yellowstone, parallel to Powder River, to an abandoned Sioux camp, thirty miles from Powder River, in which we found the remains of a captured and killed Blackfoot Indian.

Scouts reported a hunting party of Sioux in the direction of Powder River, in what in their opinion was a village. General Crook directed Reynolds to take eight troops with two days' rations (leaving him with the pack train and two troops to follow), and capture the village if he could find it.

At daybreak, on the banks of the river, the scouts reported the village. Preparations were made to attack.

Owing to the age and feebleness of Colonel Reynolds and the bitter feud that existed in the regiment (similar to that in the 7th Cavalry between Colonel Sturgis and his friends and Colonel Custer and his friends, that proved so disastrous at the Little Big Horn), this attack on the village on Powder River proved a lamentable failure. Reynolds disobeyed Crook's order to hold the village until his arrival, abandoning the field and retiring in the direction of Fetterman. It is perhaps better not to go into details here in regard to this humiliating failure, further than to say that several officers were tried for misconduct.

We were out of rations and other supplies, so there was nothing left but to return without successfully accomplishing the object for which we had been sent.

Through agents the Indian Department then took a hand and endeavored to quiet the Indians, but with little success. On June 18, 1875, Mr. Ed. P. Smith, the Commissioner of Indian Affairs, organized a commission to treat with the Sioux. It was composed of very distinguished men. Senator William B. Allison was the president, and General Terry among the thirteen members who met at Fort Robinson, September 20, 1875. I commanded the escort, consisting of my own and Captain Eagan's white horse company of the 2d Cavalry.

The majority of the Indians refused to enter the post, declaring they would make no treaty under duress. The commission agreed to meet in a grove on the White River, eight miles northeast of the post. Spotted Tail, who accompanied me from Fort Sheridan, warned me it was a mistake to meet outside the post, and kept his best friends around my ambulance.

The commission sat under a large tarpaulin, the chiefs sitting on the ground. Senator Allison was to make the introductory speech, and Red Cloud and Spotted Tail were scheduled to reply favorably to the surrender of the Black Hills for certain considerations.

There were present perhaps 20,000 Indians, representing probably 40,000 or 45,000 of various tribes. Probably three-fourths of the grown males of the consolidated tribes were present and might have subscribed to a new treaty in accordance with its provisions, that it be with the consent of three-fourths of the Indians, which supposedly meant the grown people, although the treaty did not so state. The Indians were given to understand that the whites must have the land, so that they became alarmed, and most of them threatened war.

Eagan's mounted company, drawn up in single line, I placed on the right of the commission, my own on the left. Allison began his address, during which hostile Indians, well armed, formed man for man in the rear of Eagan's men. "Young-Man-Afraid-of-His-Horses," a captain of a company of friendly Indians, asked permission to form his men in the rear of the hostile Indians, to which I consented.

When Red Cloud was about to speak, "Little Big Man," astride an American horse, two revolvers belted to his waist, but otherwise naked save for a breech clout, moccasins and war headgear, rode between the commission and the seated Indian chiefs and proclaimed, "I will kill the first Indian chief who speaks favorably to the selling of the Black Hills."

Spotted Tail, fearing a massacre, advised that the commission get back to the fort as quickly as possible. General Terry consulted with Allison, and then ordered the commission into the ambulances to make for the post. I placed Eagan's company on each flank and my own in the rear of the ambulances. At least half the men warriors pressed about us threatening to kill some member of the commission.

One young warrior in particular, riding furiously into our ranks, frenziedly declared that he would have the blood of a commissioner. Fortunately we reserved our fire.

A friendly Indian soldier showed him an innocent colt grazing about one hundred yards away and told him he could appease his anger by killing it. Strange to say, he consented, rode out and shot the colt dead, and the whole of the hostile Sioux retired to the main body at the place of our meeting. Thus ended the efforts of this commission to formulate a treaty.

Failure of both Crook's expedition and the efforts of the commission made it certain that hostilities would be resumed in the spring, so that General Terry, commanding the Department of Dakota, and General Crook, commanding the Department of the Platte, were instructed to organize large commands for the purpose of pursuing and punishing all Sioux found away from their reservations.

The Commissioner of Indian Affairs instructed his agents to warn the chiefs to call in all Indians away from the reservation, notifying that all found away would be punished. This only excited the war-like young bucks and caused them to move in the early spring as far west as they could go. At that time the buffalo were driven by encroaching settlements and the railroads from their southern grazing grounds into the country west and north of the Sioux reservation.

Crook first met the Indians in a slight engagement on Tongue River, Montana.

Terry, meanwhile, so separated from Crook by distance and hostile Indians as to prevent communication, had searched for the hostiles on the north. He discovered their trail on the Yellowstone at the mouth of the Rosebud, and organized an expedition under General Custer with the entire 7th Cavalry to pursue it.

General Crook's expedition is described in detail (Appendix, 400), save what occurred after his separation from General Terry's command.

The hostile Indians separated, some going to Canada and others turning eastward. General Crook determined to follow the latter, depending entirely on pack mules for transportation. With scanty rations, he undertook a long and distressing march through the dry and barren country, with little knowledge of its streams and trails. Both men and officers became restless and many of the horses were shot for want of sustenance.

When near the Missouri River, Crook turned southwest toward the Black Hills, crossing the North and South Cannonball rivers. Here many officers and men became dismounted, and it was feared they might perish for want of rations. There was no game, many ate horse flesh, and had no knowledge of woodcraft, course, or direction.

On the 8th of September, as I was bringing in the rear squadron of the command, having shot seventy horses that day, General Crook, in consultation with General Merritt, directed me to select one hundred and fifty of the best men and horses from my regiment, take Chief Packer Moore, with fifty pack mules, to Deadwood, in the Black Hills, and bring back supplies to the command. His last words were that should I encounter a village I should attack and hold it. It was nine o'clock before I could collect my command, and I left so hurriedly that no medical officer was sent with me. The night was very dark. I took with me Grouard, one of the best scouts we had, especially proficient in woodcraft.

Although there were no stars and insufficient light to see the surrounding land, somehow Grouard took us in the right direction. About midnight he lighted a match and showed me the fresh tracks of ponies on the banks of a little lake. We were close to the Indians. It began to rain as we lay down, holding the lariats of our horses, and it was with difficulty that we obtained a little sleep.

It was still raining at daylight, but we were early up and off, seeing by the mountain ranges we were going toward the Black Hills.

In the afternoon Grouard signaled a halt, saying we were near an Indian village. He had observed Indian hunters with their ponies packed with game. We were on the banks of a small stream, which Grouard said was near Slim Buttes. We hid under the banks and cottonwood trees, drenched with cold rain, until three in the morning, when I determined to attack. I did not know its strength, but was willing to take my chances in view of General Crook's positive orders.

Moving as close to the village as possible, I left the quartermaster, Lieutenant Bubb, with the pack mules and twenty-five soldiers. My plan was to dismount fifty men under Crawford and fifty under Von Luettwitz, retaining twenty-five mounted, under Schwatka, to charge through the village and drive the ponies away as soon as we were discovered, when Crawford would attack them on the right and Von Luettwitz on the left.

The Indian ponies near the village discovered us by smell and stampeded into the village. Schwatka charged through the village, driving the horses as far as he could, and Crawford and Von Luettwitz carried out their instructions and drove most of the Indians pell mell from their tepees, which were laced on the side facing us. These lacings, being wet, were so hard to untie that the Indians cut their way through on the other side of the elkskin tepees and ran to the rocks on the opposite side of the stream, taking only their arms with them.

Von Luettwitz, standing near me on a slight elevation, was shot through the knee; I caught him as he fell. We found the village rich in fruit and game, and I despatched three couriers at intervals, to inform General Crook that we would hold the village until he came.

The Indian Chief, American Horse, was mortally wounded in the stomach. With some of his followers, mostly women and children, he took refuge in a cave in a ravine, where they entrenched themselves with the soft clay. There were fifty tepees in this village and probably two hundred and fifty Indians, mostly warriors. Grouard got into conversation with some and tried to persuade them to surrender, but they said that they had dispatched runners to the main body of the Sioux, less than eight miles distant, and would hold out until they were relieved.

The leading part of Crook's command, those with the best horses, arrived about 11.30. The rest of his command appeared soon after, at the same time the Indian forces arrived to relieve their distressed comrades. They came in great numbers, but when Crook deployed almost an equal number, the Indians retired and we held the village.

Some of my men, entering the village, discovered a little girl three or four years old, who sprang up and ran away like a young partridge. The soldiers caught her and brought her to me. She was in great distress until I assured her, by petting her and giving her food, that she was in no danger, when she became somewhat contented.

After General Crook's men had persuaded the Indians hidden in the cave to surrender, there being many killed and wounded among them, I and my orderly took this little girl down to see the captives and the dead. Among others, the soldiers had dragged out the bodies of two fine looking half-breed squaws, only partly dressed, bloody and mangled with many wounds. The little girl began to scream and fought the orderly until he placed her on the ground, when she ran and embraced one of these squaws, who was her mother.

On returning to my station on the hill, I told Adjutant Lemly I intended to adopt this little girl, as I had slain her mother.

The Indian chief was taken to one of the tepees and the surgeon told him he would die before midnight. He accepted his doom without a blanch or shudder, and soon died.

Crook told me to take the same command and at daylight proceed to the Black Hills and execute my mission. Before starting, Adjutant Lemly asked me if I really intended to take the little girl. I told him I did, when he remarked, "Well, how do you think Mrs. Mills will like it?" It was the first time I had given that side of the matter a thought, and I decided to leave the child where I found her.

We arrived at Deadwood at nine the next night. Everyone was in great excitement, because communication with the outer world was shut off by the surrounding Indians. All readily assisted me in collecting supplies sufficient to load the fifty pack mules. With fifty head of cattle, we met Crook's command, the second morning, forty miles distant. They were in practically a starving condition, having subsisted on the ponies I captured at Slim Buttes.

Some time in June, 1914, the historian of South Dakota, Mr. Doane Robinson, sent me a volume in which he published the reports of the Battle of Slim Buttes, and also a map of the battle-ground by the State engineer, which purported to give in detail the topography in Section 27, Township 17 north, Range 8 east. On examining it, I could not recognize it as representing the location.

Meanwhile, Mr. W. M. Camp, editor of the Railway Review, had called on me to get some details of this fight, stating that he was writing a history of the Indian War of 1876. Showing him Mr. Robinson's book, I told him that, having no faith that he had made the proper location, I had invited General Charles Morton, who was present at the fight, to go with me in July and try to find the true location, and asked him to go with us, which he readily consented to do.

We invited Mr. Robinson to accompany us to the battle-ground in order that the question of location might be definitely settled. He agreed to join us on the train at Pierre at midnight on July 14th. Mr. Robinson failed to keep his engagement, but, at Belle Fourche, his son, a boy of about twenty years old, reported to us, stating his father had asked him to go with us. He was of no assistance, however, as he knew nothing about the matter, and did not seem interested in it.

After several days' search, we found the location described in Mr. Robinson's history in the map before referred to, but neither General Morton nor I could reconcile the topography represented on the map with the location as we remembered it. There were no evidences of a fight, no rifle pits, which we remembered well to have made, and which could not have been obliterated. We spent several days trying to find the true location, but were eventually compelled to abandon the search, the conditions being exceedingly unfavorable to the investigation because of poor roads, rains, and excessively hot weather.

Mr. Camp and I both corresponded with General Charles King, also present at this battle, and who Mr. Robinson claimed had furnished him with the map from which he made the location. General King replied that he had never furnished Mr. Robinson with a map sufficient to make the location and, after examining the map in his book, said it was not the correct location.

I am now in receipt of a letter from Mr. Camp, dated June 21, 1917, in which he informs me that he went on another expedition and, after considerable search, found the true location on June 19th, in Section 10, Township 18 north, Range 8 east, which is on Gap Creek, one of the main branches of Rabbit Creek, about three miles from Reva Gap, three-quarters of a mile from Mr. W. W. Mitchell's house, and nine miles north of Robinson's location. Mr. Camp found the rifle pits and many other convincing evidences of the fight, including numerous empty shells, much broken pottery and other Indian utensils, all of which corresponded to my own and other reports of the battle.

Crook stayed in the Black Hills recuperating for several weeks, when, the campaign being closed, the whole command proceeded to Fort Robinson, where it was disbanded and the various organizations sent to their proper posts. I was transferred to Camp Sheridan, where Nannie joined me and where Chief "Touch the Clouds," of the Minneconjous, came in and surrendered (Appendix, 412).

During our second stay at Sheridan, many interesting incidents occurred. Spotted Tail gave a dog feast in Nannie's honor, which she gladly attended and danced freely with the squaws, to their great delight. They boiled many dogs in large kettles, but Nannie did not have the courage to partake of the feast, which she ever afterwards regretted.

One afternoon a Sister of Charity from a Kansas City convent drove to my quarters with a novice, stating that she had been sent to me by General Mackenzie, then commanding Fort Robinson. She was on a mission to procure subscriptions for the erection of a hospital at Kansas City.

Sister Mary remained with us for several days. A very intelligent and entertaining woman, she was a welcome guest to both Nannie and me. Expressing a desire to see Spotted Tail, we prepared a little entertainment and invited him to the house, together with a few ladies and officers, Lieutenant Schwatka, who afterwards became famous, being one. The refreshments consisted of cider, cakes and apples.

Spotted Tail appeared in full Indian dress, accompanied by one of his wives and his daughter, Shonkoo, an interesting girl of seventeen. Sister Mary, dressed in the conventional robes of her order, conversed with Spotted Tail through the interpreter for some time before we passed the refreshments.

After all present had been provided with a glass of cider, Sister Mary danced gaily to the center of the room and announced that she would like to clink glasses with the great chief Spotted Tail. Upon hearing her request, Spotted Tail, quite as gracefully and gaily, danced up to her. This wild country could hardly show a stranger spectacle than a Sister of Charity, in her peaceful robes, and a savage warrior, in his war-like paraphernalia, clinking glasses!

The conversation lasted for some hours, the squaw and her daughter saying little. Finally it occurred to me that it might be interesting to Sister Mary to take this young girl back with her to the convent, and I made the suggestion to her. Her eyes sparkled with delight as she said that it would be a feather in her cap. "Is it possible that we can arrange it?" she asked.

On making the suggestion to Spotted Tail, his face also beamed. He would like nothing better than that his daughter should live among the white people and learn their ways and customs, and he had great confidence in the Sisters of Charity. While the matter was thoroughly discussed by Sister Mary and Spotted Tail, I watched Shonkoo and her mother.

The mother appeared delighted, but Shonkoo was expressionless. I suggested to the interpreter that it might be well to see what the daughter had to say, but when this was communicated to Spotted Tail, he said, "That is all right. She will go."

I arranged to furnish the transportation to the railroad, a distance of about one hundred miles. They would be ready

to depart in three days, Spotted Tail stating that he would
bring his daughter then to my quarters and place her in charge
of the sister.

The morning the start was to be made, everything was ready
but Shonkoo. In her place came a message from Spotted Tail
to Sister Mary and me to the effect that Shonkoo had eloped
the night before with a young Indian by the name of Lone Elk,
and Sister Mary returned to her convent despondent, empty
handed, and minus the feather in her cap, so far as her efforts
to civilize Shonkoo were concerned.

DETAIL TO PARIS EXPOSITION

In 1876, being senior captain of cavalry and expecting promotion, I obtained six months' leave of absence, but, on organization of General Crook's expedition to the Powder River I surrendered my leave until the Sioux trouble should be ended. When I returned to Camp Sheridan, the six months' leave was renewed, and we started for Washington. I met General Crook at Fort Laramie. We stopped a day or two before proceeding in our ambulance toward the railroad at Cheyenne. We were twelve miles from Laramie when the Adjutant General, Nickerson, overtook us, with a message from General Crook, who had not known of our departure, stating his appreciation of my services during the campaign, adding that he felt under more obligations to me than to any other officer in the campaign, and that if there was any official favor possible for him to obtain, I had only to ask. Sure of my majority in a short time, I could see nothing to ask that he might procure for me, but, after Nickerson departed, Nannie assured me that she could find something, and jokingly referred to her remark while in Arizona that she was going to Europe with me some day. So, when we arrived in Washington, she said, "There is to be an international exposition in Paris next May, 1878. Why don't you ask the General to recommend you for a detail there?" I took her advice and made application to be so detailed, to the Secretary of War.

Colonel Reynolds, of my regiment, had been retired, and Colonel Devin, whom I had never met, joined the headquarters at Fort D. A. Russell.

I sent my application to the Secretary of War through the adjutant, Johnson, who knew my history, supposing that General Crook would endorse it favorably. But, in spite of the fact that everybody in the regiment knew I would be promoted before my leave expired, the papers were endorsed by the Colonel, "Respectfully forwarded disapproved. This officer's services are needed with his company." It was successively endorsed by General Crook at Omaha, General Sheridan at Chicago, and General Sherman at Washington, "Respectfully forwarded disapproved."

These advices to the Secretary seemed to me unfair. I was introduced to him, and told him I had been unfairly treated. He encouraged me to explain, which I did, adding that I had served in my proper command more constantly since I entered the service than any officer in the army. I knew little of the record of my colonel, but I asked to have our records examined, and that if he had not been absent from his command two days to my one I would withdraw my application; but that if I were correct I asked to have the colonel's unfavorable endorsement and those influenced by it ignored. A day or two afterward the Secretary sent for me. "I am more surprised at the result than by your statement," he said. "It is short of the facts, and I shall consider the endorsements valueless; but," he added, "why do you suppose the President will send an attaché to that exposition?"

"Mr. Secretary," I replied, "because he ought to. The President sent McClellan and other attachés to previous expositions, such as the Crystal Palace Exposition in London. Officers who have served in the Civil and Indian Wars are as much entitled to such benefits as General McClellan." The next day a note from him stated the President had decided to appoint three attachés, one from each arm of the service. This announcement in the press immediately prompted numerous applications, but Secretary McCrary assured me my appointment would issue shortly.

Nannie and I sat at a table at the Ebbitt House next to that of General Sherman. As we went in to dinner that day, General Sherman stretched out his hand to Nannie, saying, "Mrs. Mills, I want to congratulate you." Nannie diplomatically replied, "What for?" though she knew well. "Why, you are going to Paris. The President detailed your husband as military attaché to the Paris Exposition today." Nannie replied, "I thank you, General Sherman." General Sherman then stated in his frank and noble way, "Don't thank me, Mrs. Mills; I had nothing to do with it."

These details show Nannie was my inspiration. She approved of every move made in the matter and was more elated than I at the result.

We sailed in March, 1878, on a Cunard steamer. My insurance policy required that I obtain permission to visit a foreign country, but at the offices of the Knickerbocker I was told that the company would issue such a permit only if I agreed to forfeit my policy should I enter any city in which there was an epidemic. I told them to "go to," that I would live longer than their company, and surrendered my policy, on which I had paid eleven assessments.

Within three years their company went into bankruptcy, and I am still living!

We had an uneventful passage, although very distressing to Nannie on account of sea-sickness. During a two weeks' stop in London we visited Nannie's relatives, Mrs. Langworthy, at Guys House, Maidenhead, near Windsor Castle. The Langworthys were delightful people and our acquaintance a very agreeable experience, although it began in a rather embarrassing way.

Neither of us had much experience in "high society," or had the money to flourish in it. We carried to Guys House no other clothing than that in our traveling bags. At the depot, a great retinue of lackeys clad in knee breeches, and coach and baggage wagon apparently waited for some great personage. But Mr. Edward Langworthy, the son, introduced himself, and asked for our luggage, when we rather shamefacedly confessed that we had only our two valises.

We were dressed simply, like most Americans, but we had America's courage, and met the situation without much chagrin. The Langworthys dressed for dinner, but we had to make the best of what we had. We had a bedroom lit by candles and without fire, although it was March and the weather very cold.

In the ante- room the next morning I saw a large wash-tub in the middle of the bare floor, two-thirds full of water, and a chair containing some towels and soap. I remarked, "Nannie, look at that. Do they expect us to bathe in that cold room in that cold water? I will not do it."

Nannie replied, "Well, I am too proud to have them think we do not wash," and, seizing the soap, she made a lot of lather and sprinkled water on the floor to leave conclusive evidence that we really were civilized.

Mrs. Langworthy asked me, "How do you get about in London?" I replied that we used the omnibus, as Nannie thought the "Hansom cabs" unsafe, and refused to ride in them. Mrs. Langworthy said, "You shouldn't do that. Only tradespeople and banker's clerks ride in omnibuses."

Before going to Paris my commission as major in the 10th Cavalry arrived. A military tailor made me a uniform, which, with the gay attire Nannie bought in both London and Paris, satisfied Mrs. Langworthy on our second visit, made after returning from Paris, that we Americans could do right after all! We enjoyed our visits in their beautiful house, a fine English estate, and always recalled our acquaintance with our delightful English relatives with much pleasure.

We were in Paris at the opening of the exposition, where we met the other attachés. Among the Americans we met Lucien Young, a very interesting naval officer, in whose carriage Nannie and I rode to the opening. Our uniforms conformed much with the Prussian style, especially my helmet. Leaving the exposition immediately behind the Prince of Wales' entourage, the French took us for Germans, and looked upon us very coldly. Some bright Frenchman, discovering on my helmet the words, "E Pluribus Unum," called out to his countrymen that we were Americans, when we received almost as many cheers as the Prince of Wales himself.

Invited by President McMahon to a review of thirty thousand cavalry, I was informed that a French captain would have a mount for me in the Bois de Boulogne. There were eight

American officers in Paris, most of them in official capacity, and when I arrived they were all there. As the senior, they insisted I approach the French officer. Speaking little French, I was somewhat embarrassed. But with the assurance of an American, I called out to the dapper young French artillery officer, "Good morning, captain; do you speak English?" "No, I do not," he replied, "but I speak American, which is much better. I spent four years as military attaché in Washington, the most beautiful city in the world."

It is needless to say that his diplomacy made us all his friends.

As Nannie had anticipated, this year's service at the Paris Exposition was the greatest practical and instructive education of my life. A practical skilled mechanic, I understood the intricacies of mechanics, and here in one building was assembled all the latest and most novel machinery of the world. The sewing machine was then in the height of its progressive construction. England, hitherto the foremost nation in machinery construction, was fast losing its place to America and France. The English machine was distinguished by its clumsy, angular and heavy parts and the difficulty of keeping it in order. The French machines were better, but the American machine stood first in all that made it handy, graceful, symmetrical and useful. And so it was with all the other machinery. Electric light and power was in its infancy, but here, as in all else, the best appliances for its use were American.

I started out in the hope of learning a great deal from the foreign nations in my conceived invention and construction of a woven cartridge belt and other web equipment, which I felt sure could be made as strong and of as firm consistency as leather, and much better than leather because it was lighter, more flexible, did not require oiling, and was less likely to break in the process of wetting and drying when exposed to the weather. However, after visiting factories in France,

England and Germany, I found that they knew less about weaving such fabrics than we did in America.

Nannie and I traveled much during our stay abroad.

France had been humiliated by Germany's conquest and exaction of the then unheard of indemnity, but she was not despondent. In the dining room of our boarding house, 44 Rue de Clichy, were two female figures on pedestals representing Alsace and Lorraine, tears streaming down their cheeks; and when the proprietress, Madame Thierry, would speak of them the tears would roll down her cheeks, too. The sympathy of Americans was generally with France.

In Germany we found a remarkable condition. In one sense unspoiled by her great victories, so cheaply bought, and the acquisition of so much wealth in indemnity, the nation was just starting two propagandas. One was to organize productive industry and encourage the sciences and arts, with the object of making their nation foremost as a commercial producer. At the same time, Germany planned to carry her products to the four corners of the earth, in which, for forty years, she was entirely successful.

The second, as unholy and unrighteous as the first, was praiseworthy, was militarism, in which the rulers of the nation sought to make the profession of the soldier universal, with the deliberate and cold-blooded purpose of conquering the rest of the world, as Alexander, Hannibal, Cæsar and Napoleon had planned before. Germany had in view also the creation of a navy which could overcome England's, so she might rule the world on both land and sea. But for the heroism and self-sacrifice of the little kingdom of Belgium, with only eight millions of people, they would have succeeded.

We saw many idle soldiers lying on the grassy parapets of their forts smoking, while near them women dressed in rags carried dirt in wheelbarrows to form additional parapets. Nannie instinctively foresaw the future. She even then denounced those people as barbarous and inhuman, and for the rest of her life she hated bitterly German militarism.

In England we found the people divided into numerous classes, royalty, nobility, gentlemen, tradespeople, and common people. Many of these latter, for want of the ambition and self-reliance necessary to bring about success, had become sordid and drunken.

There were hundreds of street cars in Paris and its environs broad-mindedly labeled "American Railway," but hardly one in England.

In Manchester (then a larger city than New York), an apparently intelligent Scotch policeman, recognizing me as an American, proudly pointed to a brand new street car with one, horse, and remarked, "I suppose you don't have anything like that in America?" When I replied that every city in the United States having twenty thousand population had a street car system, he evidently regarded me as a sort of American Baron Munchausen.

The upper classes relied upon their control of the sea by the largest navy in the world, indirectly to extort taxes from their millions of subjects in their vast possessions, governed without their consent. Suppressing ambition for democracy and restraining maritime commerce of other nations, is perhaps not as cruel and barbarous as the intended control of the world by Germany, but is quite as unrighteous and has been and still is detrimental to the progress and advancement of weaker peoples.

Of all countries we visited, Switzerland seemed to possess the best free democratic government and the people were the happiest. They looked you in the face with a cheerful smile wherever you met them and were content with their condition, as they have been for over three hundred years.

The difference between Europeans and Americans we found to be marked. For instance, on one of the Lake Geneva passenger steamers from Vevey to Geneva we found a thousand passengers, composed about equally of Americans, English, French, Germans, Spaniards, and Italians. While talking to a well-dressed American of perhaps twenty-five years of age, a band of about thirty Italians appeared on the upper deck, where most of the passengers were assembled.

Most of the passengers, especially the English, would not speak to each other without a formal introduction, so social greetings were few. When the band had played a few minutes, this American took off his hat and placed a handkerchief over it and carried it through the crowd, remarking, "Something for the band, please." He approached every passenger on deck. Europeans stared, astonished at the action of this man from the "Woolly West," but Americans smiled encouragement. He obtained probably the largest contribution the leader had ever received. He proceeded to the band and every man and woman was gazing at him in perfect silence when he turned over the handkerchief to the leader, until some American clapped and every American joined in. We were all proud of our countryman.

At 44 Rue de Clichy our son, Anson Cassel, was born on November 19, 1878. He was our joy for the next fifteen years. His birth delayed our return until March, 1879, when we took passage on a Cunarder. In Washington I received orders to proceed to the headquarters of the 10th Cavalry.

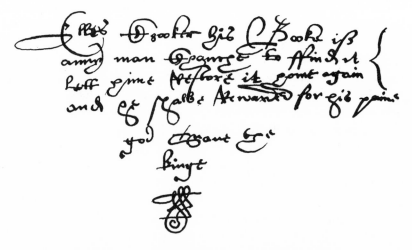

INSCRIPTION IN NANNIE'S FAMILY BIBLE, DATED 1614.
INHERITED FROM HANNAH HIPPISLY MARTIN.
TRANSLATED AND IN MODERN HANDWRITING, IT READS AS BELOW:

Ellis Crooker: his book; if
any man chance to find it;
let him restore it home again
and he shall be rewarded for his pains,
God save the King!

Out West Again

We traveled to Fort Concho, Texas, an uncomfortable and unprepossessing post, by ambulance from San Antonio, arriving April 11, 1879, and I served with the 10th Cavalry (colored) for twelve years, and was executive officer for Colonel B. H. Grierson, commanding the post, regiment and district under General Ord, department commander.

A big-hearted man, the only experience Grierson had in military affairs was as a general of volunteers, with which he was successful. With no experience in the regular army, even the best intentions did not fit him for the required discipline. He left the details of the post and regiment entirely to me, signing only papers which went to his superiors. He was too prone to forgive offenses and trust to promises for reform, which rendered the discipline and reputation of the regiment poor.

In May, 1881, Indian troubles took me with a squadron of four companies to Fort Sill. Nannie accompanied me the 225 miles, and there, on October 22d, our daughter, Constance Lydia, a joy and comfort to us both, was born. She was only eight days old when we were ordered back to Concho, making that trip, as we had the previous one, by wagon transportation, Nannie with her baby and little Anson riding in the ambulance.

In July, '82, the headquarters of the regiment was transferred to Fort Davis, when we again made a 225 miles journey with wagon and ambulance transportation.

Fort Davis was dry and cool, a most pleasant climate, but as hostile Indians occasionally made raids on the citizens, as at Fort Concho, we were kept busy. Fort Davis is near El Paso. My interests took us frequently to that city. Among other activities, jointly with Judge Crosby I built the largest hotel then in Texas.

April 1, 1885, the regiment exchanged stations with the Third Cavalry in Arizona. We made that long and distressing march

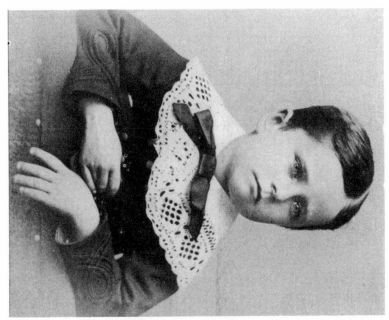

LITTLE ANSON AT FIVE AND ONE-HALF YEARS.

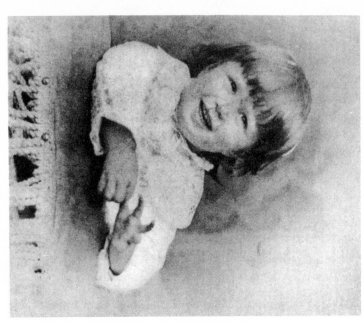

CONSTANCE AT TWO AND ONE-HALF YEARS.

Street in El Paso in Its Deserted Days, About 1870.

also with wagon and ambulance transportation. Arriving at El Paso in a terrible sand-storm, we found the Rio Grande unfordable. The only bridge crossed into Mexico three miles below the New Mexican line. According to international law, we could not pass over Mexican territory without the consent of the two governments, so we were delayed a week most uncomfortably, awaiting the tedious international interchanges to enable us to cross. We finally arrived at Deming (in a terrible sand-storm), meeting most of the troops of the 3d Cavalry there.

I was ordered to Fort Thomas on the Gila River, next to Yuma, the hottest post in the republic and the most sickly, excepting none. It was one of the most desolate posts in which we ever served. The valley was very low and hot. The mountains on each side of the river were some six or seven thousand feet higher than the valley and only about six or eight miles apart, so what little rain there was fell on these mountains.

I have often seen a heavy storm pass across the river from mountain to mountain, and watched almost a cloudburst of rain falling from the immense height only to be absorbed by the arid atmosphere before it reached the valley. Here many of our soldiers died in an epidemic of a very malignant, burning fever, which the post surgeon, Dr. Edward Carter, was unable to check. Informed that if we had ice the doctor could save many lives, I made requisition for an ice machine to cost three thousand dollars. It was twice returned by the War Department disapproved, the principal reason being that the Quartermaster General and the Surgeon General could not agree which department should pay for the wood to run the engine!

Exasperated, I appealed to General Sheridan personally. General Sheridan gave the two chieftains his opinion of them in such strong language that the appropriation for the machine was soon furnished, the first authorized in the army.

Our little daughter Constance was taken with the disease,

and Dr. Carter told us that she might not recover without ice. I wired Colonel Shafter, commanding Fort Grant, half way to the railroad seventy miles away, and he supplied me with two hundred pounds, rolled in blankets, within twelve hours. The day after the doctor reduced my daughter's temperature and she recovered.

While at Thomas the Northern Apaches went on the war-path, Geronimo and his wild followers devastating the settlements and killing many men, women and children, whom we buried in the post cemetery. This war lasted two years before our troops drove the Apaches into Mexico and, by agreement with the Mexican Government, followed them there, capturing Geronimo.

Contract Surgeon Dr. Leonard Wood, now the senior major general in the United States Army (who at one time attended my family), volunteered to act as surgeon in the expedition into Mexico, carrying his kit on his back while commanding a company of friendly Indians, which he did excellently. For this General Miles, commanding the department, became much attached to him.

To carry water into the post I had set the men to work building ditches, and also planted several hundred trees, which began to grow well. General Miles, visiting the camp on inspection, told me I deserved a better post. He relieved General Grierson from Fort Grant and placed me in command of that seven-company post. General Grierson recommended its abandonment for want of water, but General Miles said he knew I could get water from the mountains and make Grant one of the best posts. He supported me in requisitions for all the material and money I needed.

At a cost of sixteen thousand dollars I put in a most excellent water and sewage system, with a cement-walled lake in the middle of the parade ground, sixty by two hundred feet. Heretofore the parade ground and the officers' yards were bare of grass because of the extreme drought and the millions of ants which ate the grass. We put fountains all over the post,

My Family and Commanding Officer's Quarters, Fort Thomas, A. T.

PICNIC UNDER COLUMNAR CACTUS NEAR FORT THOMAS, A. T.
READ, MILLS, MRS. VIELE, WHIPPLE, NANNIE, LITTLE ANSON, CONSTANCE, FREEMAN.

capable of throwing water one hundred feet high, as the reservoirs had four hundred feet pressure. I established a small water motor which sawed all the wood and ran all the machines in the carpenter shop.

General Miles visited the post after my work was completed and issued a very complimentary order which gave me a standing throughout the army as one capable of meeting unusual difficulties in my line.

Grant was in a most beautiful climate, about four thousand feet above the sea, with Mount Graham six thousand feet higher, three miles away. The climate, trees, foliage, flowers and rapid streams of this mountain were much like the Adirondacks, so we built a small log hut camp there for the ladies and children.

Nannie's description of a visit to this camp is better than any I can write.

In Camp, Near Fort Grant,
July 18, 1888.

My Dear Mother:

We left the post at a little after two on Saturday afternoon. Anson had a big mule to ride, little Anson had a horse led by an orderly, I had a pony with Constance on behind me. I was astride. We soon had to ascend and of all the trails you could imagine! I could not have undertaken it if I had seen it. I would just as lief ride a pony upstairs, indeed *rather,* for if he fell I should not have so far to go, but on the trail if the pony had made a misstep in some places we should have gone helter skelter down a long way. I thought it was quite dangerous, but Anson would not let me dismount for he said if I walked once I would not want to ride, and indeed I could not have walked far, for we began to rise so rapidly that one gets out of breath soon. We zigzagged up the steepest places and at last reached the top, where it is perfectly lovely, the ground is covered with grass and some of the most beautiful flowers I have ever seen, and such quantities. There are loads of trees,

194

LITTLE ANSON'S COMPANY AT FORT GRANT, CONSTANCE IN CENTER.

Anson   Constance   Willie   Corbusier

principally pines. When we go back we shall have to walk about three miles, for it is very dangerous to ride down such steep places. We are all good walkers, however, and can do it nicely. I would not have missed coming up for anything, for the ride was an *entirely* new experience and one that I shall never have again. It is perfectly lovely in the camp, and though this is the rainy season and we have rains every day, it only lasts a short time and the sun soon dries things up. Yesterday it hailed.

When we reached the top of the steep road, we were about 8,000 feet above the sea, but we then began to descend in order to camp near water, so we are only about 7,000 feet or a little more above the sea. Graham peak, which is 10,600 feet elevation, is six miles from here and easily reached, that is, it is a perfectly good and safe road, but steep, and on account of the altitude the air of course is rarified and one so soon gets out of breath. We are going there in a few days, after we get used to the altitude. We all have immense appetites, and though our feet are wet sometimes for hours, take no cold.

I am so sorry Anson had to go down to Tucson, for it is extremely hot there. I think we shall soon know where we are going, and when. I forgot to say that Anson came up with us Saturday and went down Monday. Our camp is about six miles from the post, and it takes three or four hours to come, so you may know how steep it is. We are all in tents, as the log cabin that Anson had commenced is not yet finished. Our party consists of Mrs. Corbusier, her five boys, Mrs. Viele and her sister (a young lady) myself and two children and the chaplain. Across the pretty little brook which runs through the camp are four more tents occupied by several sergeants' families, and lower down the creek are the soldiers, who are felling trees and building the cabin. I forgot to say we have two cooks in our party, very necessary adjuncts when one considers the numerous and healthy appetites.

Your loving daughter,

NANNIE.

Commanding Officer's and Adjacent Quarters at Fort Grant.

CAMP ON THE MOUNTAINS,
July 22, 1888.

MY DEAR MOTHER:

We have been here a week yesterday, and notwithstanding it has rained every day, we have had a good time. The rains do not last long and it soon dries up. There are the greatest quantity of beautiful flowers here. I have a large bouquet in my tent about fifteen inches in diameter and taller than it is wide. We have had bear meat, a young fawn and wild strawberries. The nights are if anything too cold. We have taken several tramps, one of them to an old hunter's camp. He comes over to see us often and enjoys the break in his loneliness. He is alone in his camp except for a dog, which is almost as dear to him as a child, and two or three ponies. He is going to show us the way to the top of the mountains. He came over to see us last night and sat by the big log camp fire, and while we popped corn regaled us with numerous tales, all of which I took with a grain of salt.

You would be surprised to see how comfortable we can be in camp with a very little. I have turned a box on one side for a book case, put another on top where I keep my writing materials, over it all I have thrown a large towel, and with the bunch of flowers I spoke of on top, it looks very well. I have another box for washstand, another for clothes, and with nails driven in the tent poles to hang clothes, medicine bag, little looking glass, canteen, etc., things are quite shipshape.

Your loving daughter,

NANNIE.

FORT GRANT, A. T.,
August 4, 1888.

MY DEAR MOTHER:

We were up in the mountains when I last wrote you. Anson came back from the court he was on and he and the doctor came up on the mountain. We went the next day on horses and

Our Sitting Room at Fort Grant, A. T.

burros to the summit of Mt. Graham. It was about four miles from our camp, and is ten thousand six hundred feet above the level of the sea. We wrote our names and put them in the tin can left by the surveyors. Anson and Constance Lydia both wrote their own names. It was a very pleasant trip. I rode a burro, astride, of course, as I shall never ride any other way. Anson is going to take my picture as I appeared. Anson came up to the camp on Friday. On Saturday we went to the summit. That same evening, in a pouring rain, a courier came in bringing a copy of dispatches from San Carlos saying six Indians had gotten away and the troops were after them. Of course we could not tell but it was the beginning of another big outbreak. The commanding officer of Fort Grant said he had already sent out some pack mules and might have to send out all the rest, but if we wished to come down to the post next day he would send us what animals he could spare. We immediately decided to come down to the post, for in case of an outbreak, the Indians could easily take our camp. We left the camp about two o'clock Sunday afternoon. Anson was mounted on a horse with Constance behind him. I had a big white mule with little Anson behind me. We rode about a mile and reached the steep part of the trail where I was afraid to ride down. Indeed the whole party, about thirteen of us, dismounted and walked down the steepest part. We could in places look down on the post which looked so green, like an oasis in the desert. Mrs. Viele, Constance and I walked for about two miles, as we did not care to ride over places steeper than a pair of stairs, but the rest mounted before we did. We reached the post about six o'clock, pretty tired. The next day, Monday, I was stiff and tired, but everything in the house needed straightening up.

Tuesday Anson told me that General Miles would be here on Thursday. As the new commanding officer very kindly said we could keep this house till his wife came, thus saving us the trouble of a move, we had to entertain General Miles.

We straightened up the house and expected him about eleven o'clock Thursday morning, when lo! he drove in at *seven* in the morning, before we were out of bed. We hurried to dress, and as he expected to go right on to San Carlos immediately after breakfast, I told Sallie to cook the chickens for breakfast that we had intended giving him for dinner. Breakfast was late, of course, as General Miles took a nap and a bath, and it was ten o'clock when we were through. I hurried to fix him a box of luncheon to take with him, and they would have started immediately but some telegram came which decided him to wait for further news. We sent to the butcher's for a roast of beef, as we had eaten up the chickens intended for dinner. He had no meat fit to roast, so Sallie chopped it up and made a meat roll. We had dinner at five o'clock, General Miles, Colonel Pearson and Mr. Jerome taking dinner with us. The latter is a cousin of Lady Randolph Churchill. We had soup, fish, claret, meat, vegetables, olives, champagne, pudding and coffee, a dish of flowers in the center of the table and flowers in the finger bowls. I should have had a salad, but there was no oil in the commissary. After dinner I rearranged the lunch, and they got off. I told General Miles he was like a flea, no one ever knew where to put one's finger on him.

He laughed and said, "About as disagreeable as one, also." He told lots of funny stories and was very pleasant. He praised the post which Anson has improved so much and which certainly looked at its best, all beautifully green, the lake full of clear water, the fine fountains playing and the sun shining through them. General Miles showed Anson an endorsement he had made on an official paper regarding him (Anson) which was extremely complimentary. In fact, he could not have said more, as he praised him to the skies.

I hope the Indian business will be settled soon. I was so sorry to leave the mountains. It was delightful up there, and we intended to stay three weeks longer. We were there only two weeks. It was so cool at nights we had to have a big fire

Summer Camp on Mt. Graham, Near Fort Grant.

202

Nannie and Constance at Fort Grant, Artificial Lake in Background.

and sleep under several blankets, indeed one or two nights I slept under four blankets and a buffalo robe.

Your loving daughter,

NANNIE.

At this time, anticipating promotion, I took leave and, selling most of our belongings, we went to Boston. Here we bought a carload of household goods, shipping it by the Santa Fe. The car was burned at Deming, but the railroad company had insured it and we recovered the full value of our new goods. But among the losses which could not be valued was Nannie's diary, which she had kept in detail for eighteen years and from which she expected to write a book. That was one of the discouragements we faced in planning mutually to write our reminiscences.

In May, 1889, I was assigned to duty at Fort Bliss, Texas, as supervising engineer under Colonel Nettleton of the Geological Survey. I remained until April, 1890, when as lieutenant colonel of the 4th Cavalry, with three companies of that regiment, I was stationed at the Presidio, San Francisco, as executive officer under Col. W. M. Graham of the 5th Artillery.

This large post, adjacent to a very large and interesting city, was the most enjoyable station we ever had. The children enjoyed it, Anson going to school and Constance having a good teacher at home.

Numerous balls, dances and other amusements in addition to strenuous duties, kept us all busy and healthy. Here, again, we had the good fortune to have Dr. Leonard Wood, then a regular army doctor, as our family physician.

Col. W. R. Shafter commanded Angel Island in San Francisco Harbor and he, Colonel Graham and I constituted the first board under the new law for examination of officers for promotion. It was a *very lively,* and, I think, an efficient board. We examined some thirty-three officers.

When some members of the 4th Cavalry murdered a citizen, at regimental headquarters, Walla Walla, I was sent to command the regiment, the colonel being suspended for neglect. We liked Presidio, so this move was a disappointment. To our surprise we found Walla Walla among the most pleasant, agreeable and efficient posts at which we had ever been stationed. The officers and ladies were unanimously harmonious and the regiment, notwithstanding the bad reputation it had for this murder, was in every way the best disciplined and efficient I had ever served in.

Nannie, as usual, was one of the leaders in all the entertainments, which were patronized not only by the ladies and officers of the post, but by an equal number of citizens from the beautiful city of Walla Walla, at that time the wealthiest town in proportion to its population in the country.

The command was an interesting one because of the great number of semi-civilized Indians in the vicinity who were trying hard to make an honest living under great disadvantages. The citizens did not credit them with good intentions because of their inability to make a living out of the soil. They were driven from pillar to post, but always came to the army for relief, trusting, as all our North American Indians have always trusted, in the officers.

In July, 1892, with our two children, we made a most enjoyable tour of Alaska, by way of Seattle and the steamship "Queen," through the inner deep water channels with their still water and surrounding mountains covered with inexhaustible cedar. We visited dense forests of timber near Sitka, where the warm Chinook winds carry sufficient moisture to keep them damp through the entire year, so that no forest fires ever occur. The moss accumulated over fallen trees, which did not decay. Huge trees several hundred years old grow upon others, as large and as ancient, though dead. Fallen logs preserve so well that many are as available as the standing trees for lumber. Cattle live the year around on this constantly growing moss.

We stopped at Wrangell and Juneau, and spent some time at Sitka, visiting Treadwell, the great silver mine. We stopped

FATHER AND SON AT 58 AND 13. TAKEN AT FORT WALLA WALLA.

a couple of days to see the wonderful Muir glacier, traveling several miles over the surface of the solid ice mass. Twenty-seven miles long and several miles wide, it moves gradually downward to the sea by force of gravity, averaging seventy feet per day. As it moves, this great mass tears from the solid granite below huge masses of rocks, and pedestrians can hear the crushing of the rocks. On reaching the salt water, which is very deep, the ice begins to soften and disintegrate, and periodically falls in great shales, sometimes two miles in length and nine hundred feet deep, into the water, only two hundred feet being above the water line.

The captain stood off two miles from the glacier for us to see a berg break off, which happened in the afternoon. We could plainly see this immense body of ice fall into the water. It careened, disappeared, broke into many parts and finally appeared on the surface as bergs moving out to sea. The waves caused by this immense movement of ice rocked the ship as if we were in a storm.

I was promoted colonel of cavalry, not assigned, while I held command of the 4th. On the colonel's restoration, in February, 1893, I was assigned as colonel of the 3d Cavalry at Fort McIntosh, and joined February 28, 1893, where I had as adjutant Thomas B. Dugan and as quartermaster John T. Knight, both efficient officers.

The Garza Mexican troubles on the Rio Grande were then in full force, and my regiment was assigned to duty along the lower Rio Grande, leaving two companies of infantry at McIntosh.

Numerous bands of Mexicans, half from Mexico and half from the United States, committed depredations, stole property and killed Americans all along the river to Brownsville. This so-called Garza war kept my troops busy marching, and in the difficult effort to punish them we lost a number of men.

Another disturbing element between the two countries was the formation of large islands in the river. The shifting stream produced these "bancos," as they were called, which, when two or three hundred acres in extent, were claimed by the more excitable and lawless of both sides. They were used as a refuge by smugglers and other criminals denying the jurisdiction of both countries.

One of the bancos, Banco de Vela, was used by an American as a pasturage for about three thousand sheep. The Mexican customs authorities put the herders in jail and took the sheep into Mexico, as confiscated under their revenue laws. In retaliation the sheriff of the Texan county put the Mexicans found on the banco in jail.

Colonel Minero, commanding the 4th Mexican Cavalry, at the city of Reynosa, was opposite Banco de Vela. My regiment, the 3d U. S. Cavalry, was drawn up on one side to prevent further arrests and probable conflicts between the contending parties. This situation caused the organization of the Boundary Commission, of which I was later a member. (Text, 281.)

Ordered to relieve the 2d Cavalry under Colonel Wade, my regiment arrived at Fort Reno, June 24, 1893. I had always stated that if I ever became colonel and the authorities gave me an insignificant command of but one or two companies, the band and the laundresses, I would apply for retirement. A few days after reaching Fort Reno, one company was detached, leaving me but two companies of my own regiment. I wrote General Miles, commanding the department, my official and personal friend, that as regulations held me responsible for the efficiency and discipline of my regiment, I would prefer to take advantage of my right to retire on thirty years, unless I could be furnished with at least half of the regiment. For that purpose I asked six months' leave.

The general replied that he would, if it were possible, furnish me the half or the whole of my regiment, but the conditions were such that he could not. When I applied, he recommended my leave. Nannie, with Constance, had preceded me to Worcester, where I went to make arrangements to retire and devote my attention to my cartridge belt factory there.

But General Gresham, who knew of my familiarity with the banco troubles, told me the President had decided to appoint a Boundary Commissioner, and offered me the post. Supposing that it would only last a year or two, and knowing that I was well acquainted with the people of both sides and the nature of the questions involved, I decided to accept. Then it was discovered that I could not lawfully do so, unless I resigned my army commission, as no one could hold two government positions. The Secretary told me he was so anxious I should take the place, he would procure a resolution from Congress authorizing me to accept it as a colonel of cavalry, with pay and allowances as such, which he did. I entered upon this duty, not expecting it to last long, or to become a general.

As I look back over my military career I am impressed with the changes which time has wrought in the size of the military establishment. When I was made a colonel, there were but seventy-two colonels in the line, although forty-five States, represented by ninety senators, were then in the Union.

When I was made a general officer there were but nine general officers in the line of the army; while at that time the President of the United States had eight cabinet officers.

Since leaving active service I have retained my interest in military affairs, and have been so intimately connected with military orders as to be an ex-commander of the Loyal Legion, an ex-commander of the Order of Indian Wars, and am an honorary member of the Indiana Society of Engineers.

Brevet Commissions in the Army

Prior to the Civil War the Government established a satisfactory system of brevets, conferred on officers who distinguished themselves in action, so regulated that rights to promotion of those commissioned in special corps might not be infringed, while allowing the beneficiary to exercise rank and command by authority of his brevet whenever placed on duty with a mixed command. Thus, when a company of artillery and one of infantry served together, a junior captain with the brevet rank of major might assume and exercise command. (When a Captain I so exercised the rank of brevet Lieutenant Colonel, over a real lieutenant colonel by priority of date.) During the Civil War, however, the conferring of brevets was so overdone by political and other influences that in one or two instances a captain in a noncombative corps acquired the rank of major general. The situation was so absurd and confusing that Congress passed a law declaring that under no circumstances should a brevet be exercised for rank or command. This rendered brevets practically worthless. The army became dissatisfied and secured another method of rewarding distinguished service, medals of honor, but this, also overdone, is becoming unsatisfactory.

As time passed those modestly breveted outgrew all their brevets, while those immodestly breveted were generally of the noncombative corps stationed about Washington. In 1892, a bill was introduced in Congress to allow the restoration of the brevet "uniform" and "address."

I wrote the following protest:

HEADQUARTERS, 4TH CAVALRY,
FORT WALLA WALLA, WASHINGTON,
April 12, 1892.

TO THE ADJUTANT GENERAL,
    U. S. ARMY,
        WASHINGTON, D. C.

SIR: In the matter of Senate Bill No. 2699, for the restoration of brevet "uniform" and "address," I beg to make the following suggestions, and request that they be referred to the Committee on Military Affairs in the United States Senate, for such consideration as in its judgment they may seem to merit.

That all officers holding brevet commissions, whether above or below their present grade, may wear the insignia of their highest brevet rank on each side of the coat collar. Those conferred for gallantry in specific actions, on a red ground and those for faithful or meritorious service, not in action, on a white ground.

The reasons that impel me to this action are as follows:

It is well known that about the close of the war, brevets in many cases, by reason perhaps of propinquity to power, were given in such extravagant profusion as to destroy in a great degree their value to those of the deserving, and it goes without saying that as a rule a greater proportion of these highest grades by the promotions of time have worn out by covering over with other commissions a greater proportion of the modestly breveted.

It is also true that an officer holding a brevet below his present grade, and conscious of equal merit with his comrade who holds one above his present rank, will take equal pride in wearing the evidences of its appreciation if he be permitted to do so, especially if he can show that it was won in battle.

The proposed bill, however, as I understand it, will not

permit him to do either, and will, I fear, rather tend to confuse by putting on the shoulder rank without command, with no easy method of determining the actual rank or right to command.

To illustrate the effect that this bill, as proposed, would have on the Army, that is, on the officers on the active list, a reference to the last Army Register will show a total of 391 field officers in the entire Army, most of whom hold brevets below their present grade, and would be ignored by the present bill; all but 67 of the 391 hold brevet rank above their present grade, distributed in corps throughout the Army, as follows:

Adjutant General's Department	9
Inspector General's Department	0
Quartermaster's Department	10
Subsistence Department	8
Medical Department	7
Pay Department	3
Engineer Department	6
10 Regiments of Cavalry	8
5 Regiments of Artillery	7
25 Regiments of Infantry	9
TOTAL	67

It will be observed that of the 67 total, the Line of the Army have but 24, while the Staff have 43; and as a rule, even in the Staff, the noncombatant corps lead in honors.

Of this total of 67 field officers, in the entire active Army, holding brevets above their actual rank, 26 hold the brevet rank of General, and of these the Line of the Army has but six, while the Staff Corps have 20, and of these 20 Generals in the Staff Corps the Adjutant General's Department has 6, the Quartermaster's Department has 5, and the Subsistence Department has 6.

I have the honor to be

Very respectfully, your obedient servant,

ANSON MILLS,
Lieutenant Colonel 4th Cavalry,
Commanding Regiment.

As a result, Senator Sherman, chairman of the military committee of the Senate, advised me he had induced the Senate to withdraw the bill, which it had already passed.

In Washington Again

Asked to select the secretary to the Boundary Commission, on recommendation of Adjutant General Ruggles, I picked Mr. John A. Happer, a beardless youth of twenty, a minor clerk in the War Department. The Secretary doubled his pay to comport with the importance of the position, and Mr. Happer at once procured what he considered to be suitable personal attire, which included a fashionable cane and very sharp-toed buff shoes. Walking down the street with me, he remarked, "Colonel, why don't you *wear* a cane?"

I replied, "For the same reason that you wear one."

"How is that?" he asked, "I don't understand."

"Well," I replied, "you don't need a cane, and vanity impels you to wear one. I need a cane and vanity impels me not to wear it."

Later, on our first visit to El Paso, at La Coste, beyond San Antonio, he saw some Mexicans loading cotton. Calling to me from the car door, he said, "Colonel, do please come here. What induces those men to wear those foolish sharp-pointed hats?"

"Well," I replied, "I suppose they were moved by the same logic that induced you to buy sharp-pointed shoes."

Soon after, the inherent good sense I knew him to possess when I selected him, led him to abandon both cane and shoes, and he has become a prominent and successful citizen of El Paso.

After President McKinley's election, General Miles asked me if I intended to apply for promotion. I replied that I never applied for anything unless I thought I had more than an even chance of getting it, but that, if anyone high in authority would give me that assurance, I would. "I believe you have more than an even chance," he answered. "There is but one colonel I will recommend before you, and that is Shafter."

I made the application the next morning. Adjutant General

Ruggles made a detailed statement of my official services which I took to my friend, General Flagler, telling what General Miles had said. He promised me his help. In his office I met my classmate, General Merritt, then commanding the Department of the East in New York, who stated, "Mills, there is but one thing for me to do. When I return to my office I will also recommend you." I was soon promoted, but, according to the resolution of Congress appointing me Boundary Commissioner with the pay and allowances of colonel of cavalry, I had no additional pay for the nineteen years I served on that duty, holding the rank of brigadier general and receiving only colonel's pay.

Nannie and I, with our two children, stopped at the Richmond Hotel, in Washington, while we looked for the home we intended to rent or purchase. Senator White, now Chief Justice, also lived at the Richmond. Standing in the office one day, when Nannie entered and asked the clerk for her key, I saw Senator White was near her. She turned in her usual dignified manner to enter the elevator. Not knowing my relation to her, Senator White asked the clerk, "Who is that lady?" When he replied, "Mrs. Mills," Senator White said, "She is the most beautiful woman I ever saw."

While in El Paso on boundary business I received a telegram stating that Anson was seriously ill with appendicitis and was being operated on. I took the first train for Washington and arrived Sunday morning, but too late. Anson died during the night, February 25, 1894. He had been taken suddenly sick the Sunday previous, but, not knowing as much about the disease as they do now, the doctors deferred the operation until too late. It was the great sorrow of our life, and we could not help resenting all the rest of our lives the sad fate of one so young and promising.

Carefully preserved among his mother's papers is a letter from our son to me, and my reply to him. Shortly before she died, Nannie brought these to my attention, saying she thought them of sufficient worth to merit publication, considering that

NANNIE.

This graphic map illustrates how constantly Nannie followed me after marriage throughout my military service.

MAP
SHOWING
POST AND STATION ASSIGNMENTS
OF
ANSON MILLS, U.S.A.

SCALE OF MILES

NOTES:—
ALONE, AT POST OR STATION----△
ACCOMPANIED, AT POST OR STATION, BY MRS. MILLS-○
POSTS OR STATIONS OCCUPIED ON SECOND ASSIGNMENT -△- OR◉
NUMBER OF STATIONS OCCUPIED DURING 25 YEARS AFTER MARRIAGE
(1868 TO 1893) 26; DISTANCE TRAVELED (CHANGE OF STATION ONLY)
DURING SAME PERIOD, 25,808 MILES.

LITTLE ANSON AT TWELVE YEARS.

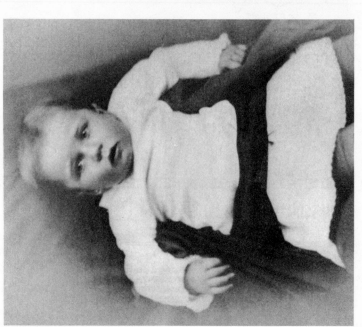

LITTLE ANSON AT SEVENTEEN MONTHS.

the boy was but fifteen when he wrote, but three weeks before he died. I append the two letters here:

HOTEL RICHMOND,
WASHINGTON, D. C.,
February 4, 1894.

MY DEAR FATHER:

I received your letter of the 27th with the letter from Walla Walla, and am very glad to hear from you. I hope that the boundary work will not take as long as the Mexican commissioner thinks.

The newspaper gave a list of the West Point cadets who failed in the last examination, and I was glad to see that Carl was not in the list. I guess Carl will be able to pull through if he works hard.

I am getting along quite well in school, but I wish that the teacher would rush a little as I think that we are not progressing as rapidly as we might. I got excellent in the carpenter shop last month and as I couldn't have gotten any higher than excellent and there were only a few boys who received marks that high, I think that I have done pretty well. I am on good terms with the carpenter and always try to do what he says and he helps me along and is very nice to me.

The weather is very cloudy and rainy today and I hope that it will clear off soon. We went to see a play called "The Senator" last Saturday and enjoyed it very much. I saw Grover and Mrs. Cleveland in one of the boxes. Last night Mamma went to a reception at the White House and shook hands with Grover, it was the last card reception of the season and Mamma says that there was a very large crowd there.

This afternoon Mamma, Tootsie and I went out to Tacoma to see the Martins, they seem to think that Carl is all right, and I think Nellie expects to make a visit to West Point in the summer when Carl will be a 3d classman. I have made the acquaintance of two boys here in the hotel, but one of them went away yesterday so there is only one left. We generally play cards in the evening and have a good deal more fun than if we were by ourselves.

The other day I went to the dead letter office and saw the clerks sorting out the dead letters. They have show cases in which they put all the extra curious things that pass through their hands. They have live rattlesnakes and everything you can think of.

Mamma called on Mrs. Happer a few days ago and Mrs. Happer said that there has only been one meeting of the club since you left and I guess that is why they have not taken me there yet. Caldwell wrote me a letter the other day and said that you stopped to see him when you passed through San Antonio. Caldwell seemed greatly pleased with his new house and I hope that he will get along all right.

Nearly all the boys around here want to go in the Navy, but I am going to stick to the Army. I don't see how anybody could prefer the Navy to the Army, but each fellow has his choice and if they want to go to the Navy it will leave that much more room in the Army for me. I am still anxious to go on that big game hunting trip to Maine and I guess this fall I will have to go on a good hunt if nothing turns up to mar it.

Uncle Tom has made me a new belt for my rifle and it is a very good one. As it is time for me to go to bed I will close. We all send our love and hope that you will be back soon. I remain,

Your loving son,
ANSON C. MILLS.

EL PASO, TEXAS,
February 11, 1894.

MY DEAR BOY:

I have just received your long letter so nicely typewritten and can not tell you in words how interesting it is to me to learn so many things of you and from you, for my hopes and fears are now more centered in you than in anyone else in the world; not that I love Mamma and Sister less or that they are deserving of less interest, but from the fact that (as you are now old enough to understand) as the world goes more is expected of boys and men, so that if I were to die suddenly the future of both Mamma and Sister would depend much upon you. So do not fail in every way possible to arm your-self for this responsibility should it come.

My mother died when I was about your age and left me the oldest of nine children, and while I did the best I could I had much care, but as Father lived to manage the business I did not have as much as you may have if I go.

I am glad you are getting along well at school for that is more important to you than all else just now, in fact, for the next five years. Don't be impatient for the teachers to go along faster. You do well enough if you keep up with the course, only strive to be thorough and understand all well that you go over so that if you go to West Point,—as I intend you shall when you are twenty, if you then still desire to,— that you may not be rattled.

I am glad you put the "C" in your name for if you had been fortunate enough to have seen and known your grandfather Cassel for whom it stands you would never fail to put it in. He was one of the best looking and most graceful men I ever saw, as straight as an arrow, with quick gait and quick speech, but few words, and liked by everybody and so correct in busi-ness that the cashiers in the banks would doubt themselves before doubting him. According to the laws of heredity you should inherit some of these qualities and I have thought sometimes I have already seen them in you, though it is hard to see the man in the boy, lest I had known him as a boy, which, of course, I did not.

Of course, you are as likely to inherit the traits of my father whom also you were unfortunate not to know at an age when you would appreciate, but he also had none that you need fear the development of in yourself, nor had either of your grandmothers.

I want you to read carefully the enclosed clipping on "Individuality," and mark the words underscored, for I think you can now understand the thoughts and ideas of our bright namesake. I think it is true, as he says, that heredity counts a great deal, perhaps not as much as surroundings and teachings, and I think, too, that he might have added that all three, heredity, surroundings, and teachings come mostly from the mother and there is where your great good fortune lies, if you improve it as you should and I think you will.

I want you to mark well what he says about individuality. Don't be restrained from doing things that seem sensible just because a lot of machine made boys say it is not the thing, nor do things not sensible because they say so. I have often regretted that I did not let you sit up all night at Fort Grant for fear it may in all your after life repress your individuality in thoughts and actions, for almost everything that man does or refrains from doing is from an instinct or teaching, like the parent talks, and not from brave independent and noble impulse of thought and reason like Paul Revere or Franklin, Cushing, Jefferson, Lincoln, Jackson, and Edison, who did new things useful to man.

I hear that Judge Maxey went hunting at Brownsville the other day and that the party killed three deer. We will look out for them when we get down there and tell you how it is.

Kiss both Mamma and Sister for me and tell them I will write to them both soon, though it is a great labor now that I am without my typewriter.

Your affectionate father,

ANSON MILLS.

The day before Anson's death, Nannie asked him what he wished she should say to me from him when I arrived, when he replied:

"Tell him I can't show how much I like him. I'm not strong enough. It will look as if I didn't like him. Tell him I love him very much." Of which she made a memorandum which I still have.

After eight months we purchased No. 2 Dupont Circle, on the most beautiful park and in the best social surroundings of the city. My position in the diplomatic service led us into the best society in Washington; we were invited everywhere we wanted to go, and were able to entertain all those who invited us, so that Nannie was able to exercise her abundant ability in making friends. We had at our house during the next twenty years several hundred interesting people of the army, navy, marine corps, senators and members of the different embassies, who were our guests.

One of Washington's greatest attractions was the opportunity it gave of renewing old friendships. We were always glad to welcome such guests as Gen. and Mrs. Freeman, Col. and Mrs. Corbusier, Col. and Mrs. Shunk, Miss Florence Cassel, and many others, old and new friends.

Early in 1894 Nannie joined the Washington Club, which she greatly enjoyed and of which she was a governor at the time of her death. She was also on the board of managers of several hospitals, and belonged to many charitable societies.

Washington was our permanent residence for the next twenty-three years, although Nannie and I, with Constance and our relatives, spent some time in Chihuahua, Santa Rosalia, Monterey, Zacatecas, Aguas Calientes, Guanajuato, Guadalajara, Mexico City, Jalapa, Puebla, Orizaba, and Queretaro, all in Mexico. (See graphic map U. S. and Mex., page 216.)

It was my professional duty to go to some of these places two or three times, the better to qualify myself by learning from the Mexicans views relating to the important boundary question. After she had heard of the simple character of the people and the interesting antiquities and customs of the country, Nannie always wanted to go with me.

While at Aguas Calientes, bathing in the hot springs, Nannie,

OUR WASHINGTON RESIDENCE.

(Text, 223.)

knowing the embarrassments of military courts in determining when an officer was drunk, brought me a copy of an inscription she had found on the wall of her room, probably left there by one seeking recovery from delirium tremens and at the same time preparing a test for the consideration of the members of the next court before which he might be brought.

"Not drunk is he who from the floor
Can rise again and still drink more,
But drunk is he who helpless lies
Without the power to drink or rise."

Spending most of our time in Washington, we found members of both Houses of Congress were much misunderstood by the people. They are constant hard workers with small salaries and almost universally honorable, honest men, and not, as many people believe, as they do of the army and navy, idle and uninterested in the government's welfare. Public sentiment has compelled many legislators to abandon the profession for another where they are better understood and better paid.

Among these noble men, I want to pay a tribute to a few of the finest statesmen the country has seen since the War of the Rebellion; men who trimmed their sails to no passing breeze but stood steadfastly for that public policy which would in their opinion bear best fruits for the great republic in the future. First among them, I put President Cleveland, Senator Hoar and Senator Root.

Cleveland, I consider the Washington of his time. When special classes of labor, having in their trust the railroads, the principal utilities of the whole people, declared their purpose to strike and by force and violence make their class the ruling class, the President issued his famous executive order that "if it took all the money in the treasury and all the soldiers in the army to carry a postal card from New York to San Francisco, the card would be delivered."

Unfortunately this glorious example had no power in later

PRESIDENT GROVER CLEVELAND.

PRESIDENT WILLIAM McKINLEY.

SENATOR GEORGE F. HOAR.

229

years, when self-styled statesmen with greater opportunities
cowered before a similar threat and surrendered the liberties
of a majority of the people.

Hoar was the Franklin of his period.　The Spanish War so
inflated our military reputation "because a wretched kern we
slew" as to cause a frenzy for "World Power"—when conquest, exploitation and subjugation of other lands and other
peoples with their trade and commerce after the manner of
other world powers was proposed.　Hoar valiantly sought to
prevent this fatal mistake by requiring that "the Constitution
should follow the flag."　He was defeated by but one vote
(I think) in the Peace Commission, in the Senate, and in the
Supreme Court.　There is nothing more pathetic in history
than his remark when called upon to assist in an appropriation for the restoration of Plymouth Rock, "Plymouth Rock
was washed away by the loss of these votes."

Root, the Hamilton of his occasion, when chairman of the
recent constitutional convention of his great State, sought to
reform its criminal and civil jurisprudence, so that its courts
should be instruments for the detection and punishment of
crimes and disorders rather than for technical avoidance of
that righteous end.

Though these three great statesmen failed of complete success, their noble and self-sacrificing example must surely inspire others.　Meanwhile, "in the sunset of life which gave
mystical lore," they have said figuratively to the American
people as did Roman gladiators in another arena, "Caesar, we
who are about to die salute you."

Many high school graduates have no better conception of
the meaning of Jefferson's "Declaration of Independence" and
the "Constitution" of Washington and Franklin than of the
book of Mormon.　They do not realize what our liberties cost,
and how easy it is to lose or, once lost, how difficult it is to
recover them.

On March 5, 1810, Mr. Jefferson wrote to his friend Governor
Langdon of Virginia:

"While in Europe, I often amused myself with contemplating the characters of the then reigning sovereigns of Europe. Louis the XVI was a fool, of my own knowledge, and despite of the answers made for him at his trial. The King of Spain was a fool; and of Naples, the same. They passed their lives in hunt= ing, and dispatched two couriers a week one thousand miles to let each know what game they had killed the preceding days. The King of Sardinia was a fool. All these were Bourbons. The Queen of Portugal, a Braganza, was an idiot by nature; and so was the King of Denmark. Their sons, as regents, exercised the powers of government. The King of Prussia, successor to Fred= erick the Great, was a mere hog in body as well as in mind. Gustavus of Sweden, and Joseph of Austria, were really crazy; and George of England, you know, was in a straight=waistcoat. There remained, then, none but old Catherine, who had been too lately picked up to have lost her common sense. In this state Bonaparte found Europe; and it was this state of its rulers which lost it with scarce a struggle. These animals had become without mind and powerless; and so will every hereditary mon= arch be after a few generations. Alexander, the grandson of Catherine, is as yet an exception. He is able to hold his own. But he is only of the third generation. His race is not yet worn out. And so endeth the book of Kings, from all of whom the Lord deliver us, and have you, my friend, and all such good men and true, in his holy keeping."

The Kaiser found Europe in a similar condition in 1914. England, Germany, Austria, Russia, and Italy had emperors by divine right, with royal families, lords and nobles, most of whom were either moral or physical and mental degenerates. The later George is so imbecile as not to require a straight-jacket, as did his predecessor, and the Kaiser, a moral degen-erate, sought only to play the rôle of Napoleon. When all Europe seemed in a peaceful and prosperous condition, he, by his foolish cablegrams, sought to distract George's and Nich-olas' attention from his planning, while the secretive diplomats of England, France, and Russia on one side, and Germany,

Austria and Italy on the other, blindfolded their people by many vari-colored state papers, and backed them over night into war, of which they knew nothing until armies were moving. Had proper publicity been given by any interested nation, war would not have ensued.

Our government, too, was somewhat responsible, in that we placed before our war college a statue of that greatest of moral degenerate rulers (not excepting Nero) miscalled "Frederick the Great," thus giving his successor, the Kaiser, to understand we approved his militarism. Strange that our people permit this statue to remain.

What the war is about the world's people have no intelligent conception. Yet unless the American people educate themselves to an intelligent understanding of the hazard of their liberties, we may become too entangled to extricate ourselves.

Every American should ponder these things and ask whether our citizenship has not become so diluted as to endanger the perpetuity of the great republic, and whether it is not now necessary to return to the high schools and colleges the careful study of the Declaration of Independence and the Constitution. Another great law-giver of three generations past, Dr. Lyman Beecher, evidently had in his sunset of life "mystical lore" to see these present shadows. I submit his words here for the people who may read this to ponder, and for study in the schools.

"We must educate! We must educate! Or we must perish by our own prosperity. If we do not, short will be our race from the cradle to the grave. If in our haste to be rich and mighty, we outrun our literary and religious institutions, they will never overtake us; or only come up after the battle of liberty is fought and lost, as spoils to grace the victory, and as resources of inexorable despotism for the perpetuity of our bondage.

"We did not, in the darkest hour, believe that God had brought our fathers to this goodly land to lay the foundation of religious liberty, and wrought such wonders in their preservation, and raised their descendants to such heights of civil and religious liberty, only to reverse the analogy of His providence, and abandon His work.

"No punishments of Heaven are so severe as those for mer= cies abused; and no instrumentality employed in their inflic= tion is so dreadful as the wrath of man. No spasms are like the spasms of expiring liberty, and no wailing such as her convul= sions extort.

"It took Rome three hundred years to die; and our death, if we perish, will be as much more terrific as our intelligence and free institutions have given us more bone, sinew, and vitality. May God hide from me the day when the dying agonies of my country shall begin! O thou beloved land, bound together by the ties of brotherhood, and common interest, and perils, live forever—one and undivided."

There were others following close on to the great men I mention; some I know more or less intimately, such as William McKinley, Charles W. Fairbanks, and Joseph Cannon and Champ Clark, in the legislature; in the army, Generals Sherman, Sheridan and Miles stand out, and in the navy, Admirals Dewey and Schley—all of them American patriots of the very highest order.

Many amusing incidents in our social life come back to me as I write. At a dinner given by Mr. Romero, the Mexican Ambassador, Mr. Cannon escorted Mrs. Mills to the table. I heard her say of some peculiar Mexican dishes, "Mr. Cannon, where do you suppose these come in?" He replied in his quaint and curious way, "Mrs. Mills, I spent my first twelve years in Washington trying to find out how they did things, and now I don't care a *dom* how they do 'em."

At a stag dinner of some eighteen guests at my house, Minister Wu Ting Fang sat at my right, and opposite sat Lieutenant General Young. General Young proposed the health of his host. All sat down save the Chinese Minister, who, after a pause, exclaimed, "Gentlemen, I think General Young has forgotten something." Young, not well acquainted with him, looked astounded. After a pause, the Minister went

Your Friend
Champ Clark.
To Gen. Anson Mills

To my friend Gen'l Anson Mills with my Compliments.

Oct 9th 1917.

J G Cannon

ADMIRAL GEORGE DEWEY.

ADMIRAL WINFIELD SCOTT SCHLEY.

on, "I am a Chinaman, but I spent four years in London, two in Madrid, and I have been here now in America a short time. I know something about civilization, and know that no man ever got up this dinner. I propose the health of the hostess." The wit and humor of the Chinaman were loudly acclaimed. He became well acquainted with Nannie, visiting her frequently, and entertained her with interesting stories of his experiences at home and abroad. In turn, she was able to interest him in our large experience in the vicissitudes of the army and travel generally.

As evidence of Nannie's superior capabilities in administering household affairs it should be mentioned that she kept two servants, Menger Caldwell and Sally Caldwell, his wife, for eleven years, from 1882 to 1893, and at Washington, Dora Miller Kelly, fourteen years, from 1896 to her death in 1910, and her brother, Martin V. B. Miller, seventeen years, from 1900 to date. (Cut, 241.)

All these servants were so capable and satisfactory that their long service seems to warrant the appearance of their pictures in this narrative.

Our daughter, Constance, attended the excellent schools in Washington, grew up, and soon entered society, when our house was visited by a host of young people of both sexes. After enjoying this interesting period, she became engaged to a young officer of artillery, Winfield Scott Overton, and two years later, they were married at our home, on the 30th day of April, 1903.

Captain Overton graduated from West Point just before the Spanish War. He served in the Philippines and was seriously wounded at the battle of La Loma, March 25, 1899. He remained in the hospital in the Philippines for some time, and has been operated upon several times since, but never fully recovered, and in June, 1908, he was compelled to retire from the service. They have three beautiful children, Hannah Elton, six; Constance Elizabeth, four, and Mabel Helen, three years old. (Cut, 240.)

CAPTAIN W. S. OVERTON WITH NANCY

CONSTANCE MILLS OVERTON.

Our Grandchildren, Hannah Elton, Constance Elizabeth and
Mabel Helen Overton in 1916.

MENGER CALDWELL.

SALLY CALDWELL.

MARTIN V. B. MILLER.

DORA MILLER KELLY.

MILLS MEMORIAL FOUNTAIN, THORNTOWN.

In 1908 Nannie and I visited my birthplace, Thorntown, Indiana, a beautiful but sleepy town of about two thousand inhabitants. An epidemic of typhoid fever was raging, caused by poor drainage and a layer of impervious clay about twenty feet below the surface, which caused contamination of the wells.

A prominent minister requested me to donate a library to my native town. Thinking more good could be done by building a pure water system, I said that if the town would maintain a fountain monument to the memory of my father and mother, I would build a water and sewer system.

A town meeting accepted my proposition. I employed Mr. Charles Brossman, a civil engineer, to draw plans and superintend the building of an excellent water system, which pumped pure water from far below the impervious clay, carrying it to an elevated tank sufficient to supply the whole city with water; also the main sewers of a system to carry off the impure drainage; and to erect a fountain in memory of my parents.

When the work was completed, the town gave a celebration in my honor, which I attended, together with my family and many of our relatives on both sides. About ten thousand people were present. I made a few remarks, presenting the works to the city, and my daughter, Constance, unveiled the fountain. Many speeches were made, the principal one by Mr. A. Morrison, representing that district in Congress.

The water-works and sewer system have proved a great convenience, and added to the health of the city. So far the city has kept its faith in maintaining the fountain beautiful, clean, flowing, and in neat repair.

In Washington we invested a large sum in U. S. two-per-cent bonds, the proceeds of the woven equipment business. The peculiar laws relating to the reserve of national banks forcing these bonds to a six per cent premium, we disposed of them at a profit. With this money we bought property at Penn-

Captain Carl Anson Martin.

Miss Kathleen Cassel Kline.

sylvania Avenue and Seventeenth Street and erected the first steel-frame perfectly fireproof building in Washington.

After retirement, while I was conducting the cartridge belt factory at Worcester, Nannie spent much of her time in Gloucester, Mass. In 1910 she bought property on a rocky ledge eighty-four feet above and a half a mile from the sea and built a fireproof residence. In writing her sister Katie, she said, "We have called our place 'Bayberry Ledge,' a very suitable name, for it is on a ledge of rocks and has lots of bayberry bushes on it. Anson has deeded it to me, and it is the dearest spot I know in the world." For seven years, until her death, Nannie spent most of her summers here cultivating flowers and enjoying the freedom of the country life, where, too, she entertained many of her relatives and old army friends during the hot seasons, among them General John M. Wilson, my classmate, Miss Waller, General and Mrs. Geo. M. Sternberg, General Wm. H. Bisbee, Mr. and Mrs. Keblinger, Mr. and Mrs. Batchelder, Mr. and Mrs. Follett, and our favorite nephew, Captain Carl A. Martin, and our favorite niece, Miss Kathleen Kline.

By 1912 the only piece of property I had remaining in El Paso became so valuable that I tore down the two-story building then on it, and built a monolithic cement building twelve stories high, containing no steel beams, the concrete being held in place by steel rods interspersed through the walls, columns, floors and roof. There is no wooden floor in the entire building from basement to turret, even the wash-boards in the rooms are made of cement and on all sides not exposed to parks the windows are fireproof. This was said to be the first building of the kind erected in the United States, and, so far as I know, it is still the only one of that magnitude.

Mills Building, Washington, D. C.

MILLS BUILDING, EL PASO.

NANNIE'S RESIDENCE, BAYBERRY LEDGE.
(Text, 245.)

BRIGADIER GENERAL JOHN M. WILSON (CLASSMATE).
(Text, 245.)

Faithfully your friend
Charles W. Fairbanks
To Gail Mills

(Text, 233.)

Consolidation of the El Paso and Juarez Street Railways

When the Santa Fe, Mexican Central, Texas & Pacific, and Sunset Routes were completed to El Paso, about 1880, the five thousand people of El Paso, and eight thousand of Juarez, organized four street railways, two in El Paso (one on El Paso Street and one on Santa Fe Street), connecting with the two similar Mexican roads on the Juarez side at the middle of the Stanton and Juarez Street bridges. Stock in these roads was subscribed in the East, but each road had a president, four directors and other officers, all of whom, to be popular with the public, made deadheads of the officials of the two cities, policemen, collectors of customs, revenue officers, and so forth. There was, therefore, great maintenance expense and little revenue for the stockholders, and the equipment soon degenerated into a most impoverished condition. When it became necessary to assess stockholders or go into bankruptcy, Senator Bate, from Tennessee, a personal friend, complained to me that he and his wife had twenty-five thousand dollars in stock of the El Paso street road. He was unable to pay his assessments and, as El Paso was said to be my town, he thought I ought to do something to relieve him. We went to El Paso and he had some stormy interviews with the managers of his road. Suggesting the possibility of a consolidation of the four roads, I told him that as I had the confidence of the Mexicans as well as the Americans of the two cities, if he was willing to come with me, we might encourage the stockholders in New York to give proxies for a majority of the stock.

We saw the principal stockholders in New York, one of them a cousin of J. P. Morgan, obtained proxies for a majority of the stock and power of attorney to represent the stockholders in the consolidation of the four roads.

The El Paso street road was advertised for sale under foreclosure. Authorized by its stockholders to purchase, I did so, and then obtained from the Mexican stockholders and others in El Paso proxies for a majority of the stock in the other roads. Calling a meeting of each of the four roads, I proposed a consolidation into one company, making the circuit through both cities, to be styled the El Paso and Juarez Traction Company, with charters from the States of Texas and Chihuahua. Governor Ahumanda of Chihuahua and the Governor of Texas both granted the charters. The four companies made a statement of their financial condition and expressed willingness to merge in the new international company. It had a capital of two hundred thousand dollars, distributed to each company in proportion to their annual gains for the past five years. The directors of the four companies elected officers for the new company. Messrs. Z. T. White, Jos. Magoffin, John A. Happer, Max Weber and I were elected directors, and by them I was elected president. There was some disagreement as to the stock to be allotted the Santa Fe Street Company, and the officers to be elected, so Messrs. White, Maxon and Gordon declined to enter the consolidation. It was agreed to run the roads jointly, but the Santa Fe company kept its own organization. The four companies were run under our management as one road, all deadheads were cancelled and the company soon prospered.

At this time Stone and Webster of Boston offered to buy the company at its stock valuation, two hundred thousand dollars, and, after some delay in correspondence, the sale was accomplished. The new company at once put in an electric system and it has since grown to be one of the best car companies in the United States, well managed, with two million dollars capital, and some sixty miles of road.

It can be justly claimed, I think, that this was a most material development for the cities of El Paso and Juarez. Too much credit can not be given those who joined me in the project, Messrs. Magoffin, Happer, Weber, and others. Printed proceedings of this consolidation may be found in the El Paso Library.

The Reformation of El Paso

The American War of the Rebellion and the Mexican Maximilian War left El Paso and Juarez almost destroyed. Neither recovered until the advent of the several railroads in 1881, when thousands of men, good, bad and indifferent, were attracted by the easier access by rail. Many had good intentions, but many were of that noisy, lawless character that usually drifts to cities under such conditions. Gambling, especially among the Mexicans, was soon a leading amusement on both sides of the river, and the saloon and red light districts for many years gave the two cities the just reputation of being among the most disorderly and lawless in the country.

No mayor could be elected unless he harmonized with and fostered all three of the above mentioned elements—some mayors lived in the red light district. Notwithstanding that righteous and well intending people were in a majority, the bravest of them were unable for many years to work any reformation, business and professional men being ostracised when demanding reform. Many cruel murders were committed, but it was impossible under the dominance of the three bad elements to procure convictions.

An experience of mine with an El Paso jury about eight years prior to the reformation will illustrate the task these reformers had.

While defending a suit for some $11,000 for liens on buildings, I received two anonymous notes asking me to bribe the jury. I handed them to the judge that he might make an example of the case. While he and the lawyers in the case were in consultation in chambers, a message was sent that a man wished to see me at a certain place. Suspecting the author of the notes, I suggested that if the Judge and attorneys approved I would try to entrap him. All consented, remaining in chambers until I returned. Compton, the "end man" of the jury, was the man who sent for me, and suggested that I pay him $3,000 for a favorable judgment, stating he had

HORACE B. STEVENS.

JOHN A. HAPPER.

W. WILBUR KEBLINGER.

FRANK R. BATCHELDER.

canvassed the jury and a majority had agreed. I replied that as a business man I could not part with so large a sum on the guarantee of one man. I asked to see them all privately, two at a time, after 9 p.m., at my room at the Sheldon Hotel. Compton agreed.

I told the Judge this, and placed myself at his disposal.

Calling in Sheriff Ten Eyck and Court Reporter McKelligon, he told them to report at my room at 8.45, and follow my instructions.

I secreted them behind a folding bed in a corner. When Compton came, he started to search the room. But I told him if he wanted to do business with me to sit down and do it, asking peremptorily where the second man was. He was down stairs, and when Compton brought him up I asked them to state plainly what they could do. Hunt, the other man (reputed to be a brother of Sarah Althea Hill, who married Judge Terry) (Text, 338), handed me a paper with the names of all the jurors with the sums a majority had agreed to receive, some as low as $50. I placed the paper in my pocket and after a little further talk to make sure they had been well heard, told Compton to bring up the next man. But he never returned.

This was Saturday, and all concerned were pledged to secrecy, but when Judge Willcox called court to order on Monday morning, there was not standing room to be had! The Judge said:

"Gentlemen of the Jury: Since last session the defendant in this case has handed me certain letters which I desire to read to you. The first appears to have been filed in the post office, El Paso, on the 20th day of June of the present year, and is as follows: 'Mr. Mills, if you want to win your case you must fix the jurymen in this case liberally or you will lose. A friend.' The second is as follows: 'Mr. Mills if you are going to do anything do it quick and have it money and nothing else. Go to the man at the west end of the jury box. It must be money or you will lose. A friend.' "

The judge asked each juryman if he knew anything of
the letters. All denied any knowledge, the end men most
vehemently.

Called to the stand, I told my story, omitting mention of the
witnesses. When I read the amounts to be paid each juryman,
a most respectable salesman and neighbor of mine who was
named at a very low price, cried out, "For God's sake, Judge,
stop this! My parents are respectable people, and when they
read this it will break their hearts!"

In the midst of my narrative Compton violently declared,
"You are a —— damned liar." The sheriff forced him back
into his seat. Compton and Hunt were sworn, and denied all
that I had stated.

The sheriff and court reporter then corroborated my report
of the conversation which they heard concealed behind the
bed.

Asked if they wanted to be heard again, Compton and Hunt
hung their heads, Compton only replying, "No, it's no use;
they were behind the bed."

The Judge announced a mistrial, honorably discharging all
members of the jury but Compton and Hunt, who were confined in jail to await the action of the grand jury. True bills
were found against them and they were tried, convicted and
sent to the penitentiary.

This narrative is compiled from official records of the case
which I possess.

Returning home one Sunday from a walk down El Paso
Street, Nannie said, "Anson, we had thought to make El Paso
our home, but if you do, you will have to live alone. I saw
nothing but saloons and gambling dens with the cries of
gamblers and singing of women among them!"

Not until 1905 did strength enough appear to overcome the
lawless, when Horace B. Stevens (Cut, 254) took the matter in
hand, assisted by such brave and self-sacrificing men as J. A.
Smith, W. S. McCutcheon, R. B. Bias, William H. and R. F.
Burges, H. D. Slater, Rev. Henry Easter, Felix Martinez, Waters

Davis, Millard Patterson, W. M. Coldwell, Frank Powers, U. S. Stewart, and many others. Success was not attained until after many public meetings, Waters Davis becoming the head of an organization for that purpose. Mr. A. L. Sharp was elected to the legislature and at the request of his constituents procured a bill closing the gambling houses by injunction. This bill was prepared at the suggestion of Richard Burges by Judge W. M. Coldwell, and stood all court tests.

All these reformers were foremost among the builders of the now great city. J. A. Smith, who began with its beginning and never faltered either in successes or honest failures, either in statesmanlike politics or brave progressive business enterprises, is particularly a noteworthy figure. H. B. Stevens and Waters Davis, in this long fight, not only sacrificed their financial interests, but risked their personal safety.

The reform movement was so successful that El Paso today is one of the best governed cities in the United States. Notwithstanding the addition to its population during the past two years of fifty thousand United States soldiers (well disciplined men, however), it has stood the test of good, safe government.

MEXICO

Youthful knowledge of our war of 1847 with Mexico, and a residence of four years at El Paso, where I employed many Mexicans in the construction of buildings and surveying, gave me a great interest in its government, its people and affairs generally. History told me Cortez in his conquest destroyed a civilization better than his own, leveling to the earth a beautiful city of five hundred thousand inhabitants, and rebuilding one less beautiful by the enslavery of its people, reduced from civilization to abject serfdom by Spanish authorities. For two hundred years these people suffered cruel wars before their efforts to acquire independence were successful. Later, Mexico was again victim of foreign nations, and finally America, too, was guilty, as I believe, of making a needless and unrighteous war upon her in 1847. In evidence, I quote the following from page 53 of Grant's Memoirs:

"For myself, I was bitterly opposed to the measure, and to this day regard the war which resulted as one of the most unjust ever waged by a stronger nation against a weaker nation. It was an instance of a republic following the bad example of European monarchies in not considering justice in a desire to acquire additional territory."

The peace treaty promised we were to pay Mexico many millions for territory acquired by force, but much of this money was withheld until a commission of our own people determined how much be finally kept in payment of claims alleged to be due our citizens—the pretext for the war. This commission could not find claims enough to exhaust the money withheld, so much of it was given back to Mexico.

My brother, W. W., lived on the border for fifty years, ten of which he was consul in Chihuahua. Another brother, Edgar Allen, after spending twenty years on the Rio Grande border, lived and traveled in various parts of Mexico in different business capacities from 1886 to 1901. He was employed at Escalon, the City of Torreon, Culiacan, the capital of Sinaloa, and the City of Jiminez, traveling through the states of Sinaloa and Durango to Jiminez, then to Sombrerette, and then to Gutierrez and state of Zacatecas, thence to Chihuahua. He found Mexico a tranquil nation with a people satisfied with their government; where a great majority of the foreigners were likewise satisfied with the government and their treatment, and where the people were glad to see foreigners and treated them well.

From all foreign nations, however, but principally from our own, came a disturbing element of ne'er do wells, itinerant visitors awaiting a hoped-for conquest and exploitation of that country to get their innings. Somewhat lawless, these people did much for which they would be arrested at home. Occasionally they were arrested by Mexican authorities. Many brought money procured from friends and relatives at home to enable them to establish themselves in a new country. They spent it rapidly, became troublesome, got into difficulty with the officials and made loud complaints to our government. These, perhaps, did not represent one-fifth of the American residents in Mexico.

Another class on the border of Texas, Arizona and New Mexico, were native citizens of Mexican descent, born on American soil, but good citizens of neither country, and continually in trouble with one or the other. Together with lawless Americans these fostered trouble from year to year.

Of the probable fifteen million inhabitants of Mexico, at least eleven million are pure Indians, with no admixture of Spanish or other foreign blood. These Indians are much as when Cortez found them, few speaking Spanish or any other common language, but speaking at least fifty-five different Indian languages. They have never taken any interest in what is known to us as politics; have no desire to vote, and do not know what it means. Yet they are, or were, as contented and happy as other peoples, satisfied with their governing classes, and as kind and gentle in their intercourse with each other as the people of the average nation.

More Mexicans, or people of the Mexican race, lived on
the American side of the border in Texas, New Mexico,
Arizona and California than on the Mexican side, because no
American markets are available to Mexican producers. They
could not afford to pay the duty required to enter the American
market and compete with producers on the American side, so
that most produce was raised on the American side to which
adjacent population gravitated.

As a citizen in Mexico, an officer on the border in Texas,
and as boundary commissioner for twenty years, I can testify
Mexico possessed a tranquil government, and that my wife
and family felt as well protected from violence on the streets
of the great cities as they would have felt in the United States.
My brother, W. W., also found in his official connection as
consul, that this state of affairs existed.

In October, 1909, President Taft and President Diaz, by
mutual agreement, met for greetings and congratulations at
El Paso and Juarez, and gave each other dinners on each side
of the river. Physically splendid men, it is a compliment to
each to say they resembled each other, both in physical
appearance, in language, and in gesture. In Juarez, I was a
guest of the Mexican Government; in my diplomatic capacity,
I sat near both Presidents, who were seated vis-à-vis. In
their speeches the two Presidents seemed to vie with each
other in congratulations on the good relations and tranquil
governments on both sides of the border. The hundred guests
in the great hall of the custom-house heard them with profound interest and respect. No one could doubt the sincerity
of each; yet in a few months the two nations were practically
at war. How it came about will be a mystery forever, but
there is no disputing the fact that the rebellion against Diaz
was organized, armed and equipped on the American side.

When the trouble began six years ago, as boundary commissioner, I advised the Government that our neutrality was
so inadequate, or laxly administered, or both, that nearly all
the insurrectos then in arms in Mexico were organized in the

United States, and practically all the arms and munitions of war were unlawfully or at least unrighteously introduced from this country. Living in El Paso during much of the hostilities, I knew that many secret service men, detectives and others in the employ of the Government, were seeking something. But neither I, nor so far as I know, either of my brothers were ever approached regarding conditions in Mexico.

The original Francisco I. Madero, said to be of Jewish descent, as a young man lived near Matamoras, when General Taylor crossed the Rio Grande for Monterey. The army was unable to procure wagon transportation, and Madero suggested pack animal transportation to General Taylor as more feasible because of difficult sandy roads. Our Government gave Madero large contracts to transport the baggage and supplies of Taylor's army to Monterey and Saltillo, by which he accumulated a considerable fortune. After the war he received large concessions from the Mexican Government.

The family was very prolific, Francisco I having twelve or thirteen children, Francisco II about the same number, and Francisco III, presidential candidate, having many, as did nearly all his brothers, sisters, uncles and aunts. When the revolution against Diaz broke out, the Madero family embraced four or five hundred souls, nearly all more or less wealthy. Madero II was a Diaz supporter, as were about half his brothers. The rest were adherents of Madero III. The family is now dispersed and many have died.

I was personally acquainted with Francisco Madero III, and his father, Madero, Jr., was an extreme agitator similar to our Debs. The greatest qualification friends in each case claimed for their candidates for the presidency was that they had been confined in jail by their two countries for violations of laws!

Mr. Madero stated in all sincerity that he hoped to be to his country what Washington was to mine. I never met Mr. Debs, but I dare say he had similar ambitions and with about the same reason! Debs received relatively as many American votes when candidate for president as Madero did when he claimed election.

Our assistance given to such men as Madero, Orosco, and Villa in driving Diaz, the greatest ruler Mexico ever had, from his tranquil government to exile, set back for fifty years the advancement that Diaz had given in his twenty-seven years of authority. Until Mexico discovers another such noble man as Diaz, it will never have the tranquil and stable government it had. Some day Mexico will erect a monument to his memory as resplendent as that of Guatemozin or Montezuma. Were it not that our country is now so absorbed in the greater war in Europe, our jingoes might ere this have caused another war of conquest, subjugation and exploitation in Mexico.

I also knew Huerta personally. A graduate of their military academy, an officer of forty years' service in the army, I do not believe it possible that he had guilty knowledge of Madero's murder.

EQUITABLE DISTRIBUTION OF THE WATERS OF THE RIO GRANDE

Because settlements in Colorado and New Mexico appropriated so much water from the Rio Grande in the flood season the river ran dry before it passed through the arid region around El Paso. Thus grapevines and fruit trees perished, and because it was impossible to cultivate vegetables, wheat, corn and other cereals, the settlers on both sides of the river were abandoning the country. In 1888, the city council of El Paso asked me to devise some remedy for their distress.

I recommended the construction of a dam three miles above the city, where the formation in the valley gave ample room for immense water storage. At the council's request I went to Washington and presented a statement of their distress to the Secretary of State.

I saw Mr. Bayard on the 9th of December, and on the 10th, at his request, presented the following communication:

EBBITT HOUSE,
Washington, D. C., December 10, 1888.

SIR: Agreeable to promise at our interview this a.m., I have the honor to submit the following general outline of my projected scheme for an international dam and water storage in the Rio Grande River, near El Paso, Tex., for the control of the annual floods and the preservation of the national boundary to the Gulf, and for other purposes.

The Rio Grande, 1,800 miles long, rises from an unusual number of tributaries in the very high altitudes of southern Colorado and northern New Mexico, where the rain and snowfall is extraordinary, and the ice formed therefrom in the long winter enormous. As it flows southward the precipitation gradually decreases for 600 miles, when the Mexican boundary is reached at El Paso, Tex., where there is neither snow nor ice, and but 8 inches annual rainfall; from thence 1,200 miles south to the Gulf of Mexico the rainfall is only sufficient to compensate for the loss by evaporation (which latter is very great), and for these reasons the river has but few tributaries and no increase of flow below El Paso.

The annual floods, caused by the melting of snow and ice in the mountains, take place in May and last for about seventy-five days, during which period the average flow may be estimated at 200 yards in width by 2 yards in depth, with a velocity of 5 miles per hour, although in recurring periods of about seven years it is much greater. During the remaining two hundred and ninety days of the year the average flow is perhaps not over 30 yards wide by 1 yard deep, with the same velocity; and in the same recurring periods, in the intervals between the high tides, the river goes dry for months, as it is at this time—or at least has no current, with not enough water in the pools to float the fish.

There is at present popular opinion that this want of water comes from its diversion by the numerous irrigating canals lately taken out in Colorado and New Mexico, and while it is problematical what effect this may have, if any, I am of the opinion that most of this water returns to the stream again, either through the atmosphere, by evaporation and precipitation, or by the earth, through overflow and drainage, as from personal observation I know that these seasons of flood and drought were of about the same character thirty years ago.

After leaving the mountains the river passes through low valleys of bottom lands from 1 to 12 miles wide and from 4 to 8 feet above low-water level, of a light, sandy alluvium formed during annual overflows by sedimentary deposits from silt, which the water always carries in a greater or less degree.

In meandering along the Texan bank of the river as a

land surveyor, from the New Mexican line to a point below Fort Quitman, in 1858, 1859, and 1860, I observed that the deposit was from one-half inch to 3 inches annually, that during the floods the bed of the river was constantly changing by erosion and deposit, and that in regular cycles it shifted from one of its firm rocky or clay banks to the other, as the deposits had raised the side of the valley through which it then flowed above the level of the opposite side. Generally this change took place slowly, by erosion and deposit of matter entirely in suspension; but frequently hundreds of acres would be passed in a single day by a cut-off in a bend of one channel, and sometimes the bed would suddenly change from one firm bank to the other, a distance of perhaps 20 miles in length by 6 in width. For instance, when surveying "El Canutillo," a valley a short distance above El Paso, the river was moving westward, and about the middle of the valley, which was some 6 miles wide. Old Mexicans who had lived in the vicinity informed me that in 1821 the river ran close along the eastern bluff, where its bed was plainly to be seen, as was also a less plainly outlined bed along the bluffs on the opposite side, where the river flows at this date, and gives evidence of returning abruptly to the eastern bluffs again at the next greatest high tide, to its old channel along the bed of the track of the Santa Fe Railroad.

In another case, more recent and extensive, in the great valley below El Paso, some 12 miles in width and 20 miles long, the river, as was plainly evident at the time I was surveying the land, had made a sudden change from the bluffs on the eastern or Texan side to the western or Mexican side of the valley.

Mexicans who had been residents continuously in that vicinity informed me that this change took place in 1842.

Again, in 1884, in this vicinity, the river swept suddenly from the Mexican side, crossed the Southern Pacific Railroad, and destroyed both track and bed for a distance of 15 miles, stopping traffic for a period of three months and causing the removal of the road to hills above the valley.

Though these are the most extensive changes that came within my personal observation, similar ones are being made annually, from El Paso to the Gulf, which not only prevent the settlement and development of such of the lands as are sufficiently above the overflow (were the banks and boundaries secure), but by reason of the river being the national boundary between the United States and Mexico for over 1,200 miles, cause fatal embarrassments to the citizens and officials of both Republics in fixing boundaries and titles to lands, in preventing smuggling, collecting customs, and in the legal punishment of all crimes and misdemeanors committed near the supposed boundary line, it being easy at almost any point in its great length to produce evidence sufficient to raise a reasonable doubt in the minds of the jurors as to which side of the line the arrest was made or the act committed.

At the last session of Congress the House passed a joint resolution (No. 112) requesting the President to appoint a commission, in conjunction with a similar one from the Republic of Mexico, to consider the matter above referred to. While surveying these lands in 1858, and prospecting for a crossing of the Rio Grande for the Memphis, El Paso and Pacific Railroad, which was then projected—and in fact in course of construction—I examined the pass about three miles above the present city of El Paso, and discovered that it had solid rock bed and walls, the latter but about 400 feet apart, and that the valley above which came close down to the spur of the Rocky Mountains which crossed the river and formed the pass was from 4 to 8 miles wide, with a fall of about 4 feet to the mile, so that it would be an easy matter to build a dam in this pass and create an immense lake.

The water coming through this pass for ages has deposited at its lower end a great mass of rocks, over which is formed rapids with about 12 feet fall, and the aborigines of prehistoric ages made use of this to carry the water on to the lands below, no one knows how long ago, but it is known that the Mexicans have used it for two hundred years under most disadvantageous and unsatisfactory circumstances.

I have witnessed, each succeeding year, hundreds of Mexicans piling loose stones on the top of this drift of rocks to raise the level to that carried away by the floods of the preceding year; and it has been estimated by a Federal engineer sent from the City of Mexico, that, had the labor thus expended been reduced to silver, the dam could have been built of the solid metal. The difficulty has been and always will be that there is neither bed rock nor solid earth in the bottom or banks, each being composed of quicksand.

In other places in the valley temporary willow dams 1 or 2 feet high are made at convenient places, and the water carried several miles below on to the lands that are above the usual overflow; but these dams are carried away annually and have to be rebuilt, and frequently the river bed moves miles away from the mouth of the ditch or acequia, rendering it useless; but even if these difficulties in carrying the water from the bed of the river to the lands are overcome in the usual manner, it is evident that by reason of a great overflow, say, every seventh year, and a dry river in a like period, no system of irrigation for the Rio Grande can prove satisfactory that does not embrace a grand storage system sufficient both to restrain, to a great extent, at least, the tidal flow and maintain a constant annual flow, especially since the great immigration and settlement in its valley is constantly doubling the demand for water.

Being on leave of absence in the city of El Paso recently,

where I was a citizen before the war, having surveyed the
first plat of the town and being well known to most of its
citizens, I was invited by the city council to submit to it a
plan for water supply and irrigation that would overcome
the difficulties above referred to.

It at once occurred to me that as the Rio Grande was
the joint property of the two nations, and especially as
the Mexicans had used its waters since time when "the
memory of man runneth not to the contrary," that any
plan to be acceptable and satisfactory must be international in character, and the works, both before and after
completion, under the joint federal control of the two
nations, the more so as riparian rights in this country, so
far as regards irrigation, are not well defined by law, and
could be best brought about in this instance by treaty
stipulations between the two countries.

The matter of restraining the tidal flow by storing the
water, and thus protect the constantly changing national
boundary, occurred to me—if it could be introduced into
the project—as likely to secure encouragement and substantial aid in money from both governments.

And further, that El Paso, being now a city of over
11,000 population, and having every prospect of being a
large manufacturing city at no distant day—there being
no place within 500 miles likely to compete with it—the
subject of water power ought also to enter into the problem, which of necessity is of such vast proportions as to
require all incidental aid possible to attach to it to insure
its success.

It will be apparent, from what has been written, that
the Rio Grande is one of the first magnitude, not only in
length and breadth, but for short annual periods in devastating flow of waters, and that its general characteristics,
as compared with other rivers with reference to irrigation,
are so abnormal as to require different or more heroic
treatment.

I therefore projected a scheme which may be briefly outlined as follows:

To build a strong dam of stones and cement—say, 60 feet high—in the pass before referred to, and by submerging about 60,000 acres of land now subject to overflow and of little comparative value, create a vast lake 15 miles long by 7 wide, with a probable storage capacity of 4,000,000,000 cubic yards of water; place gates on each side of the river in the dam at the 50-foot level for wasteweirs and irrigating canals to supply each side of the river and keep up a flow in its bed which would bring the water in the canals 70 feet above the streets in the cities of El Paso and Juarez, respectively.

The gates at the 50-foot level would give an available reserve of water of 10 feet over the entire surface of the lake—over 2,000,000,000 cubic yards—which would be exhausted during the long season of little flow for the purposes of irrigation and other needs, as well as maintaining a constant stream in the river beds so arranged as to exhaust the reserve about the period of annual flood, which would be checked and held in reserve for the next season of little flow, and in this manner produce a comparatively constant and unvarying flow of water for each entire year below the dam, redeeming many times the number of acres submerged above in the lake from overflow below, and fixing permanently the national boundary, the banks of the river, as well as the boundaries and titles to private lands, and making it an easy matter to collect duties and prevent smuggling, detect crimes and misdemeanors generally, arrest and punish criminals, as it is along other national boundaries.

The assumed flow given for the 75 days of high-water will give about 6,500,000,000 cubic yards, and that for the remaining 290 days 1,500,000,000, making an aggregate annual flow of 8,000,000,000 cubic yards. If we allow 2,000,000,000 of this for loss by evaporation and other wastes, which former in this dry atmosphere is very great, perhaps 80 inches, we have 6,000,000,000 cubic yards remaining. This should be divided into three equal parts, one for each side of the river, for irrigation and other needs, and the third for overflow, through water motors, to furnish power to the future manufacturing cities on each side and to maintain a constant flow in the river below to the Gulf, as would no doubt be demanded by the people there as their right ere they would permit the scheme to be carried out.

The 2,000,000,000 cubic yards falling a distance of 50 feet over the dam, estimating the weight of a cubic yard of water at 500 pounds, and 1 horse-power the energy required to lift 33,000 pounds 1 foot in a minute, would expend energy equal to over 10,000 horse-power for 8 hours every day in the year, and produce a constant stream in the bed of the river 26 yards wide by 1 foot deep, running with a velocity of 5 miles per hour, to say nothing of the probability that the greater part of the other two-thirds would find its way again to the river bed through the earth and air, the whole flowing in a steady, continuous stream to the mouth of the river, to be used as required at any season of the year, instead of, as is now the case, three-fourths of the entire mass of the annual flow going rapidly to the Gulf in the short period of 75 days untaxed.

Estimating the amount of water required for annual irrigation at 20 inches, the water reserved for that purpose would be sufficient for 100,000 acres on each side of the river—all that could be reclaimed from the desert for 100 miles below.

To carry out this project I recommended to the people on each side of the Rio Grande that they petition to the executive authority of their respective nations for the creation of a joint commission to draw up the necessary treaty stipulations to protect the work and the rights of all interested in them, the fundamental feature of which should certainly be that each nation should have the right to divert no more than one-third of the flow at any period, and that one-third of the flow should be maintained in the bed of the river; and that this international commission have charge and control of the work after completion as well as during construction.

That the legislative authorities of the two nations be asked to appropriate, after complete investigation and estimates have been made, money sufficient to complete the work, probably $100,000 for the dam proper, $100,000 for the condemnation of the 50,000 acres of land to be submerged, and $100,000 for the removal of some 15 miles of the road-bed of the Atchison, Topeka and Santa Fe Railroad to bluffs above the old bed of the river, where the track now lies, subject to annual damage, and sooner or later total destruction, unless removed.

It will also be apparent that the waters of this great lake will be clear and fresh, the silt held in suspension in the current of the river being precipitated as soon as it enters the still water of the lake, doing away with the great trouble and expense now necessary in keeping the canals and ditches cleansed of sedimentary deposits, and a further great benefit derived from using water reduced in temperature by exposure for months in a warm climate far below that used in the early spring, which comes in three days from snow and ice and is immediately applied to the young and tender sprouting plants, chilling and checking their growth.

I know of no point in the Rio Grande between Albuquerque and the Gulf of Mexico where nature has provided both the natural basin and rim for a lake of such great dimensions, for, indeed, it can be made 100 feet deep if desired, and it may be questioned whether a depth of 60 feet, with 10 feet reserve to draw from, will afford sufficient storage to control perfectly the tide at its highest flow.

This project was well received by the people and has been earnestly discussed in the public press of the locality ever since with general approbation and a disposition to endeavor to carry it out as quickly as possible. The only question exciting any general distrust is that the sedimentary deposit in the lake, it is held by some, will shorten the life of the reservoir by filling the lake at such an early period as to render the scheme of doubtful expediency, and opinions differ very widely upon this subject, which is, indeed, a problematical one, and can only be determined, even approximately, by actual measurements of a great majority of the annual flow, for the quantity of sediment changes with flow and season.

That the bed of the river will eventually be filled, of course, is only a matter of time, but whether in fifteen or one hundred and fifty years can only be ascertained by prolonged, actual measurements; but even if filled in the near future it seems to me that the difficulty may be overcome by raising the dam, unless, indeed, that should be required too often.

The matter has already been referred to Major Powell, chief of the Geological Survey, who has sent Captain Clarence Dutton, of his Department, to El Paso to investigate and report on the feasibility of the scheme; but as the initial steps, should it be pronounced feasible, must come from your Department in the nature of international treaty stipulations, I have thought it proper to thus early acquaint you with the grand project.

I beg to refer you to Hon. Mr. Lanham, member of Congress from Texas, who is acquainted with me personally and my projected scheme.

ANSON MILLS,
Major Tenth Cavalry, Brevet Lieutenant Colonel,
United States Army.

The SECRETARY OF STATE,
Washington, D. C.

In April, 1888, at the instance of Major Powell, I had received orders from the War Department to report to the commanding officer at Fort Bliss, with instructions to lend whatever aid I could to the Interior Department and its Geological Survey party, investigating the redemption of irrigable lands in the Rio Grande Valley.

Major Powell also wrote, asking me to act as advisory agent of the survey, and to give it my opinions and advice regarding this work, as well as to supervise a gauge station they were to construct for measuring the annual river flow, evaporation, etc.

The Geological Survey was authorized to investigate the feasibility of reclaiming arid lands by dams and water storage. Colonel E. S. Nettleton, of Denver, Colorado, was appointed supervising engineer of the southwestern district, and I was appointed his assistant, as supervising engineer of the district of El Paso, with money to employ engineers and other assistants to make plans and estimates for the proposed international dam at El Paso. With Mr. W. W. Follett, one of the best hydraulic engineers in the United States as my aid, I proceeded to carry out the work as speedily as possible. The Senate Committee on Irrigation, of which Senator Stewart was Chairman, intended to visit El Paso later and examine the location, plans, specifications and estimates, so that, if approved, they could recommend an appropriation to construct it.

While engaged in this investigation an apparently unrelated incident occurred which had a most unfortunate effect upon our labors.

The Secretary of War, Mr. Proctor, ordered me to Fort Selden.

Here an irrigation company, represented by Mr. W. H. H. Llewellyn, held a revocable license to construct a canal through the Selden Reservation. The Mexican citizens, assembled in force with arms, had forbidden the workmen to construct the canal, and I was to make a thorough investigation

MAJOR JAMES W. POWELL.

COLONEL E. S. NETTLETON.

W. W. FOLLETT.

as to the trouble, and report to the Secretary personally in Washington.

After two days investigation I found the canal company charter authorized them to build their canal through and over the community canals of the settlements along the river, in use for over one hundred years, and compel the Mexican farmers to pay water rent for new canals. The farmers, having prior right to the use of the water, objected.

In Washington, the Secretary proposed a hearing on February 2, 1889, and asked a written report from me, to be read at the meeting, in which I recommended the license be revoked.

Senator Reagan, of Texas, the delegate from New Mexico, Mr. Llewellyn, and many others interested, were present at the meeting. After reading my report and a full hearing of both sides, the Secretary revoked the license and instructed the commanding officer of Selden to remove Llewellyn's workmen from the reservation. Mr. Llewellyn grew violently angry at me, and on my return to the hotel I found the following note:

THE EBBITT HOUSE,
Washington, D. C.,
Feb. 2nd, 1890.

DEAR MAJOR:

I have wired Messrs. Davis and Morehead to have their people keep out, that if there is no new ditch at Las Cruces there will be no new dam at El Paso.

W. H. H. LLEWELLYN.

Davis and Morehead advocated the El Paso dam.

When the committee reached El Paso, August 20, 1889, Major Powell, Colonel Nettleton, Mr. Follett and I explained our plans in detail. They and the members from that district and Mr. Lanham, who was much interested in the project, all approved.

Meanwhile the Mexican Government demanded compensation from the United States for the appropriation by American citizens of the waters of the Rio Grande, to which Mexico claimed prior right. A bill was introduced in both Houses of Congress making an appropriation for the construction of the El Paso dam by the United States, provided Mexico relinquished all claims for indemnity in return for half the water to be stored.

This bill was thoroughly discussed in both Houses of Congress during the session of 1889 and 1890, and was apparently satisfactory to all parties concerned, and it was generally supposed that it would pass. On April 26, 1890, having finished the duties required of me, the War Department relieved me and I rejoined my regiment.

When it was evident the United States was committed to building a dam at El Paso and dividing the water with Mexico, Dr. Nathan Boyd, of New Mexico, obtained a charter from New Mexico to build a similar dam at Elephant Butte, one hundred and twenty-five miles above El Paso, with the apparent intention of holding up the waters of the Rio Grande and the United States Government and compelling it to supply water to Mexico through his company. (See Colonel Engledue's address to the stockholders of Boyd's company, p. 343, vol. 2, Boundary Commission Proceedings.)

The Mexican Government protested in 1896, stating that before they could accept their share of the water to be stored by the proposed international dam at El Paso, as indemnity for their loss of water taken out on the upper river, investigations should ascertain whether there would be sufficient water in the Rio Grande to supply both dams. If not, measures should be taken to restrain the projectors of the Elephant Butte dam from using waters to which Mexicans had prior right.

This protest was referred to me by the Secretary of State, who asked my opinion.

I reported that in my opinion that it would be unsafe to rely on a sufficient flow to restore to Mexico the water to which she claimed prior right unless the Elephant Butte corporation could be restrained from the use of such water. Suit was instituted by the Attorney General to enjoin the company. So began a contest which lasted for many years, going three times to the Supreme Court of the United States, before the Elephant Butte Company was permanently enjoined from constructing their dam.

These complications delayed both projects for several years. A protocol, dated May 6, 1896, between the Secretary of State, Richard Olney, and Ambassador Romero, directed F. Javier Osorno and myself, Boundary Commissioners for Mexico and the United States, to continue the investigation and report on the following matters:

First, the amount of Rio Grande water taken by the irrigation canals constructed in the United States.

Second, the average amount of water in the river, year by year, before and since the construction of the irrigation canals.

Third, the most feasible method of so regulating the river as to secure to each country and its inhabitants their legal and equitable rights and interests in said water.

Captain George McC. Derby, U. S. Engineers, was ordered to report to me, and Señor Don J. Ramon de Ibarrola, engineer on the part of Mexico, was ordered to report to Mr. Osorno.

The Commission worked diligently on this investigation until November 25, 1896, when it reported its opinion that the most feasible means of attaining the ends desired was to construct the dam and reservoir projected by Mr. Follett and myself under the investigations made by the Geological Survey, provided Mexico could be protected in some way which would prevent the taking from the Rio Grande by dams and water storage of water to which she had prior right. I was authorized by the Secretary of State to formulate with Ambassador Romero a draft of a treaty to that effect, which we accomplished, submitting copies to the Secretaries of State of both nations.

The two nations were willing to consummate the proposed treaty. Congress appeared to be ready to appropriate the necessary money but, again, the unexpected happened. Making violent charges against me to the Secretary of State, Dr. Boyd demanded that President McKinley dismiss me from the Boundary Commission or he would defeat his re-election by his control of two or three western States; and threatened to horsewhip Secretary Hay if he did not do his bidding. Mr. Wilkie, of the Secret Service, reported Dr. Boyd to be a dangerous man, so he was denied further personal conferences in the State Department. (I knew nothing of this for years afterwards.) Boyd then strove to influence Roosevelt (who had become President) against me and the international dam. Mr. Roosevelt, without consulting the Commission having the project in charge, placed it in the hands of Mr. Newell, of the Reclamation Service, with directions to build the dam at Elephant Butte. After some delay another treaty with Mexico (concerning which I, though still Mexican Boundary Commissioner, was not consulted), was effected for building the dam at Elephant Butte. By the terms of this treaty Mexico is to receive a share of the water to be stored by the dam and relinquishes all claims for indemnity for the diversion of the waters of the upper Rio Grande by American citizens.

As Llewellyn threatened, there never was a "new dam at El Paso," largely owing to himself and Boyd. After twelve years, at a cost nearly four times as great as estimated for the international dam at El Paso, the Elephant Butte dam is complete; but it is doubtful whether it will ever be of any great benefit to the valleys near El Paso because of the great distance over which the water has to be carried through arid wastes. Full details may be found in my published reports under the head of "Equitable Distributions of the Waters of the Rio Grande, Vol. 2."

JACOBO BLANCO.

MEXICAN BOUNDARY COMMISSIONERS
(Text, 300.)

F. BELTRAN Y PUGA.

JOINT U. S. AND MEXICAN BOUNDARY COMMISSION.
CUNNINGHAM, HAPPER, MAILLEFERT, CUELLAR,
DABNEY, MILLS, OSORNO, CORELLA.

Boundary Commission

I have already explained how this Commission came to be formed and how I was appointed and entered upon the duties as sole Commissioner on the part of the United States (Text, 207). I have also explained the relation of the Commission to the international dam for the equitable distribution of the waters of the Rio Grande, the subsequent Commission by protocol of Commissioner Osorno and myself for the same purpose (Text, 263), and the later Commission for the equitable distribution (Text, 273).

The duty of the International Boundary Commission, briefly stated, is to apply the principles agreed upon by the two governments in the boundary treaties to the varying conditions caused by the kaleidoscopic changes in the current of the Rio Grande.

The boundary treaties of 1848 and 1853 make "the middle of" the Rio Grande the boundary, while the treaty of 1884 provides that the boundary shall "follow the center of the normal channel * * * notwithstanding any alterations in the banks or in the course" of the river "provided that such alterations be effected by natural causes through the slow and gradual erosion and deposit of alluvium and not by the abandonment of an existing river bed and the opening of a new one." Article II of this same treaty provides that "any other change, wrought by the force of the current, whether by the cutting of a new bed or when there is more than one channel by the deepening of another channel * * * shall produce no change in the dividing line."

The treaty of 1889, which established the International Boundary Commission, provides that "when owing to natural causes, any change shall take place in the bed of the Rio Grande * * * which may affect the boundary line, notice of that fact shall be given by the proper local authorities * * * on receiving which notice it shall be the duty of the said Commission to repair to the place where the change has taken place or the question has arisen, to make a personal examination of such change, to compare it with the bed of the river as it was before the change took place, as shown by the surveys, and to decide whether it has occurred through avulsion or erosion for the effects of Articles I and II of the convention of November 12, 1884."

The Commission was organized January 8, 1894, in the office of the Mexican Consul, in El Paso, as follows:

On the part of Mexico:
        Jose M. Canalizo, Commissioner
        Lieut. Col. E. Corella, Consulting Engineer
        Salvador F. Maillefert, Secretary

On the part of the United States:
        Col. Anson Mills, Commissioner
        Frank B. Dabney, Consulting Engineer
        John A. Happer, Secretary

The Commission recommended rules for its future government, which were approved by the Secretaries of State of both governments. Before we completed the first case referred to us, Commissioner Canalizo died, and F. Javier Osorno was appointed as his successor.

September 28, 1894, the full Commission again met at El Paso and proceeded to an examination upon the ground of the cases of Banco de Camargo, Banco de Vela, Banco de Santa Margarita and Banco de Granjeno.

These so-called bancos were formed by a combination of "slow and gradual erosion" coupled with "avulsion" in the following manner: Where the river passes through low alluvial bottoms with banks of fragile consistency and slight fall the channel continually changes from right to left, eroding the concave bank and depositing on the convex. This occurs in low as well as high water, though the changes are more marked during high water stages. These erosions are greatest where the water in a tangent from a curve strikes the bank at an acute angle, ceasing when the angle becomes so obtuse that the water is readily deflected by the consistency of the bank. When the curve forms a circle the radius of which is dependent on the consistency of the earth and the volume and velocity of the water, erosions practically cease and the river turns upon itself in a circle and forms a "cut-off," leaving the land thus separated (called a banco) somewhat in the form of a pear or gourd, with the stem cut by the river's current at the moment of separation. (See cut of the double Banco de Santa Margarita. Proceedings Boundary Commission, Vol. I, p. 191.)

In many cases through ensuing changes in the channel an American or Mexican banco would be entirely cut off even from the river and wholly surrounded by land within the jurisdiction of the other country.

The origin of these bancos was so different from our expectations that both the Mexican Commissioner and I, after deliberate consideration, concluded that their process of formation, their form and constantly changing character, could not have been contemplated by the conventions creating the treaties of 1884 and 1889. We both suggested to our governments the reconsideration of Articles I and II of the treaty of 1884, as far as they related to these bancos, to the end that provision might be made for transferring all such bancos to the sovereignty of the United States or Mexico according as they lay on the American or Mexican side of the present river channel, without disturbing the private ownership as it might be ascertained.

This treaty was negotiated and ratified in 1905 and has since then worked to the satisfaction of both governments and resulted in the "elimination" of perhaps 75 of these bancos and the maintenance of the international boundary line in the center of the running river.

Some of the difficulties under which the Commission did much of its work on the lower Rio Grande will appear from the following incident which occurred while the Commission was considering the case of the Banco de Granjeno, near Havana.

The day before the Congressional elections in Texas the Mexican Commissioner joined our camp on the river. Coming by carriage through Havana, he observed a procession of grotesquely clad Americans and Mexicans carrying a flag and beating drums. Mr. Osorno's first experience with United States election methods, the several hundred people in the little town of not more than 20 or 30 inhabitants excited his curiosity as to where all these people had come from. As Reynoca was a large city on the Mexican side, he suspected that many of them were from Mexico. A portly Mexican, much resembling Sancho Panza and clad very much after his style, carried the flag.

The Joint Commission had summoned nine witnesses to appear at our camp the next day at 9 o'clock and testify in the case. But the witnesses did not appear.

Two hours later a messenger from the village stated the witnesses were indisposed from the excitement of the night previous and would not be over until later in the afternoon. At 4 o'clock we observed a party headed by this identical flag-bearer. Not speaking English, he addressed himself to Mr. Osorno, stating that he had been summoned as a witness.

The Commission Regulations prescribe that the witnesses shall be sworn by the Commissioner representing the country of which the witness is a citizen. Asked to state his country, the flag-bearer said he was a Mexican citizen. Mr. Osorno looked astonished.

"Then, you a Mexican citizen?" he asked.

"Yes, sir," answered Sancho Panza.

"Did not I see you at Havana in Texas, yesterday, carrying an American flag?"

"Oh, yes, sir."

"How does it come that you would carry an American flag in Texas if you are a Mexican citizen?"

"Oh, it was election time."

"Election time," said Mr. Osorno; "what have you to do with elections in Texas?"

"Oh, we all go over there for elections!"

Understanding the habits of the frontier people better than Mr. Osorno, I suggested asking if he had voted. Rather reluctantly Mr. Osorno said:

"Did you vote in Texas?"

"Oh, yes, sir."

"Well, how can you be a Mexican citizen if you vote in Texas?"

"Oh," said Sancho, "if you don't believe I am a Mexican citizen I will show you a certificate of my consul!" pulling out a paper signed by the Mexican Secretary of the Boundary Commission, formerly Mexican Consul at Brownsville, certifying he was a Mexican citizen.

Though Mr. Osorno was a lawyer and well versed in international law and custom, he was much perplexed but finally administered the oath. During the course of the examination of the other nine witnesses examined we found six claimed to be Mexican citizens though admitting they had voted in Texas the day before, which explained the fact that although the registered voters in that county numbered but 650, the Democratic majority footed up over 1,200!

The population along this part of the river, on both sides, speak Spanish almost exclusively, and their habits, sympathies, and general characteristics are entirely Mexican. The people are the poorest and least progressive of any I have ever seen, except the North American Indians. The extreme drought for the seven preceding years had made them poorer than for generations, and their numbers were. less than for the past hundred years. Most of our witnesses were unable to tell their ages, or where they had lived during particular years. Most claimed citizenship in Mexico, but voting rights in the United States.

The jurisdiction of the Commission included a great variety of cases involving questions as to location of the boundary lines as affected by changes in the channel of the river, "elimination" of the bancos, unduly projecting jetties or other obstructions in the channel of the Rio Grande, marking of international bridges, question of artificial cut-offs in the river channel, etc., etc.

The nature of the Commission's work can perhaps best be explained by treating two important and typical cases in some detail.

The Horcon Ranch case grew out of an artificial cut-off of the river channel. The Rio Grande at the Horcon Ranch near Brownsville, Texas, formed two loops. (Cut, 288.)

The natural course of the water appeared to be about to form a cut-off at A, whereby the upper loop would have been eliminated. The result would have been to deprive the American riparian proprietors on the upper loop of the water they had theretofore enjoyed for irrigation.

Among these was the American Rio Grande Land and Irrigation Company, which had a large pumping station at B, on the upper loop. To counteract the threatened danger the American proprietors, after vainly striving for months to prevent the cut-off at A by defensive works, dug an artificial channel at C, across the neck of the lower loop, straightening the river, relieving the pressure at A and averting the threatened disaster to the company's pumping station. This deprived Mexican riparian proprietors, on the lower loop, of the water they had been accustomed to use and to which they were entitled. The boundary treaties expressly forbid such artificial cut-offs and provide that they shall not affect the international boundary.

The Mexican Government brought the case to the Commission, which promptly held the cut-off a clear violation of the treaty. Not feeling clear as to its power to take the necessary remedial measures, the Commission reported its findings to the two governments and asked for instructions. The American State Department approved the findings, but thought the Commission had fully discharged its duty, and that subsequent proceedings should be taken in the ordinary courts. It asked the Department of Justice for an opinion. The Attorney General concurred in these views and at the instance of the State Department brought a suit in equity in the name of the United States against the American Rio Grande Land and Irrigation Company, asking a mandatory injunction to compel the defendant company to restore the river to its original channel, or, as an alternative, for the conveyance of land in the upper loop owned by the company to the Mexican riparian proprietors so they might have a river frontage, together with the payment of compensatory damages to these proprietors and both compensatory and punitive damages to the United States.

The President of the American Rio Grande Land and Irrigation Company, Mr. Edward C. Eliot, of St. Louis, and its general counsel, Mr. Duvall West, now a Federal District Judge, were men of the highest type. When the matter was brought to their attention they recognized the correctness of the position of the government. By agreement between the representatives of the Government and these gentlemen, the company admitted the cause of action and the truth of the material allegations in the government's bill, and submitted to the alternative relief prayed. An order was accordingly entered by the court which not only adjusted the matter to the satisfaction of the Mexican Government and the Mexican citizens interested, but brought home to the people of both countries along the river the intention and power of the two governments to live up to their treaty obligations. (For full particulars see the pamphlet published by the Boundary Commission, which gives all the important papers in the case, including the proceedings both before the Boundary Commission and before the Federal court.)

Further to illustrate the work of the Commission, I call attention to Chamizal case at El Paso, Texas. The Chamizal tract is a body of land of some 600 acres south of the channel of the Rio Grande as it ran when surveyed by Emory and

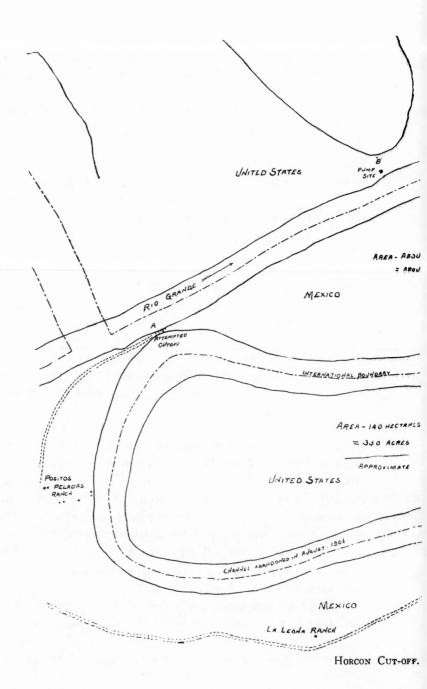

UNITED STATES

PUMP SITE • *B'*

AREA - ABOU
= ABOU

RIO GRANDE →

MEXICO

A
ATTEMPTED
CUTOFF

INTERNATIONAL BOUNDARY

AREA - 140 HECTARES
= 350 ACRES

APPROXIMATE

POSITOS
or PELADAS
RANCH

UNITED STATES

CHANNEL ABANDONED IN AUGUST 1906

MEXICO

LA LEONA RANCH

HORCON CUT-OFF.

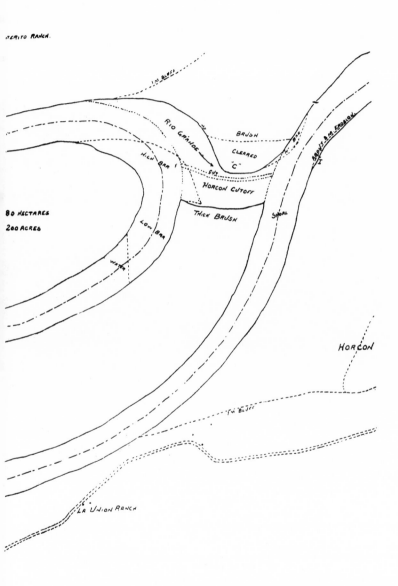

(Text, 286.)

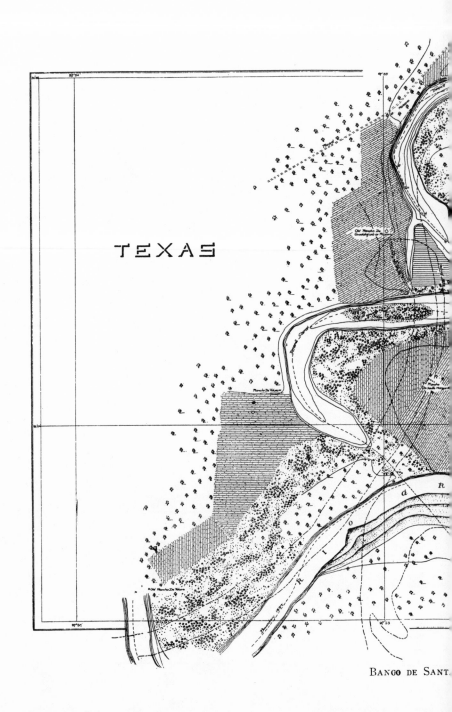

TEXAS

BANCO DE SANT

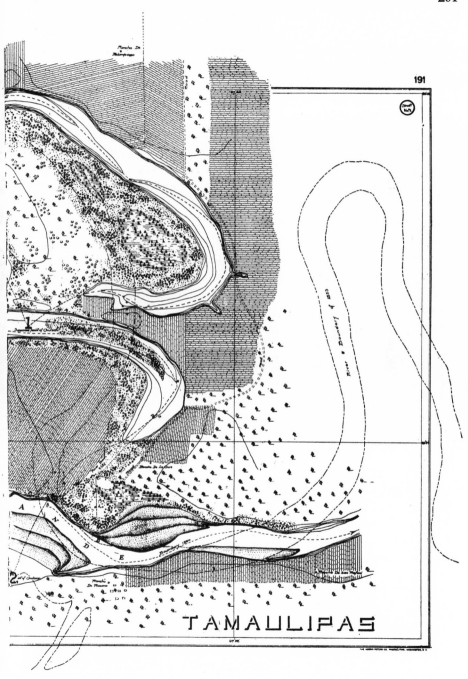

MARGARITA. (Text, 283.)

Salazar in 1853 and north of the present river channel. In 1894 the Chamizal case was referred by the Mexican Foreign Office to the Commission on the complaint of one Garcia, a Mexican citizen, who claimed to own land in the Chamizal tract which had been cut off from his holdings on the Mexican side by the change in the course of the river.

The question at issue, under the provisions of the boundary treaties, as formulated by the American Commissioner and accepted by the Mexican Commissioner at the session of the Commission on November 6, 1895, was "whether or not the river in its passage moved over the land by gradual erosion from the Mexican bank and deposited on the United States bank, as described in Article I of the treaty of 1884, or by sudden avulsion, by cutting a new bed or deepening another channel than that which marked the boundary."

The case was tried at El Paso by Commissioner Osorno and myself; Messrs. Maillefert and Happer being the secretaries of the Commission, and Messrs. Corella and Dabney consulting engineers. We limited the witnesses to four of the most trustworthy of the older inhabitants on each side. Their testimony showed there was no basis for any claim that there had been any avulsion or cutting of a new bed. The change in the channel was clearly erosive, although at certain or rather "uncertain" times and places during floods the erosion had been much more rapid than others, and had been visible to the naked eye, since as the lower substratum of sand was washed out, the upper layer of clay along the concave or Mexican bank would cave in, sometimes in considerable chunks. The building up of the convex or American shore, however, had always been imperceptibly gradual.

The Mexican Commissioner reduced his argument to the following syllogism:

"Major proposition: Any change other than slow and gradual does not alter the boundary line (Article I of the Convention of November 12, 1884).

"Minor proposition: Since the change of the river in the

case denominated 'El Chamizal' *was not slow and gradual,* but, on the contrary, violent and at periods of time of unequal intermissions (which has been fully demonstrated above).

"Conclusion: Thence, the change of the river at the lands of 'El Chamizal' does not alter the boundary line marked in 1852 by the International Boundary Commission (Article II of the Convention of 1884)."

I held that the treaty "clearly specifies but two classes of changes in the river," namely, erosive and avulsive, and that "any other unspecified change, as is implied in the major proposition of the syllogism of the Mexican Commissioner, we have no authority to consider, but that our respective conclusions must be in favor of one or the other, as specifically stated in the treaty."

I furthermore held that:

"The syllogism of the Mexican Commissioner must be rejected, not only because its minor proposition is not proven, but because it is abundantly disproven by every witness who testified in the case save Serna."

I further pointed out that in my opinion:

"* * * If the change at El Chamizal has not been 'slow and gradual' by erosion and deposit within the meaning of Article I of the treaty of 1884, there will never be such a one found in all the 800 miles where the Rio Grande, with alluvial banks, constitutes the boundary, and the object of the treaty will be lost to both governments, as it will be meaningless and useless, and the boundary will perforce be through all these 800 miles continuously that laid down in 1852, having literally no points in common with the present river save in its many hundred intersections with the river, and to restore and establish this boundary will be the incessant work of large parties for years, entailing hundreds of thousands of dollars in expense to each government and uniformly dividing the lands between the nations and individual owners, that are now, under the suppositions that for the past forty years the changes have been gradual, and the river accepted generally as the boundary, under the same authority and ownership; for it must be remembered that the river in the alluvial lands, which constitutes 800 miles, has nowhere today the same location it had in 1853."

Commissioner Osorno and I disagreed on the proper construction of the words "slow and gradual, erosion and deposit of alluvium" rather than on matters of fact. No decision could be rendered and the disagreement was reported to our governments, where the matter remained in a diplomatic state until 1910, when it was again referred to the Commission, enlarged for this case only by the appointment of a (presiding) commissioner, a Canadian jurist, to be selected by the two governments. The case was again brought to trial in El Paso in 1911, with the Commission constituted as follows:

Hon. Eugene Lafleur, of Montreal, Canada, Presiding Commissioner.

On the part of Mexico—
> F. Beltran y Puga, Commissioner.
> E. Zayas, Consulting Engineer.
> M. M. Velarde, Secretary.

On the part of the United States—
> Anson Mills, Commissioner.
> W. W. Follett, Consulting Engineer.
> Wilbur Keblinger, Secretary.

The two governments were represented as follows:

On the part of Mexico—
> Señor Joaquin de Casasus, Agent.
> W. J. White, K. C., of Montreal, Canada, Counsel.
> Seymour Thurmond, of El Paso, Associate Counsel.

On the part of the United States—
> William C. Dennis, Agent.
> Walter B. Grant, of Boston, Mass., Counsel.
> Richard F. Burges, of El Paso, Associate Counsel.

In the second trial, Mexico advanced a wholly different theory from that developed in the diplomatic discussions between the first and second trials. Mexico now maintained that the boundary treaties of 1848 and 1853 had laid down a "fixed

William C. Dennis.

Richard F. Burges.

CHAMIZAL ARBITRATION COMMISSION.
BURGES, DENNIS, GRANT, MILLS, LA FLEUR, PUGA, WHITE, CASASUS, THURMOND.

line" between the two countries in the centers of the channel of the river as surveyed at that time by Commissioners Emory and Salazar, which boundary line remained immutable irrespective of any subsequent change in the course of the river, whether erosive or avulsive, until this was changed for the future by the treaty of 1884. Mexico contended this latter treaty was not retroactive but applied only to river changes taking place after 1884.

Driven to concede that in this view the treaty of 1884 had really no meaning, Mexico insisted the two governments were under a misapprehension when this treaty was negotiated, that it was inoperative and that the general rules of international law governing river boundaries had no application because the Rio Grande was in a technically legal sense not a river at all, but merely an intermittent torrential stream.

The United States denied that the boundary treaties of 1848 and 1853 established a fixed line, and contended the treaty of 1884 was retroactive in any event, and applied to the Chamizal dispute, and that this treaty was merely declaratory of the general rule of international law. Furthermore, the United States claimed the Chamizal tract by prescription.

The case was argued during sessions of the Commission extending over a month. The presiding Commissioner, Mr. Lafleur, rendered an opinion holding squarely against the Mexican contentions with respect to a fixed line and the non-retroactivity and non-applicability of the treaty of 1884. His discussion of these subjects is detailed and masterly. After holding against the American claim based on prescription, he appeared to assume that the treaty of 1884 contemplated some *tertium quid* aside from erosion and avulsion, which might perhaps be called "violent" erosion and which had the same effect as an avulsive change, namely, to leave the boundary line in the abandoned bed of the river. Applying this latter doctrine he found the erosion at the Chamizal tract from 1852 to 1864 had been gradual within the meaning of the treaty of 1884, and therefore the boundary during this period had fol-

lowed the river, but that the floods of 1863 brought about a
violent erosion, whereby the boundary line was left in the
middle of the bed of the river "as it existed before the flood
of 1863." He therefore awarded that portion of the tract
between the channel of 1852 and the channel of 1864 before
the flood, to the United States, and the remainder to Mexico.

The Mexican Commissioner filed a separate opinion dissenting from that part of Mr. Lafleur's opinion relating to the
fixed line and the retroactivity and applicability of the treaty
of 1884. Overruled on these points, Mr. Puga felt himself
justified in joining with the Presiding Commissioner in construing the treaty of 1884 and therefore united in the award
dividing the Chamizal tract between the two countries along
the line of the river bed as it existed before the flood of 1864.

I filed an opinion dissenting from that portion of the Presiding Commissioner's opinion construing the treaty of 1884.
I held the Commission was not empowered by the two governments to divide the Chamizal tract but was called upon to
render a clean-cut decision in favor of one or the other government. I recorded my conviction that it would be "as impossible to locate the channel of the Rio Grande in the Chamizal
tract in 1864 as to re-locate the Garden of Eden or the lost
continent of Atlantis." And finally I pointed out, as I had in
1896, the impossible situation which would arise if any attempt
were made to apply the principles of the majority opinion in
other cases, concluding as follows:

"The American Commissioner does not believe that it is
given to human understanding to measure for any practical
use when erosion ceases to be slow and gradual and becomes
sudden and violent, but if this difficulty could be surmounted,
the practical application of the interpretation could not be
viewed in any other light than as calamitous to both nations.
Because, as is manifest from the record in this case, all the
land on both sides of the river from the Bosque de Cordoba,
which adjoins the Chamizal tract, to the Gulf of Mexico (excepting the canyon region), has been traversed by the river

since 1852 in its unending lateral movement, and the mass, if not all of that land, is the product of similar erosion to that which occurred at El Chamizal, and by the new interpretation which is now placed upon the Convention of 1884 by the majority of this Commission, not only is the entire boundary thrown into well-nigh inextricable confusion, but the very treaty itself is subjected to an interpretation that makes its application impossible in practice in all cases where an erosive movement is in question.

"The Convention of 1910 sets forth that the United States and Mexico, 'desiring to terminate *   *   *   the differences which have arisen between the two countries,' have determined to refer these differences to this Commission enlarged for this purpose. The present decision terminates nothing; settles nothing. It is simply an invitation for international litigation. It breathes the spirit of unconscious but nevertheless unauthorized compromise rather than of judicial determination."

Of course, I dissented from the award. When the award and the opinions of the three Commissioners were presented at the final session of the Commission, the United States agent made a formal protest on substantially the same grounds I had taken. My dissenting opinion and the protest of the American agent were sustained by the Department of State and the United States has declined to admit the validity of the award. The whole matter has therefore become the subject of diplomatic negotiations, which it is believed are progressing satisfactorily.

It is as much to the interest of Mexico as of the United States to reach an arrangement whereby the Chamizal tract divided from Mexico by the channel of the Rio Grande 'as it now runs, shall be definitively admitted to be American territory, because it forms an integral part of El Paso, upon which thousands of citizens have their homes.

During my service as Commissioner, Mexico was represented by four Commissioners: Mr. Canalizo, whose death has already been noted; Mr. Osorno, who participated in the first trial of the Chamizal case, and who subsequently resigned; Mr. Jacobo Blanco, who died after serving seven years, and Mr. Fernando Beltran y Puga, who sat at the second trial of the Chamizal case and remained with the Commission until our activity was suspended and he removed from office by the Madero government, leaving me the sole survivor of the four Mexican Commissioners.

These gentlemen were all equal in legal and judicial attainments to similar officials of our own government. They sought always to attain righteous decisions, and I think succeeded in the many cases that came before us.

Of my associates on the American section of the Commission, Messrs. J. A. Happer and Wilbur Keblinger, Secretaries, and P. D. Cunningham and W. W. Follett, Consulting Engineers, deserve special mention. Mr. Cunningham unfortunately lost his life in the service of the Commission through the overturning of his boat in the rapids of the Rio Grande near Eagle Pass in July, 1901. Messrs. Happer, Keblinger and Follett rendered invaluable service during many years, Mr. Follett in spite of a painful illness which would have incapacitated most men for work. Mr. Happer resigned to go into business in El Paso, where he has become a leading citizen. Mr. Follett died shortly after retiring from the Commission. Mr. Keblinger is serving with distinction as United States Consul at Malta.

Our proceedings were published in both languages, and the evidence, maps, plans and monuments were explained not only in scientific but in popular language, so that officials, surveyors, lawyers and judges of each country could readily understand the location of the boundary. (See Volumes 1 and 2, Proceedings Boundary Commission, Treaties of 1884 and 1889, and Equitable Distribution of the Waters of the Rio Grande, Roma to the Gulf, reports and maps, and many other reports on the same subject.)

I have presented copies of all my printed reports and maps

and all proceedings published by both governments with respect to the Chamizal Arbitration, to the El Paso Carnegie Library, together with many reports and maps of the Barlow Commission and the Emory Survey, with the understanding that they will be kept as reference books subject to the examination of all interested.

During the sixteen years of our active service (the revolution in Mexico in 1911 having put an end to our activities), the Commission tried over one hundred cases of all kinds, disagreeing only in the Chamizal case, and preserved the peace and quiet of the entire Rio Grande border for these long years to the satisfaction of both governments and the people of the two nations.

Late Saturday afternoon, January 31, 1914, without any previous warning, I received by messenger a letter from Mr. Bryan, the Secretary of State, peremptorily dismissing Mr. Wilbur Keblinger, the Secretary of the American Section of the Commission, and appointing as his successor John Wesley Gaines, a discarded member of Congress, the bare mention of whose name to his former colleagues proved "a source of innocent merriment."

Mr. Gaines presented his appointment as secretary to me on Monday morning, stating he had been appointed associate Mexican boundary commissioner with me, and that he had been directed by Mr. Bryan to act as chairman.

He suggested I turn my books over to him, after the manner of a policeman who seizes a suspected culprit in the hope of finding stolen goods in his possession.

I informed Mr. Gaines that, while I recognized the legality of his appointment as secretary, I had theretofore been allowed to choose the American secretary of the Commission. As I had not asked for him, I told him he could go home and I would send for him when I wanted him in that capacity. I would not acknowledge him as an associate commissioner, as I was the only commissioner authorized by treaty, and told him he could inform the Secretary of State I would have nothing to do with him in that connection or his attempted authority over me as chairman.

Mr. Keblinger and I had already been summoned to appear before the Foreign Affairs Committee of the House at ten a.m. that day. I telephoned the Secretary of State for permission to take Mr. Keblinger with me as the official secretary. Mr. Bryan sent for me (it was the first time I ever saw him) and stated that there was no objection to my taking Mr. Keblinger as an individual, but I could not take him in an official capacity. I protested he had always appeared with me and greatly assisted me in my explanations to the committee; he was an honorable man and I felt the Secretary could not be aware of the great injustice he had done him. I told Mr. Bryan that Keblinger was too proud to appear voluntarily while under such unjust humiliation.

Finally the Secretary announced he might go with me temporarily in an official capacity. He turned upon me, and, "by questions dark and riddles high," charged me with prostituting my high public trust for purposes of private gain.

I told him I had served my government for fifty years as an army officer and in various capacities and in different departments of the government, and under eight of his successive predecessors in office—Secretaries Gresham, Olney, Sherman, Day, Hay, Bacon and Knox—without ever receiving from any one such language, and that I would not submit without resenting it. I invited him to put his best sleuths on my trail. While I was anxious to separate myself from official connection with him, I had been taught in the army it was not honorable to resign under charges. I told him I would not resign until he was able to state that his investigation found nothing wrong in my twenty years' administration under the State Department. I did not believe he could induce the President to dismiss me, and I told him I believed he had been deceived by such men as Dr. Boyd, who, during the administration of nearly all of his eight immediate predecessors had persistently made charges against me verbally, in writing and in published pamphlets. None of the Secretaries under whom I had served had thought it worth while even to notify me officially of these charges. I only learned about them in detail during the latter part of Secretary Knox's administration, when I found Dr. Boyd had several times been investigated by competent officers of the Department. Chief Wilkie, of the Secret Service, had reported him a dangerous man, when he had threatened in writing to horsewhip Secretary Hay. Thereafter he was denied the privilege of personal conferences with the Department.

Notwithstanding these explanations, Mr. Bryan appeared before the Foreign Affairs Committee, with Mr. Gaines, on the 5th. After a two days' hearing, in which I was questioned and cross-questioned regarding all my transactions for twenty years as Commissioner, my hearing closed with the following, which is quoted from the official report of the hearing:

"Gen. Mills: Mr. Chairman, I crave about three minutes, in which I hope to clarify this whole subject.

"I have met you here for the last twenty years. I have met also the committee in the Senate. And I have always been treated with such courteous consideration by the Department of State that I was encouraged to believe that my work was satisfactory, and it was desired that I should continue, especially so as after about sixteen years' service I was selected without solicitation by the Department as a member of a high commission to arbitrate the Chamizal case, and also that my dissenting opinion from a majority of the judges in that case was approved by the Department and by the President in his message, and I believe it is still maintained by the Department that kept me here. Had I considered my own personal convenience I would have resigned long ago. For obvious reasons I intend now to separate myself, if I can do so with honor, from this commission, and shall not have the personal pleasure of meeting you again. I thank you very kindly personally, and as I can not anticipate or hope to meet you again officially, I bid you adieu.

"The Chairman: Gen. Mills, I want to say for the committee that nothing has been done or said by the committee to tend to reflect upon either the character of your work or your intentions in disbursing the funds in your hands.

"Gen. Mills: I appreciate that, sir.

"The Chairman: We all realize that you have done a valuable work down there, and you have done it splendidly, but certain matters developed here that we were not aware of, and that you had been led into by the State Department, and we thought it our duty to investigate them and right them, and no reflection was intended upon you or Mr. Keblinger.

"Gen. Mills: Mr. Chairman, I want to say to one and all of you that I have been treated with the utmost fairness in all of my intercourse. My troubles are not here, but in another direction." (See printed report of the committee, containing sixty-five pages.)

Notwithstanding this absolute acquittal by an American jury —there were twelve members of the committee present, all intensely interested—Dr. Boyd's old charges, rehabilitated by Mr. Bryan's apparent support, led Senator Thomas, of Colorado, to deliver a two days' speech on the floor of the Senate. (See Congressional Record of March 23 and 24, pages 5984 to 6006, inclusive.) He mentioned my name fifty-two times, including such references as "this man Mills," charging me with the most disgraceful conduct with which an American officer can be charged. Called to my attention several days after its delivery, I brought it to Senator Root's notice, asking him to confer with Senator Thomas and see if an amicable adjustment could not be had by Senator Root's explaining I had served under him while he was Secretary of State, and could not be guilty of such misconduct.

Senator Thomas stated he had his information from reliable authority, whereupon Senator Root had my rejoinder published in the Congressional Record. (See pages 13424 to 13426, inclusive, of the Record of July 18, 1914.)

Mr. Thomas replied on the floor of the Senate (see Record,

July 20, pages 13479 to 13480, inclusive), admitting he obtained much of his information from Dr. Boyd. He added, "My information comes, however, from the State Department and, until I am satisfied of its incorrectness, I shall insist that my statements are in accord with the facts."

I asked the State Department what their records showed upon the point in question. The matter was handled in the Department by the Honorable John E. Osborne, Assistant Secretary of State. He could have informed himself by a telephone conversation with an accounting officer of the Department. But he referred my letter to Mr. Gaines, who was absent. Followed delay, evasion, equivocation and confusion of the issue, the giving of unsought information about matters not in dispute, and withholding information needed for my defense, which it was the duty of the Department to give.

When finally cornered, after a four months' correspondence, Mr. Osborne wrote me the Department did not know the source of Senator Thomas' information. Mr. Osborne may have deceived himself into thinking that there was technical justification for his statements, but no one who reads the correspondence can have any more doubt as to the real situation than Senator Thomas, or as to the complicity of State Department officials in Senator Thomas' attack upon me.

When I sent the correspondence to the Senator he wrote me as honorable a letter of apology as could be expected, doing his best to let the State Department down easy, presented all the correspondence upon the floor of the Senate and asked for its publication, which will be found on pages 272 to 275, inclusive, of the Record of December 16, 1914.

I cheerfully acquit the Senator of everything except bad judgment. He felt justified by the information he received from officers of the Department to which he, perhaps not unnaturally, gave a credence proportionate to their official status rather than to their actual knowledge.

Mr. Bryan, however, has never offered any explanation. I

am reconciled to the situation, believing he could write me
nothing I would value in that connection.

The President accepted my resignation on June 24th, to take
effect July 1st, on the conditions I stated, that the Department
had found no evidence of neglect or wrong-doing on my part.

The President soon restored Mr. Keblinger to official favor.
He suspended the regulations governing the Consular Service
by executive order, in order to appoint this man, whom Secretary Bryan had summarily dismissed for alleged cause, as
United States Consul at Malta, where he is serving with distinction, and where he was recently promoted.   His defamers,
Bryan, Osborne and Gaines, have returned, voluntarily or
otherwise, to private life, while the Department of State is
once more in the hands of gentlemen qualified by their training and ability to guide the foreign affairs of a great nation.

Woman's Suffrage

From what has gone before readers will understand that Nannie and I were always fervent advocates of woman's suffrage throughout our lives, and, as far as we could with respect to the popular prejudices of the day, tried to advance it.

Because of my diplomatic service under Secretary of State Gresham, the president of Indiana University, Dr. William Lowe Bryan, honored me with an invitation to the commencement of 1911, and showed me marked courtesy. My friend, Norman Walker, of El Paso, president of the class of 1906, accompanied me from El Paso and introduced me to members of the various classes.

The Indiana University is coeducational; of the 975 students, 231 were young women. Diplomas were given the graduates in the open air in a large sugar tree orchard in the presence of five thousand persons. When the president called the first name, a young lady in graduating garb presented herself. When several more young ladies followed I asked the president if he was calling women first out of courtesy to the sex. "Oh, no," he said, "they are honor graduates." Of the five highest graduates three were women. Asked how this was accounted for, the president said, "Because they are the best students. No one should suspect any partiality is shown them by their instructors. They deserve everything given them." This reinforced me in my lifelong opinion that women, if given an equal chance, were the equal of men in all the essentials of life's successes. I could but think how my mother would have felt if she could have survived to witness that scene, and when I returned home and told Nannie, it encouraged her to take a more prominent part in the cause of woman's rights generally, and especially woman's suffrage.

In February, 1913, a meeting of suffragists was held in Washington. Mrs. Carrie Chapman Catt was our guest, and a very interesting, well informed and courageous advocate of her cause we found her, as well as a most charming woman.

We attended several of their meetings in Washington and aided them materially. The association decided to hold a parade March 3, 1913. Nannie and I were members of the advisory committee, and about ten days before the date set Miss Paul, who had charge of that paradte, told me that she was having difficulty in getting permission to march on the avenue. As I was personally acquainted with Mr. Rudolph, General Johnston and Colonel Judson, the District Commissioners, I introduced her to them. They treated her with the greatest courtesy; the chairman, Mr. Rudolph, both encouraged her and expressed his sympathy with her attempt to get permission and secure protection during the march, as did Colonel Judson. General Johnston was a little luke-warm; reasonably so, however, because he was not in favor of woman's suffrage. But they did not grant the permission.

General Johnston objected to the selection of the day before the Presidential inauguration, but others thought if permission was to be granted at all, it was better to have the two parades as near together as possible.

I advised Miss Paul to ask the Secretary of War for military protection from Fort Myer. Judson agreed, and, in his presence, Miss Paul made the application through the District Commissioners to the Secretary. Later she showed me a letter from the Secretary of War, declining to furnish the escort. Although the committee feared the parade would not be protected, most people believed the police would not so disgrace themselves as to fail to protect them from insult and humiliation, or to allow their parade to be broken up, as it practically was. Failing to get the permit from the Commissioners, Miss Paul applied to Congress, and the day before the parade Congress authorized it and made an appropriation for extra policemen. The parade was organized as systematically, as brilliantly and as efficiently as any parade of men ever held.

I believe that on that 3d day of March, 1913, woman's suffrage won its fight. Some of its members have acted foolishly since, as members of reform movements often do, but the day is won, and nothing but absolute reversion to barbarism can prevent women, as long as this country remains a republic, from having some voice in its government.

We both marched in the parade, Nannie with the home-makers. Another army officer, General Charles Morton, U. S. A., had the courage to march with his wife in this procession, as did a few Senators and members of the House. What happened is history. As it is fully related in Hearings Before Senate Committee, District of Columbia, 63d Congress, special session, under Senate Resolution 499, part first, wherein Nannie and I each testified, pages 101 to 116, inclusive, I will not relate it here.

But, notwithstanding the insults and humiliation heaped upon these brave and fearless women to the shame of many of the officials of the government, and particularly the Washington police, it was a proud day for women. Probably no marcher has ever regretted her participation in that parade, but is still proud.

Nannie enjoyed the victory to the utmost. While she continued to assist the society, she felt that the day of battle was past, and the problem would work out by the common sense of the men and women of this country, as it will.

> "Be shame to him of woman born,
> Who hath for such but thought of scorn."

It is remarkable that up to this time no candidate for President ever admitted any sympathy with woman's suffrage. Since that date, no candidate for President has failed boldly to announce (I hope sincerely) that he was whole-heartedly in favor of woman's suffrage. And I believe that in the future no candidate will fail to make this declaration.

PROHIBITION

Another cause in which Nannie and I were enthusiastic was that of prohibition, to restrain the intemperate use of intoxicants. We always kept liquor in the house and often offered it to guests, but we early learned to exclude it from the table when very young officers were present, because such an example might encourage them to form habits which they later would not be able to restrain. Unfortunately, Congress and the War Department authorized the canteen, an organization formed by the officers of military posts. Originally intended to dispense only such articles as were not furnished the soldier in the ration, clothing, and other allowances, it gradually came to dispense the strongest beverages, sometimes of a very poor and dangerous quality. Throughout the country, especially in States having anti-liquor laws, hostility to this privilege awarded to the army grew generally. Strong efforts were made to have Congress prohibit the canteen on the ground that the young soldiers, entering to buy ordinary supplies would be brought into the presence of comrades indulging in liquor and thus induced to participate.

The War Department ordered that the selling of beverages should be conducted in a separate room from that of other goods. This rule, however, was not generally obeyed. Politicians, employed by the liquor interests to circumvent the action which they feared Congress would take, would apply to the War Department to send circulars to officers of prominence asking his opinion as to whether it was to the interest of the army to allow the sale of beverages. The liquor interests selected copies of many favorable reports, together with a few of those that mildly objected, and published them throughout the country, carefully suppressing those vigorously opposing the use of liquor in the canteen. The canteen continued authorized for many years after the best judgment of the army decided against it, but Nannie and I both lived to see it entirely abolished, to the great joy and benefit of all save the conscienceless purveyor.

In like manner the highly taxed traffic was allowed among the people long after public sentiment disapproved of it, but thanks to the intelligence of Americans and the free discussion of the subject, Nannie and I lived to see it suppressed throughout much of our land. That it will soon disappear entirely, not only from this country, but from the whole world, seems assured.

Trip to Europe With General Miles

As General Miles had previously invited me to go with him to Europe, in 1906 I accepted an invitation to accompany him. We sailed on "La Provence" for France, and spent some two months in France, Ireland, Scotland, England and Switzerland, traveling most of the time by automobile.

Mr. Colgate Hoyt, of New York, president of the American Automobile Society and brother-in-law to General Miles, with his wife and daughters, Elizabeth and Anna, had invited us to accompany them on various journeys in their automobile, and we found them very enjoyable traveling companions.

Our most interesting sojourn was in Dublin, where we met the genial, strange, though interesting race of Irishmen. We were much interested in the jaunting cars, which are to this day the principal passenger vehicles of the cities of Ireland, and exclusively confined to Ireland. Curious to know why they were used there and nowhere else, we inquired, and found that the British Government, in their eagerness to collect all the taxes they could from such properties, levied a tax on vehicles per wheel, and on domiciles for window panes. To avoid this, the stubborn Irishmen would use nothing but two-wheeled vehicles and, unfortunately, they would put just as few panes of glass in their houses as possible, and this custom is carried out there to this day. The jaunting car, while not presenting to one unacquainted with it a very enticing invitation to ride, is, after all, when you become used to it, a very interesting vehicle, and General Miles and I invariably rode in them.

Our visit was at the time of the horse show and, being cavalrymen, we were interested in the exhibition and racing of the animals.

From Dublin we were invited by a Mrs. Galt-Smith, who was the owner of an old Irish castle, to visit her, and we spent some days as her guests at Kilwaughter Castle, in the north of Ireland.

Mrs. Galt-Smith took us around her neighborhood and we became acquainted with the peat bogs, which we had never seen before, where a great part of the fuel of the country was taken from dried up peat bogs, and, strange to say, the undried bogs were such that even horses became drowned when they tried to pass over them.

From there, we also visited the "Giant's Causeway," one of the geological curiosities of the world.

We passed from there through Scotland, through the country described by Sir Walter Scott, and saw in Edinburgh what is known as the "King's Inn," a national prison.

We traveled through the western part of Austria, adjoining Switzerland, where we saw the most unhappy people probably then on earth, poor and helpless, surrounded by soldiers on all sides and influenced by priests, who caused them to build wayside shrines at short distances from each other along the roads where the people would pause and make their obeisance to images. So unhappy and ignorant were these people that they would make grimaces at us while riding by in the automobile, and by gesture and physiognomy showed how much they hated those who were better situated than they were.

Returning, we visited London, stopping at the fashionable Carlton Hotel, where the people seemed less isolated from the world than on my former visit, less exalted in their estimate of themselves, and more appreciative of the progressive features of others, having adopted street cars, tunnels, elevators and electric lights, and become themselves personally more cosmopolitan, but they were still loudly English, proud of their Emperor, his empire and his royal family and accompanying dukes and nobles, so amusing to the rest of the intelligent world.

My Cartridge Belt Equipment

The invention, development and manufacture of the woven web ammunition carrier and its accompanying web equipment (which has taken the place of leather throughout the world), was my greatest material achievement. I only regret that they were not designed for construction rather than for destruction.

In 1866 our army adopted the breech-loading rifle with metallic ammunition, comparatively non-perishable by exposure to the elements. The almost cylindrical stem of the cartridge with the projecting flange on its head, made it possible to make a belt with closely fitting cylindrical loops, in which the cartridge was held in place by friction, prevented from dropping through by the flange.

When captain of the 18th Infantry, I equipped my company with my invention, using belts made of leather, with sewed-on leather loops. These did not prove entirely satisfactory. The acid in the leather acted on the copper in the shell, producing verdigris, causing the shells to stick in the belt or, after firing, in the chamber of the gun.

Belts of this character were submitted to every equipment board organized between 1866 and 1879, but so wedded were the authorities to the use of ancestral methods that no board even made favorable mention of my invention. Meanwhile, the cavalry and infantry on active service against Indians adopted these belts of this character, fabricating them themselves.

Becoming known at Washington, two ordnance inspectors were sent to inspect the equipment of the armies of General Terry and General Crook, confronting the hostile Sioux, in 1876. They reported it was impossible to compel soldiers on the frontier to use the regulation McKeever cartridge boxes, and recommended the manufacture of a uniform belt at arsenals. The Chief of Ordnance approved, and thirty

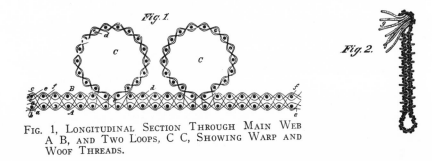

Fig. 1, Longitudinal Section Through Main Web A B, and Two Loops, C C, Showing Warp and Woof Threads.

Fig. 2, Cross Section of Main Fabric, Showing Extra Threads g, in Tube of Selvedge.

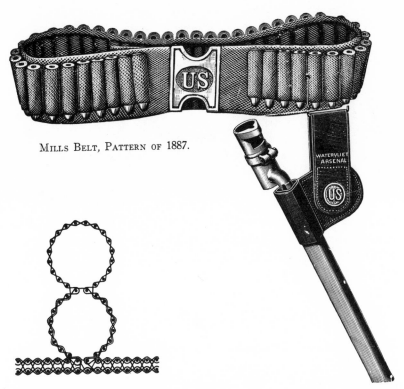

Mills Belt, Pattern of 1887.

Section Through Double Loop Belt, Showing Continuous Fabric.

MILLS DOUBLE LOOP BELT, CARRYING 90 ROUNDS,
CALIBRE .30.

MILLS NINE POCKET BELT, HOLDING 90 ROUNDS,
CALIBRE .30.

MILLS INFANTRY BELT, DISMOUNTED, MODEL OF
1910, TEN POCKETS, 20 CLIPS, 100 ROUNDS,
CALIBRE .30.

thousand sewed canvas belts were made at Watervliet. Their uniformity and the facility with which they could be procured made them more satisfactory than those previously used, but the loops were still apt to rip and enlarge.

My experience with looms as a boy, gave me the idea of weaving the whole belt, body as well as loops, in one piece without sewing the loops, uniform in size and incapable of ripping or enlarging.

In search for advice as to the feasibility of this plan, I visited the Russell Manufacturing Company, at Middletown, Connecticut, and found Mr. Hubbard in charge.

I asked if he could not help devise a method for weaving the loops on the belt. He told me that thirty years' experience in textile fabrics told him it was utterly impossible, and that I should know that every string had two ends!

"You an army officer?" he asked; "Will you get angry if I give you some good advice?"

"No."

"Do you see that building?" pointing to the insane asylum. "Well, there are smarter men than you right in that building who got there by having just such things as this on their minds too long. I advise you to get it off."

Notwithstanding his advice, I did *not* get the matter off my mind until I had accomplished my conception.

In 1878 the War Department organized a board of officers consisting of Colonels Miles, McKenzie and Morrow, Major Sandford and Captain Benham, all officers of frontier experience, to consider the best method of carrying the new metallic cartridges.

They reported unanimously in favor of the belt, adding, "In this connection the board is very favorably impressed with the means devised by Major Anson Mills, 10th Cavalry, for weaving the cartridge belt and recommends it for adoption by the Ordnance Department and their manufacture."

This report was approved by General Benet, Chief of

Ordnance; General Sherman, commanding the army, and the Secretary of War.

A few of these belts were made for presentation to the board on a hand loom manipulated by a skilled Scotch weaver, but we found it difficult to produce a web with loops of proper consistency and resilience. In spite of all we could do the web would be more or less fluffy or inconsistent (unable to retain its form), and was not satisfactory. I had more difficulty in producing webbing of proper consistency than in inventing the web belt and a loom to weave it all in the same piece. However, by procuring cotton of the very best fiber, twisted into multiple threads with such hardness of twist that neither the warp nor woof threads would break under a strain of nine pounds each, I finally produced a web with a better consistency and resilience than the best leather itself, notwithstanding the old adage that "there is nothing like leather."

Mr. George Crompton, of Worcester, the textile manufacturer, told me there was no hand machine which could not be duplicated by a power machine. So my next effort was devoted to making a power loom. I visited many textile factories in England, France and Germany, but found nothing to meet my requirements, and in a shop with two assistants I constructed the first loom, in Worcester, in 1879.

The Chief of Ordnance sent his senior officer, Colonel Hagner, to inspect the loom and report whether it was practicable to weave the loops on it. Its work was so satisfactory he recommended the discontinuance of the manufacture of the sewed belts made under his charge at Watervliet.

The Secretary of War adopted the belt for field service, continuing the McKeever box in the garrisons only. On August 24, 1895, the box was permanently abandoned and the belt became universal throughout the army.

Its superiority over all other methods for carrying ammunition are too apparent to need any general description here, but among its practical qualities may be named the easy access, the ready inspection, the instant detection of loss or

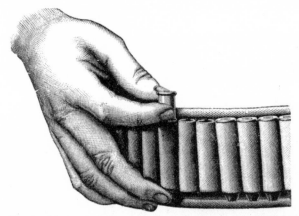

PROPER METHOD OF EXTRACTING CARTRIDGES FROM LOOPS.

CALIBRE .45 COMPARED WITH CALIBRE .30 CARTRIDGE.

CLIP OF FIVE .30 CALIBRE CARTRIDGES.

GOLD MEDAL AWARDED BY NEW ZEALAND INTERNATIONAL EXPOSITION, 1882.

U. S. Infantryman
With Mills Equipment of 1887.

exhaustion; the expressive martial purpose at sight, important in the suppression of riots, the ease with which it is carried, fitting closely to the body with weight so equally distributed as to lead the soldier almost to feel it a part of his person; the economy in weight and expense, neither being more than the leather belt to which the box, pouches, etc., of other methods were attached.

As an active army officer, I could not contract with the government to manufacture the belt.

On September 22, 1879, I offered, through the Chief of Ordnance, General Benet, to give the invention to the government if he would manufacture the belts in his department, thus advertising its worth to the sporting trade and to other nations. He preferred purchasing the belts in open market. The Gilbert Loom Company, of Worcester, agreed to furnish forty thousand single loop belts, paying me a small royalty. The forty thousand belts supplied the army for five years, so that neither Mr. Gilbert nor I received any large compensation. But we supplied a larger number to the sporting trade for different sized arms, rifles and shotguns, and so had sufficient income to keep the factory going. The Winchester Arms Company had the sole right to sell the sporting goods for five years, yet at the end of that period we received from both sources less money net than I had expended in the twelve years from 1866 to 1878 in perfecting and exploiting my improvements.

The cartridges for army belts were forty-five caliber. More than fifty loops on a belt for an ordinary man were not possible; yet, for rapid fire, it was necessary to have more than fifty cartridges on the person, and it was too cumbersome to carry two belts.

At the expiration of Mr. Gilbert's contract I entered into a contract with my brother-in-law, Mr. T. C. Orndorff, by which he was to devote his entire attention to building up the factory and perfecting the belt. He agreed that by diligent application and industry there was a fortune in the prospective improvements of the web belt and equipments and substitutes for leather, and entered heartily into the spirit of the work. He took over ten looms from Mr. Gilbert and the contract for furnishing the sporting trade from the Winchester Arms Company. I agreed to pay him an annual salary and ten per cent of the net profits. During the first three years, owing to difficulties with the trade and the Winchester Company, there were no profits; indeed, I advanced the factory a large sum of money. But he never lost courage.

Mr. Orndorff employed Captain Henry R. Lemly, U. S. A. (retired), to canvass the South American republics, and he obtained sufficient orders there to increase the net receipts. I was gradually regaining the money invested when the unexpected happened. The difficulty with Spain arose, and, on the passage of the "Fifty Million Bill," we received telegraphic orders from the Chief of Ordnance to equip a factory capable of turning out at least a thousand belts per day. The department wanted three hundred thousand belts as soon as possible. Orndorff contracted for equipping the factory for day and night work at a large expense, for which we had to go into debt.

We had about completed the order, but had delivered only two hundred thousand, when notice was sent that no further belts would be received. The ninety days' war was over! This put us in a practically bankrupt condition, a hundred thousand belts on hand and no market for them, and a large indebtedness. But we had no written contract and could not compel the government to take or pay for the belts.

Two Canadian regiments were assembling at Quebec to leave for South Africa and the Boer War. Orndorff and I concluded to make the two regiments a present of our belts. Hurriedly packing sufficient belts to equip the two regiments, he started for Quebec, October 28, 1899, consigning the shipment to Colonel Otter, commanding the contingent steamship "Sardinia-Quebec."

Arriving two hours before sailing, the colonels commanding

U. S. INFANTRYMAN, WITH COMPLETE MILLS WEB
EQUIPMENT, FRONT VIEW.

U. S. INFANTRYMAN, WITH COMPLETE MILLS WEB EQUIPMENT,
BACK AND SIDE VIEWS.

the two regiments made much of Orndorff, gave him a dinner, and formally accepted the belts with many thanks in commendation of the "blood that is thicker than water."

In 1898 Mr. Hiram Maxim, of London, England, manufacturer of the one-pound automatic gun, wanted seamless belts for feeding his gun with large cartridges. He came to our factory, examined the looms and furnished riveted models for Orndorff's guidance.

During this visit I took Mr. Maxim and his wife to the Springfield armory and introduced them to the officers, whom Maxim hoped to get interested in his gun.

Then Maxim contracted with Orndorff to introduce our belts into the British army. Furnished with a number of samples to present for trial, both he and Mrs. Maxim went before the Army Board at Aldershot, of which Colonel Tongue was president, but the British army authorities were so wedded to ancestral methods that he failed in spite of eleven years of effort.

A Mr. Leckie, associated with Maxim, obtained some small orders for belts for the colonial troops in Australia, and Captain Zalinski, a retired artillery officer, tried to sell the belts in Europe, but in spite of energetic efforts, he failed. Orndorff visited Europe and applied at the British War Office before he ever saw Maxim, Leckie or Zalinski, but received no encouragement.

Orndorff bought much cotton yarn from Mr. William Lindsey, of Boston, who became familiar with our belt by visiting General Shafter's army at Montauk. Seeing an opportunity, Lindsey solicited a contract to manufacture and sell belts to England, with exclusive rights.

We told him we had a tentative agreement with Messrs. Maxim and Leckie and, as they might claim compensation for any orders he might get, we expected him to stand between us and any claims presented by Maxim and Leckie, or either. Lindsey visited England and saw Maxim and Leckie, after which we contracted with Lindsey, binding him to expend a certain sum of money of his own in establishing and promoting the business. We loaned him a loom, furnished a skilled weaver, and sold him sufficient material to keep it going. On October 25, 1899, he sailed for England.

He possessed indomitable energy. Practically all his small fortune was invested in this undertaking of storming the British War Office, an impregnable fortress to most Americans.

The War Office soon learned that the Boers were equipped with our cartridge belt, save that they were sewed. The British troops were being defeated principally by the cumbersome, inadequate and heavy British equipment. By June, 1901, Lindsey had orders to equip the 300,000 British troops in Africa. The equipment gave such satisfaction that the War Office adopted the belt for universal use, and by the end of the year Lindsey established a large factory in London, and small ones in both France and Germany, making his venture as well as ours a complete financial success.

These factories have since been much enlarged, the buildings of the Worcester establishment now covering over two acres of ground.

The United States adopted a new magazine repeating rifle, after the Spanish War, with a thirty caliber cartridge, instead of fifty, but greater in length, necessitating carrying the cartridges in clips of five each. The loop belt was unsuited to cartridges in clips. It was necessary to replace the loops with pockets, carrying one or more clips. A bottom was woven in the pocket to keep the clips from falling through, and a flap was provided to button over the top to hold them in. Orndorff and I invented this belt. The belt usually has nine pockets, containing four clips of five cartridges each, which enables it to carry one hundred and eighty cartridges. When filled, these belts average about ten pounds in weight. It was found necessary to have attached straps, so the weight is partially carried by the shoulders.

For the marching equipment, we devised full kits of webbing so that no leather appeared in the whole outfit.

BRITISH INFANTRYMAN WITH MILLS-BURROWES
WEB EQUIPMENT.

FRENCH INFANTRYMAN WITH MILLS WEB EQUIPMENT.

Knapsack, haversack, and canteen are almost entirely of tightly woven waterproof webbing.

After the Boer War the British Government changed its single-loading rifle to a clip rifle and the double loop belts and bandoleers which Lindsey had manufactured became obsolete. The development of the pocket belt, however, enabled the foreign business to continue with a new product.

I gradually increased Orndorff's interest to thirty per cent of the profits of the business. Our long partnership was never marred by any friction or trouble. He had the harder part, as he had to submit to my dictation, I having the controlling interest. He was one of the most genial men with whom I ever associated.

After twenty-seven years' hard work, his health failed, and in July, 1901, he asked me to buy out his interest. I gave him a sum with which he was more than satisfied. Added to what he had accumulated, he had a competence greater than he needed during the rest of his life. He and his wife moved to Redlands, California, where Nannie and I visited them a year later. He was contented and happy, but he never grew strong again, and died in August, 1905. (Cut, 330.)

Twelve years ago, when I was offered enough for my factory and its good will to enable me to retire with a similar competence, I had the good sense to accept. I have not had one dollar's interest in it since September 11, 1905.

In twenty-seven years we never had a strike, never a serious discontent with any number of our employes, and we retain to this day the loyal good will of those who bought us out. The factory is still known as the Mills Woven Cartridge Belt Company, and my portrait is in the office with a legend telling of the foundation of the factory. Every article they make, now hundreds in number, is labelled and catalogued with my name.

Mr. Frank R. Batchelder, the present manager and sole controller, engaged in service with us in a subordinate capacity twenty years ago. He has made a fortune, which he has faithfully and honestly earned. He is very able and com-

Mr. and Mrs. Thomas C. Orndorff.
(Text, 329.)

petent and as long as he lives will maintain the name of the factory in all its worth and integrity.

It has been my good fortune during most of my efforts to associate myself with young men, like Orndorff and Batchelder, of happy, sociable temperaments, able and industrious. I shall always remember them for the earnest, faithful and assiduous manner in which they forwarded my interests and at the same time afforded me a happy association with them socially.

Many connected with these factories at home and abroad are making more out of them than ever I made, but I have no envy. I received more than I expected or deserved, and am perfectly content. I enjoy the reputation more than the money.

To the day of her death, Nannie felt the same gratitude. In fact, it was she who first suggested that I had made enough, and that it was time to stop.

The League to Enforce Peace

On Saturday, May 27, 1916, Nannie and I attended by invitation, the national meeting in Washington of the League to Enforce Peace. Made an honorary vice-president and member of the executive committee, I attended its monthly meetings in New York. Officials of the society asked me to aid it by public speeches or written articles, and the editor of the New York *Evening Mail* requested my views on the League for publication. I referred a copy of my letter to the *Mail*, to the President, Mr. Taft, and Dr. Lowell, chairman of the executive committee. It was approved by them for publication over my name as a member of the League, although of course not as an expression of the League itself; President Taft suggested that I send a copy to Secretary Short for publication by the League as a part of its literature, which I did.

After making changes suggested by Dr. Lowell, the article which follows was published by the *Mail*:

November 28, 1916.

To the Editor of the Evening Mail:

SIR: Your favor has just reached me.

You ask my opinion "as to what should be done at once or in the near future, and what steps should be taken by the League to Enforce Peace to help the national government create an atmosphere wherein the voice of the American people may be heard and heeded."

To the first I answer—Nothing. There are at present, counting Greece, seventeen of the most powerful and civilized nations of the world engaged in the most causeless, vengeful and barbarous of all wars known to history.

There are perhaps actively engaged twenty-five or thirty millions of the most destructive soldiers that ever trod the earth, representing perhaps five hundred millions of the earth's best civilization, whose judgment has "fled to brutish beasts," and nothing this nation or its people can do will change its course or affect its termination one iota.

In fact, we have no remedies for our wrongs, more than a bystander in a street fight, and must bide our time, meanwhile playing the Good Samaritan under difficulties as best we can, leaving the various roads to the various Jerichos devastated and unpoliced.

The art and science of war has so enhanced the means of defense and taken the pomp and circumstance from war that all the world in arms can not again conquer and abjectly subjugate an enlightened, homogeneous and loyal people of fifty millions. This war can be settled only by exhaustion of many years and a truce of perhaps a year to compose many compromises.

We have an example in our own civil war, where England, France and Austria sought to intervene, to their own mortification and regret, and where we (but one nation then as contrasted now with seventeen) were as vengeful as the present combatants; but we were all patriots, and when there came a Lincoln, a Grant and a Lee we learned to know each other better, as in due time these hundreds of millions of the very best, most civilized and most patriotic people of the world will learn to know each other better when they have developed (as they will develop) their Lincolns, Grants and Lees, "with charity for all and malice toward none."

They have "taken many captives home" (perhaps near four millions each in fair proportion), but they can not as of old by slavery "their general coffers fill"; on the contrary, their care and keep will be a great expense and burden. Meanwhile the captives will be learning the language of their foes and earnestly preaching their country's cause and their own patriotism—none entirely without reason.

Our people and nation have much mixed up the preparedness frenzy—appropriating hundreds of millions for

the best arms and munitions—paying little heed to the
"man behind" them, who also should be the best. They,
however, insult his intelligence by offering him $15 a
month, while he knows that the nation employs as many
policemen as it does soldiers, and pays (the lower grades)
from $75 to $100 per month, and as many letter-carriers
at similar rates. The soldier is as well worthy of his hire.
Statistics show the soldier's pay to be about 14 per cent of
the cost of our great wars.

Preparedness will be complete when the private's pay
is $50 on entrance and graded upward. This would be
less expensive than to "make his trade the trade of all"
by universal conscription. Desertions, recruiting stations,
guard-houses and courts martial will virtually disappear.
The very best and most intelligent single men in the
country will qualify and each captain will have a long
waiting list of men who will need little training or discipline. We shall have a democratic army from which
intelligent and efficient officers can be raised.

There is no such tangible thing as "international law."
All real laws are "rules of action" entered into and agreed
upon by communities of individual rational and soul-
possessing human beings, where each individual surrenders some of his natural rights that greater good may
come to the greater number, and where there is a latent
police force (subject to call) with a moral environment of
its soul-possessing members sufficient to make the call
and enforce its mandates.

Without these two elements of the individual human
conscience there is no community on earth so civilized and
righteously inclined as to be able to conduct in peace and
order a prayer-meeting, a bank, a fair or a public game,
but with these two elements well developed, what is
known as a "gentleman's agreement" could be carried out
by the righteous soul-consciousness of public sentiment.

So-called international law has no such elements. Its

rules are generally established by powerful nations in great wars who, in dire disaster, for self-preservation disregard and violate previously accepted rules to suit their success and also proclaim new rules not hitherto known or accepted, enforcing them to serve the same ends as far as they have the power, thus establishing precedents, leaving the wronged of the world no remedy against such might-made laws save the might-made remedy of war, and so so-called international law is created, the individual rational soul-possessing human being having no voice in its creation, repeal or enforcement.

These "precedents" are without the two essential elements, "latent police force" and "soulful moral environment," to compel observance. Hence there is no such tangible thing as "international law."

Perhaps the League to Enforce Peace would be in a better position at the close of this war to present its scheme had we adhered to the contribution of General Jackson to so-called international law. In 1818, when General Jackson with a punitive expedition after Creek Indians captured Pensacola, then under Spanish sovereignty, he arrested two British subjects, Ambrister and Arbuthnot (one a British army officer), and tried and executed them for selling arms to the Creek Indians.

This was accepted by England, then the ruling power of the world, and her predecessor, Spain, and approved by the United States.

In this present war it is obvious to all, combatants as well as neutrals, that we are luxuriously feasting on the blood and tears of all the combatants, and to some extent the neutrals. For a long time custom has approved this. Now envy and jealousy on the part of some and a conviction on the part of many that it is unrighteous, is bringing to bear upon us a widespread prejudice which will continue to increase in a progressive ratio until the war ends.

This may impair our efficiency as an advocate of a league to enforce peace.

Now, as to "what steps should be taken by the League to Enforce Peace." I know that it realizes the magnitude of its undertaking; but owing to the great international communication, general intelligence, and common interest of the people of the world, with the opportune conditions we shall have at the termination of the war—perhaps no greater an undertaking than that devolving upon Washington, Jefferson, Franklin and their associates of the convention of the thirteen former free and independent colonies, then thirteen free and independent states.

Their problem was then much as ours is today. That is to say, to form a community of individual states after the methods and manners of the communities of individual men above described, wherein each individual state was to surrender some of its minor natural rights for the greater good of the greater number.

There was then, as there are now, great misgivings and doubts even among ourselves. The rest of the world held, through the despotism of custom, the false doctrine that war was the natural state of man. Academic lawyers and diplomats held, as they do now, that there were "state's rights" and "non-justiciable interstate cases" more potent than the rights of human beings. So that outside America the scheme was ridiculed as visionary and impracticable.

Our people and the colonies (then states) had become so abhorrent of the devastation, blood and tears of a seven years' war that they decided, through the wise men of this convention, that the states would surrender to the general good the few rights "without remedies" they might have and, so to speak, charge them to "profit and loss."

This wise convention surprised the world with a constitution of "league of states" so perfect in all its detai's of "legislation," "adjudication" and "execution" (reducing the loss of rights without remedy to the minimum) that for 128 years (with one regrettable exception) the nation had played the Good Samaritan for the natural afflictions of pestilence, flood and famine to all its people of the thirteen states (gradually increased to forty-eight), meanwhile preventing the unnatural afflictions of war and keeping open and well policed all the roads to all the Jerichos within them. In the case of the exception, the force provided proved sufficient and effective to restore order and contentment.

To a rational mind giving the matter reasonable study it is hard to conceive a conclusion other than that similar results may be accomplished with a similar league of the nations of the world.

ANSON MILLS.

While there were some forty-six members of the executive committee, it was difficult to get a legal quorum of fifteen and there were never more than twenty members present, almost all from New York City or New England. It was in fact a close North Atlantic seaboard corporation.

Believing we could not organize national sentiment in favor of the League's program with so sectional a representation, I moved that the next meeting be held at Kansas City, or some other central location, to obtain a better representation of the sentiments of the whole people. I was refused a vote, but the motion was referred to the committee on management, which smothered it.

At the meetings I attended never more than fifty minutes were devoted to the discussion of an intelligent propaganda solely in the interests of the League, but there was much discussion by a few as to inducing the President, Congress, or both, to intervene in the European war. The efforts a few of us made to declare the League an organization formed to maintain a neutral attitude regarding the European war, so that when peace should come the society might have greater opportunity to carry its righteous propaganda successfully to both victors and vanquished, were uniformly referred to the Committee on Management and never heard of again.

When the United States declared war the few members of the committee present declared the League not neutral but belligerent. My view, expressed in a letter to the Secretary, was that since our Government had accepted the gage of "Trial by Combat" it was the first duty of every American to put forth every energy to attain success, postponing nobler aspirations until flags of truce should be flying from both friends and foes. To that end I suggested we postpone our next meeting until victors and vanquished alike be so prostrated with wretchedness, poverty and shame for their cruelties and barbarities, that they would lend more willing ears to the propaganda we had so much at heart. This course not being taken, I notified the Secretary, that by participating in the war as an organization, the League had in my opinion so destroyed its capacity for good that my further attendance at the Executive Committee meetings could serve no useful purpose. My resignation was accepted.

In my opinion, the League made two serious errors: First, in Article III of its constitution where it excepted "non-justiciable" cases from the control of the proposed league. It is unsafe to devise any law or rule of action which permits of too numerous or too ill-defined exceptions. If criminal law exempted non-justiciable questions from the jurisdiction of courts, no criminal, even the most heartless murderer, could be convicted. The ingenuity of lawyers could always prove some non-justiciable element entered into the crime. The same would be true of nations. Those most powerful and best prepared for war would assume greater latitude in defining what was justiciable and would show less punctiliousness in endeavoring to establish their definition than nations smaller and less well prepared. Statesmen and diplomats working in secret would easily show any question about to lead to war as "non-justiciable" and not to be presented to the international court set up by a league composed of many nations too weak to be respected by the powerful.

The second mistake was to yield, as an organization, to the allurements of "Trial by Combat," and to endeavor, as a league, to induce our nation to intervene in the present war. Members might take this course as individuals, but, when they made it the act of a league for *peace* they stultified the league, and in my opinion, destroyed any great power for usefulness the league might have in the future.

DUELLING PISTOLS BROUGHT FROM ENGLAND BY NANNIE'S GREAT UNCLE.

TRIAL BY COMBAT

PERSONAL TRIAL BY COMBAT

I hope to show a close analogy between the personal trial by combat legalized throughout Europe for many hundreds of years (now legal nowhere, practically abandoned in all civilized countries), and international trial by combat, still existing throughout the world. Describing conditions before the middle ages, George Nielson, in his "Trial by Combat," says:

"Nothing was too high for it, nothing too low. It would establish the virtue of a queen, test the veracity of a witness, or reargue the decision of a judge; it would hang a traitor, a murderer, or a thief; it would settle a disputed point of succession, give a widow her dower, or prove a questioned charter. From such high arguments as these, it descended with equal ease to discuss debts of every kind and of whatever amount, and a French monarch earned a title as a reformer when he disallowed it where the principal sum in plea was under five sous."

This legalized method of trial was used prior to any historical record, but Gundobald, King of Burgundy, in 501, established the law permanently in his kingdom, where it was continued for over eleven hundred years. Replying to the remonstrances of one of his bishops, he said: "Is it not true that the event both of national wars and private combats is directed by the judgment of God? And does not Providence award the victory to the juster cause?"

Of a later period, Nielson says:

"When the fourteenth century began, the duel had ceased to be in any real sense a living proper part of law. On the continent and in the British Isles it was alive a thousand years and more after the enactment of Gundobald."

The incident of David and Goliath was quoted by some as a divine authorization of trial by combat.

Throughout Europe, England, and even America, it was a personal privilege of men of honor, until the middle of the nineteenth century, when, to the great honor of America, be it said, the good sense, intelligence and courageous action of the American people caused its abolition.

Some claimed the unlegalized continuance of it to be necessary because of the non-justiciable questions of honor raised between disputants; also this method of trial was not available to common people, but only to what were known as gentlemen and so-called men of honor.

Until the first part of the 19th century judges on the bench, lawyers in court, and other public functionaries, supposed to belong to that small class of people "of honor" wore swords, wigs and knee breeches when officiating, after the manner of barons, squires and knights errant of the mediæval ages.

As examples of personal trial by combat, I select the four most famous duels fought in America during the fore part of the last century:

Burr-Hamilton, 1804; Baron-Decatur, 1820; Graves-Cilley, 1838, and Terry-Broderick, 1859.

Burr, Baron, Graves and Terry were the challengers, and all were skilled professional duellists, and each killed his antagonist.

At the time of their duel, Burr and Hamilton were among the foremost men of the country, Burr being Vice-President, and Hamilton perhaps the most influential politician. Burr was forty-eight and Hamilton forty-seven, conspicuous and able from boyhood. They served together on General Washington's staff when mere youths, although Washington soon found it necessary to relieve Burr. He retained Hamilton, and later made him one of his cabinet.

Though both were from New York, they headed opposite political parties. Hamilton's influence defeated Burr's appointment as brigadier general in 1789, and also his hope of securing a foreign mission. When Burr and Jefferson were candidates for the Presidency in 1800, Hamilton threw his influence against Burr and Jefferson was elected.

During these fifteen years of political rivalry Hamilton said many severe things of Burr. Rendered desperate by his successive disappointments, Burr forced a quarrel on "a trivial bit of hearsay" in a letter of a Dr. Cooper. This went the rounds of the press, stating Hamilton had said he had a "despicable" opinion of Burr. Burr sent his friend Van Ness with a letter demanding Hamilton admit or deny having expressed such an opinion. Hamilton declined to submit to such a vague and sweeping inquiry, while stating his readiness to avow or disavow any specific statement, closing his letter with the formula used by those who expected to accept a challenge if tendered. After further correspondence Burr sent Hamilton a formal challenge, which was accepted. Hamilton wrote a statement for publication after the meeting, announcing his religious and moral opposition to duelling. He stated he had no malice toward Burr, and accepted the challenge only because of the imperious custom which would destroy his public usefulness if he declined. He added that he did not wish to kill Burr, and intended to reserve his first fire in the hope that it would induce a reconciliation. If it did not, he might perhaps reserve his second fire. This declaration, of course, was unknown to the public or to Burr. In a note to his wife and six children he beseeched their forgiveness, declaring he was forced to accept by public sentiment.

They met at Weehawken, N. J., July 11, 1804. At the signal Burr fired, Hamilton sprang convulsively upon his toes, reeled —at which moment he involuntarily discharged his pistol— and then fell forward upon his face and remained motionless. His ball rustled the branches seven feet above the head of his antagonist and four feet wide of him. Hearing it, Burr looked up to see it had severed a twig. Seeing Hamilton falling, he advanced with a manner and gesture expressive of regret, but, urged from the field by his friends, without speaking he turned about and withdrew.

Public indignation in New York became violent. The grand jury found a true bill against Burr and the Vice-President of the United States fled the jurisdiction of his State.

During his remaining thirty-two years, he gradually lost the confidence of his countrymen. With no hope of achieving former ambitions, he formed the ill-fated expedition in the West known as Burr's Conspiracy, planning to abandon or dismember his own country and make a conquest in Mexico. He died in 1836 at the age of eighty, despised throughout the United States.

Baron and Decatur

Baron and Decatur were both advocates of the duello.

While in command of the U. S. Frigate Chesapeake off Hampton Roads, in time of peace, Baron was hailed by Captain S. P. Humphreys, commanding the British Frigate Leopard, and ordered to lie to and deliver over alleged deserters on board the Chesapeake. His brother officers accused him of failing to make preparations to defend his frigate when he was attacked and compelled to surrender to Captain Humphreys.

Baron called for a court of inquiry. Decatur was a member of the subsequent court martial, although junior to Baron. Before the court martial was sworn, Decatur advised Baron that he felt prejudiced against him and feared he could not do him justice, suggesting Baron exercise his right to object to being tried by him. Baron declined, and Decatur reluctantly sat on the court, which suspended Baron for five years. This he took much to heart, making frequent applications for reinstatement. One of these applications passed through Decatur's hands. When he could not recommend Baron's reinstatement, Baron took offense and threatened a challenge. Decatur replied that he felt no animosity toward Baron, but had made his endorsement through a conscientious conviction of duty. He hoped Baron would not resort to extremes, but, if he did, would feel bound to accommodate him. Baron responded with a formal challenge, which Decatur accepted.

Just before they were placed in position, Baron remarked, "Commodore Decatur, I hope when we meet in another world we will be better friends."

Decatur promptly replied, "I have never been your enemy."

The distance was ten paces. Both were excellent shots, and firing simultaneously, both fell, Baron seriously, and Decatur fatally wounded.

Baron lived thirty years, becoming the senior officer of the navy, but he never wholly reinstated himself in the good opinion of either his brother officers or the people of his country.

Graves and Cilley

Graves and Cilley were congressmen from Kentucky and Maine, respectively. Cilley, in debate in the House, reflected on the character of Mr. Webb, editor of the New York *Courier and Inquirer*, who sent a note by his friend Graves demanding an explanation. Not wanting a controversy with Webb, Cilley declined to receive the note, expressing his high respect for Graves. According, however, to the duellists' hair-line theory of honor, Cilley's refusal to receive the note from Graves implied a reflection upon the latter and after some correspondence Graves sent a challenge to Cilley, which he accepted.

They met on the road to Marlborough, Maryland, Graves attended by Mr. Wise, his second, and Cilley by his friend, Mr. Jones. The weapons were rifles, the distance about 92 yards. They exchanged two shots without effect. After each shot efforts were made to reach an accommodation, thwarted by Graves and his seconds. After the second, Graves said, "I must have another shot," and asked Wise to prevent a prolongation of the affair by proposing closer quarters, if they missed repeatedly. But at the third shot, Cilley dropped his rifle, cried, "I am shot," put both hands to his wound, fell, and in two or three minutes expired, shot through the body.

The committee of seven appointed by the House of Representatives to investigate this affair reported that early on the day on which Cilley met his unfortunate end, James Watson Webb, Daniel Jackson, and William H. Morell agreed to arm, repair to Cilley's rooms and force him to fight Webb with pistols on the spot, or pledge his word to give Webb a meeting before he did Graves. If Cilley would do neither, they agreed to shatter his right arm.

Finding Cilley was not at his lodgings, they went to Bladens-burg, where it was said the duel was to take place. It was agreed that Webb would approach Cilley, claim the quarrel, insist on fighting him and assure him if he aimed at Graves, Webb would shoot him. Not finding the party at Bladensburg, they returned to the city to await the result of the duel. A statement drawn up by Webb, signed by Jackson and Morell, and published in the New York *Courier and Inquirer,* says: "It is unnecessary to add what would have been the course of Colonel Webb if Mr. Graves, instead of Mr. Cilley, had been injured. Suffice it to say that it was sanctioned by us and, however much we deplore it, we could not doubt but the extra-ordinary position in which he would have been placed would have warranted the course determined upon." It is difficult to imagine what is here darkly shadowed, if it be not that, had Cilley survived the encounter with Graves, and had the latter suffered it, it would then have been Cilley's fate to have encountered an assassin.

A prominent politician, Graves never fully recovered from his countrymen's universal condemnation of the killing of Cilley, who had tried in every honorable way to avoid the meeting. He did not die in as great disgrace as other duellists, but the affair marred his career.

Terry and Broderick

Terry was an advocate of the duello. Broderick had previously fought with a Mr. Smith.

Terry from Texas, Broderick from New York, went to California as Forty-Niners.

Both rose to prominence in politics. Terry became Chief Justice of the State, and Broderick a senator in Congress. Later they became political adversaries, Terry pro-slavery and Broderick anti-slavery.

While at breakfast in a San Francisco hotel, Broderick read an address Terry had delivered in Sacramento. Angered by something Terry had said, he remarked to a friend, "I have said that I considered him the only honest man on the supreme bench, but now I take it all back." A Mr. Perley, an English subject, asked Broderick if he meant Terry. Being answered "yes" he at once resented the reflection on Terry. Broderick cut him short with some curt remark, whereupon Perley challenged Broderick, but the latter declined because of the political canvass then in progress. On September 7, 1859, Broderick's party was overwhelmingly defeated, and he emerged from the contest dispirited and in ill health. As soon as Terry knew the result of the election, he tendered his resignation as chief justice and sent Broderick a note by his friend Benham, demanding a retraction of the remarks overheard by Perley. Admitting the words, Broderick observed Terry was "the best judge as to whether this language affords good grounds for offense." Terry sent a formal challenge by Benham, which Broderick accepted, and on September 13th they met.

Terry had passed a comfortable night, but Broderick's friends had taken him to a house where he got little rest, and he came on the field unrefreshed and without even a cup of coffee. The pistols had very delicate hair triggers, and Terry had practiced with them. They were strange to Broderick, and he had difficulty in handling them. When, according to the custom, the seconds searched both, McKibben, Broderick's second, merely touched Terry's vest. But Benham manipulated his hands up and down Broderick's person as though he thought to discover a coat of mail. This annoyed Broderick at a time when he needed to be calm. When word was given, Broderick fired and missed. Then Terry took deliberate aim and Broderick fell, fatally wounded.

The day of Broderick's funeral public sentiment changed suddenly in the late senator's favor, and against Terry. He lost standing in his party, and although a great lawyer and a universally popular man, became something of an outcast in

California. He was indicted, but the case was transferred to another court and dismissed.

His end was violent. He had harbored resentment against Stephen J. Field, Associate Justice of the United States Supreme Court, for a certain decision unfavorable to Terry's wife, widely known as Sarah Althea Hill, and also because he had not hesitated to send both Terry and his wife to jail for resisting and assaulting a United States marshal in open court. Field's friends were informed that Terry threatened violence, and when Field returned to California after Terry's release from jail he was accompanied by a deputy marshal as body guard. Terry sought Field, entered a restaurant where Field was seated, walked directly back of him and struck the venerable justice in the face. Nagle, the body guard, shot Terry, who died instantly.

These four duels are mentioned here because they involved citizens of the highest prominence. They proved clearly to the American people that King Gundobald's law that "Providence awards the victory to the juster cause" was wholly untenable.

After the Burr-Hamilton affair severe laws were passed against duelling; but the influence and power of its advocates rendered it difficult to get an indictment from a grand jury or a conviction from a petit jury. After the Terry-Broderick duel, however, it became easy, and so many convictions were obtained that this mode of trial was permanently banished from America. Today no one could give better evidence of unrighteous and murderous intentions than to challenge another to trial by combat.

It should not be difficult to draw an analogy between this barbarous and cruel method of trying so-called non-justiciable cases and that of the great and powerful nations, which make the same false claim that differences between them are non-justiciable and only to be settled by trial by combat.

If, as the world has decided, questions of honor between individuals are justiciable, it must also be true that no question of honor between nations is non-justiciable.

National Trial by Combat

Of the present war, I want to record my conviction that, as we are in it, whether wisely or no, it is the duty of every American to help prosecute it with all his abilities until peace is attained.

But of war in general, I have much to say. As personal trial by combat has disappeared from all civilized lands, so national trial by combat will, I believe, be abolished by force of public opinion, at no very distant date.

The manner in which this, the greatest of all reforms, can best be brought about has been with me a matter of the greatest interest, to which I have given much reflection.

My profession, and Nannie's attachment to it and to me, led us to see more of humanity than falls to the lot of most. We lived in almost every State and Territory in the Union, and in several foreign countries, mingling with many races. We knew the negro, a short time as slaves, but for over fifty years emerged from bondage, as household help, as soldiers and as citizens. We learned their racial instincts, hopes, aspirations and ambitions. As closely, in service with and over them, we knew the wild Indians. We knew closely and intimately, both officially and in private life, the misunderstood Mexicans, and the Chinese and Japanese, who are so misunderstood by our own people.

This intercourse with many races taught us that men in their instincts, hopes, ambitions, passions and dislikes are much the same the world over, and that no race or nation can claim any very great superiority over any other. In the inherent desire to be of use, all have practically the same good purposes as far as environment will permit, and as it is given them to see. Those whose efforts win greater academic civilization and consequently greater power often develop a mistaken sense of duty to compel less fortunate neighbors to take on suddenly that state of civilization and progress they have been thousands of years in acquiring, arguing that it is *"Mani-*

fest Destiny" that they could do better with these people and their belongings than they could do themselves. It is a short step to the further mistaken doctrine that *"The End Justifies the Means,"* and the means is always conquest and subjugation by the doctrine that *"Might Makes Right."*

This logic consolidated the different German nations into one central power, and, under the present Kaiser, organized a militarism for the purpose of conquering and subjugating the world. Hannibal, Alexander, Cæsar and Spain's rulers, accomplished and maintained wicked and tyrannous powers for an average of 300 years. When oppression became unbearable, their subjects freed themselves by bloody rebellions.

Lately England (by destroying the Spanish Armada and building one of her own) began ruling all the seas and straits of the world, its commerce and trade "by orders in council," confiscating the mail, censoring the news of the world, and is no less arbitrary in controlling the sea and commerce by navalism than those who controlled the land by militarism.

England, however, during the last three hundred years, has been more beneficent and benevolent than any of her predecessors. The best ruler the world has ever had, she abandoned to some extent her right to rule the land by allying herself with some of the most powerful nations of the world, while maintaining rule of the seas by overwhelming navalism.

Though we are now her ally, Americans should ponder well what our position in the world will be after the present war.

Flags of truce, if they should appear today, would find about 40 millions of soldiers of the seventeen combative nations in arms, who have taken captive, in fair proportion, some 4,500,000 prisoners, who are now face to face with their captors, learning each other's language, their hopes, and aspirations and arguing, none altogether without reason, their aims in the war.

This, like the conditions of our own Civil War, presents the grandest peace table ever known to history, all having been eye witnesses, and for the most part, unwilling participants in the despotic cruelties, participated in more or less by all the armies, formulating an enduring peace without vainglorious victory in contradistinction to their secretive, vengeful rulers, the politicians and diplomats who would have no peace without vainglorious victory.

In the years to come, these unselfish arbitrators may prevail and establish the principles of a democratic peace and a confederacy of the world's nations to control it. This must come not only on land, but on all the seas and straits and in commerce, for a democratic peace is just as necessary for the betterment of humanity on the seas as on the land. An oligarchal government of the seas and straits is just as detrimental to the peace and prosperity of the world as an oligarchal government anywhere else. In the face of a peace of this character insincere and unrighteous formulations will melt away as did those of the politicians, diplomats, carpetbaggers and Ku Klux before the well formed judgment of the "Blue and the Gray" engaged in our Civil War by which we were enabled to establish an enduring peace without vainglorious victory.

Peace will leave at least 40 millions of the most efficient small arms ever known, probably 10 million machine guns of the same character; three hundred thousand cannon, large and small; thousands of war-ships, all with corresponding munitions and equipments for which the world will then have little use.

Peace will find most of these soldiers with three or four times their number employed as accessories to the army, discharged without vocation, and, perhaps, 100 million expatriated citizens, poor, helpless and starving men, women and children, wandering on the face of the earth. All these several hundred millions must be provided for in food, shelter and raiment. How to do it will be the greatest problem mankind has ever faced.

The bonded indebtedness of the world is, perhaps, today 100 billions, and after flags of truce are flying, it will necessitate, perhaps, one or two years to compose a satisfactory peace among the many nations at war; so, that before it will be practicable to disarm and free these hundreds of millions of unemployed, the bonded indebtedness will probably increase to 200 billions. If it be attempted to enforce the punitive doctrine that "to the victors belong the spoils," it is obvious that it would be wholly impossible for the victors to maintain these bonds and maintain their national armies necessary to enforce reparations and indemnities, and the world would be compelled to face at least a partial repudiation. It would take hundreds of years for the vanquished to indemnify and repair, and hundreds of billions to support the necessary armies to enforce the penalties. Whereas, if the individual nations could be relieved of the support of armies and navies, they could readily indemnify and restore themselves in twenty years, and advantageously charge the expense to "Profit and Loss."

To palliate and partially remedy this distressing situation, three courses may be presented to the American people:

First. **An alliance with the victorious nations claiming new= found democratic emperors by Divine right, hereditary royal families, lords and nobles), for the future preservation of the peace of the world. Such an alliance could hardly prove more successful in the future than similar alliances have proven in the past, and would only engender and breed similar opposing alli= ances in a comparatively short space of time, probably embrac= ing the yellow races, which would produce a similar world war, besides which it would make "scraps of paper" of our Constitution framed by Washington, Jefferson, and Franklin, and Lincoln's government "of the people, by the people and for the people."**

Second. **Apparently a better remedy: a policy of isolation carried out by building ships for coast defense only, by girding our seacoast and our international borders with a broad gauge national railway, capable of carrying the heaviest ordnance and transporting strong armies rapidly; by building emplacements, magazines and trenches, and manufacturing and storing at strategic points heavy artillery, small arms, ammunition and equipment for at least two million men; forming a regular army of several hundred thousand men with pay equal to, or even greater, than that of other government employees, to serve but one short enlistment. When thoroughly trained and disciplined,**

they would be returned to civil life subject to call in an emer=
gency. This in a few years would provide several million
efficient soldiers. With the present airplane scouts the approach
of any foe could be detected and announced so as to assemble
an army either on the land or seashore that would destroy any
possible force that could approach us. America is better situated
for such isolation than any other quarter of the globe that
nature has given to a homogeneous people, because we produce
all the necessities of life. The rest of the world would be obliged
to make terms with us for the necessities they can not live with=
out, of which fact this war is a perfect exemplification.

Third. Certainly the most promising and feasible course, if
the tyranny of the world's custom can be overcome as it has
been in personal trial by combat, is to federate all the nations
of the world under a constitution similar to the constitution
of the original thirteen States, now the greatest nation in the
world, and that of the Swiss cantons, now the oldest funda=
mentally unchanged government in the world.

This plan ought to be offered at the coming peace table with
the United States a controlling factor in its accomplishment.
We will be stronger, less impoverished, less distressed and less
bitterly antagonistic than any of the other warring nations,
with a President capable of leading his people, known to be
in sympathy with control of the world's peace.

A spontaneous call from the peace societies of America is
suggested for a convention of all the nations of the earth having
a population of three million or more, with a democratic or re=
publican government with powers derived from the consent of
the governed, to consider a confederacy of the world's nations,
to which all should be invited to enter by "knocking at the door,"
and subscribing to the constitution then to be formed.

That the nations so confederated should take over all the seas,
the Straits of Gibraltar, the Dardanelles, those at Dover and
Calais, those between Japan and Korea and the Panama Canal,
together with adequate adjacent lands, and build tunnels there=
under and maintain them free to the passage of persons and
property of all nations save those who may fail to confederate.

That this confederacy should have as its main feature the

establishment of an itinerant arbitral government with, perhaps, five capitals, say, at these straits so taken over.

The world government should consist of a Congress of not over two senators from each nation, and not over four hundred representatives, proportioned to the population of each nation, selected in the constitutional manner of each nation. The government should be executive, legislative and judicial; the executive chosen by the Senate, to choose his cabinet from the Senate. All government officers would serve a limited number of years, save the judges, who would serve for life. The government to sit five years at each capital in turn.

That the nations so confederated should take over, intern and maintain in approximate equal portions at the five mentioned points, all instrumentalities of the nations confederated for the destruction of life and property in international wars, not necessary for the preservation of law and order within the respective nations, or, required by the police force of the confederacy to guarantee to nations confederated, free passage through all the seas, straits, canals and tunnels under its control, of all persons, ships and commerce.

That the National police collect from nations who fail to confederate a toll at least equal to their proportion of the total expenses of the confederated administration.

That each nation reciprocally with others, control within their own borders, citizenship, migration, emigration, taxation, militia and police for the preservation and maintenance of their laws, but no nation, whether of the confederacy or not to be permitted to have armed vessels at sea.

Any nation, whether a member of the confederacy or not, would have the right to present a grievance, if it agreed to abide the decision of the confederacy's court. No nation, whether of the confederacy or not, would be allowed to disturb the peace of the world by entering into war with any other nation without first presenting its grievance to the world's court and obtaining permission therefrom.

Nations, like individuals, often have wrongs without adequate remedies, which are better served to the general good by waiving them to other nations as individuals do to their communities.

Honolulu

In 1915 Nannie and I spent some time at the exposition at San Francisco. Previous visits to many other international expositions enabled us intelligently to understand the superiorities of the various exhibits. We thought the best showing, outside of our own country, was made by Canada, the next best by Germany, and the third best by the Japanese.

From there we went to Honolulu, spending a month in the most interesting island of Oahu. Stopping at the Moana Hotel, we enjoyed our visit there perhaps as well as any we ever made. Numerous friends, our favorite nephew, Captain Carl Anson Martin, with his interesting wife, Agnes, among them, showed us many courtesies. We visited every place of interest, and particularly enjoyed watching the wonderful surf riding. Many journeys in the mountains showed us the sea from all directions. Captain Martin took us to Tantalus Beach, where, though we were old people, we were able to climb five hundred feet of the ruggedest part of Tantalus, a mountain some twenty-five hundred feet high, with the younger ones. I believe Nannie was as strong and vigorous and enjoyed her outing as much as she did forty years before.

The island has a population of about one hundred and fifty thousand, only seven per cent native Americans, the rest Chinese, Japanese and Portuguese. The original Hawaiians have practically disappeared from the earth as a result of so-called missionary efforts to Christianize them by presenting them with a Bible with the right hand and a bottle of rum with the left.

This mixed population presents a most embarrassing problem. Race prejudices of the few Americans who claim to control officially, politically, and socially the destiny of the island will not permit them to allow their children to attend the very efficient public schools. This creates classes as in England and other autocratic nations. By separation of growing citizens, division of the people against their so-called American rulers will soon result. People of alien nationalities, estranged from their rulers, will hardly help maintain our government. Although I have never seen our other insular possessions, I fear the same danger and embarrassment regarding the perpetuity of the republic exists there also.

Hawaii has a most interesting museum presided over by Professor William T. Brigham, of Boston, a man of about my age, who has spent most of his life on the island. He told us much of interest about the climate, animals, flowers, shrubbery and forests. On the Boundary Commission I learned to determine the age of trees by their girdles of growth, caused by the frost driving the sap down during the winter. I asked Professor Brigham whether in a tropical torrid climate where there was no return of sap to the earth these girdles existed. He showed me a cut from a large tree with its cross section polished, showing no sign of girdles. The growth is constant and solid.

On returning to the States we spent some time with our old friends in El Paso. In recognition of the part we had played in the development of the city, the city council changed the name of St. Louis Street, in front of our building, to Mills Street, a monument to our name which will outlast the building.

Conclusion

Our last visit to El Paso was on March 3, 1917, when Nannie, Constance and I went there to meet Captain Overton, who had been in San Francisco on business. We stayed for a few days with our good friends, Mr. and Mrs. H. B. Stevens. While in El Paso I had ptomaine poisoning, and was in great pain and very miserable for most of the visit. Nannie was greatly distressed, and worried about me both there and on the journey home. I completely recovered, but only seventeen days after reaching Washington Nannie was taken suddenly ill with angina pectoris, and, after a month's suffering, died on May 14, 1917.

Until this last illness she had always been well and very active, taking great interest in her home and spending much time and thought on doing good to her many relatives and friends. She had no inordinate love of life, but often expressed the fear that she might outlive her health and strength and become a care to others. Among her last words to me were, "Anson, I wanted to live four or five years more, as there are some things I hoped to do."

The End

"How strange it seems, with so much gone
Of life and love, to still live on."

APPENDIX

The Organization and Administration of the United States Army

Address before the Society of the Army of the Cumberland

Address before the Order of Indian Wars, on "The Battle of the Rosebud"

THE ORGANIZATION AND ADMINISTRATION OF THE UNITED STATES ARMY

JANUARY 22, 1897

A partial course at the Military Academy, four years' experience as a citizen of Texas—there in contact with the Army during its sorest trials—and a service of thirty-six years as a commissioned officer both in the Cavalry and Infantry (in the field without leave or sickness during the War) and at twenty-five separate and independent posts during the subsequent years, with a fair share in Indian campaigns of this latter period, has convinced me—against my will and inclination—that the Army is not now and never has been organized or administered in its own interests, the interests of the people, nor in harmony with the other institutions (national, state, or corporate) of the Republic.

These pages are written with a view of making as full and free criticism and exposition of the faults and errors as they have occurred to me, and the remedies as they have suggested themselves, as is proper for me to do under paragraph 5 of the Army Regulations, with the full knowledge that the rôle of the innovator or reformer is generally obnoxious to mankind, so given to the worship of ancestral methods in all the affairs of life, but more markedly, perhaps, in the profession of arms, the very mission of which is to maintain the order of things as they exist, so that at present I can hardly hope to have the support of perhaps even a majority of my brother officers, for the reason that they are supposed (erroneously, I think) to be the beneficiaries of the system and methods here assailed.

With this prelude and the faithful promise to "Nothing extenuate nor set down aught in malice," I will proceed with my theme without apology.

A careful study of the history of our country will show that neither the great patriots and statesmen who founded and

secured our liberties, nor those who have followed and maintained them, have ever at any time seriously considered the
subject of *a permanent military establishment*, save to declare
in the Constitution *"That Congress shall have power * * *
to raise and support armies,"* and that *"a well regulated militia
is necessary to the security of a free State,"* and providing at
various and sundry times to this date by legislative enactments
for the enrollment of *"every male citizen between the ages
of eighteen and forty-five"* as the well regulated militia, and
that each citizen so enrolled *"shall within six months thereafter provide himself with a good musket or firelock, a
sufficient bayonet and belt, two spare flints, and a knapsack,
a pouch, with a box therein to contain not less than twenty-
four cartridges, suited to the bore of the musket or firelock,
each cartridge to contain the proper quantity of powder and
ball; or, with a good rifle, knapsack, shot pouch and powder
horn, twenty balls, suited to the bore of his rifle, and a
quarter of a pound of powder; and shall appear, so armed
and accoutred, and provided, when called out into exercise,
or into service; * * * that commissioned officers shall,
severally, be armed with a sword or hanger,* and a spontoon;
and that from and after five years from the passage of this
act, all muskets for arming the militia, as herein required, shall
be of bores sufficient for balls of the eighteenth part of a
pound,"* and *"for making farther and more effectual provisions
for the protection of the frontiers of the United States."*

In carrying out these projects they adopted for the government of the troops so authorized, with very little alteration,
the Articles of War, Regulations, Pay and Allowances, and
Systems of Organization, with the Laws, written and unwritten,
then in force in Great Britain; and in the main the military
establishment of the United States for both Regulars and
Militia so remains to the present day.

Jefferson and his contemporaries had busied themselves

---

*See Cullem's "Art of War," page 26, describing the "Frank" soldier of the
Sixth Century.

assiduously before, during, and after the Revolution, in erasing from the statute books of the Colonies and the Congress, all vestige or semblance of support of a personal and despotic government, such as titles of nobility, established church, primogeniture and the entailment of estates, all of which had played so great a part in upholding cruel and despotic governments of the great nations of civilization, to the end that freeing the people from the all-powerful influence of these ruling classes, they might establish a free and permanent government, where all just powers should be derived *"from the consent of the governed"*; so that by the time of the adoption of the Constitution in 1789 they had not only destroyed all these privileged classes, but had established a government so unique in all its leading characteristics that it differed in every feature save one, *the War Department,* from any great nation known to history; complicated, yet symmetrical; its executive, legislative, and judicial powers blending—both Federal and State—in harmonious whole.

From its Supreme Court at the Nation's Capital down through its inferior auxiliaries in the districts of all the States and Territories, and in each State and Territory on down through their Supreme Courts with their auxiliaries, and still on down through the county, corporate and justices' courts in the counties and cities, there is no cause of action, civil or criminal, possessed by any party—individual or corporate— but there is a well-defined and easily accessible remedy in original, appellate, and final jurisdiction; so simple that the young lawyer just entering upon practice can, without hesitation, file his complaint in the proper direction; when once filed, though it may proceed to that of last resort—the Federal Supreme Court—there is no confusion or conflict between the judges, marshals, sheriffs, or constables, county, State, or Federal. But when these legal authorities have exhausted their power to suppress the lawless and make their call upon the executive of the nation to protect the lives and property of the law-abiding (their dearest and most sacred rights), neither the President nor the Governor, the Marshal nor the Sheriff, the officer commanding the Federal troops nor the officer commanding the State troops have any rules of law for their mutual and common guidance and government; too often local passion and political prejudice blind a just conception in otherwise good men and endanger the public safety. The Army (and its supplement—the Navy) being the only unimproved inheritance left us from Great Britain.

This Organization and Administration for the British Army was developed during the four of five centuries preceding our Revolution, for the purpose of maintaining the alleged God-given right of dynasties to rule the people without "The consent of the governed," to support large royal families, a large line of nobility with attendant trains, entailed estates, a numerous line of army officers—the latter supplanting the knights errant—who together constituted the ruling classes, distinguished from tradespeople and toilers as were the patricians of Rome from plebeians.

Earlier the armies were raised by the knights and barons; the officers from sons of the nobility who were admitted to the pomp and circumstance of regal courts; the men from the lowest class (often foreign mercenaries) hardly any of whom could read, or had any conception of individual, much less political rights, just emerging from barbarism and trained for wars where plunder was the main incentive to courage in battle.

These were men to be governed by fear alone, and not by the love of order and personal interest in its maintenance as Americans now govern themselves. With such people, rigid personal government and rules of discipline were necessary and accepted; with Americans, they are not only unnecessary, but abhorrent.

To comport, then, with the surroundings in the ruling classes and with the necessity for discipline among men so base in mercenary wars for the benefit of the ruling classes alone, the Organization and Administration were made to consist of two classes—officers and men—as widely separated as master and slave; the officer became by laws, written and unwritten, despotic and supercilious, with power even to take life without responsibility; the man servile and blindly obedient in the most abject sense, without remedies against his cruel wrongs.

It is true that at the time of our Revolution popular liberty had greatly advanced in England, but as the pay of the men was very small and the most of the service required in distant colonies, many of which were barbarous, and few equally advanced with England in civil liberties, few but the idle and vicious could be induced to surrender the rights then dawning upon them at home, and separate themselves for years from civilization, friends, and kindred; so, of necessity still, the unwritten laws were maintained, and those written did not keep abreast with those pertaining to civil liberties at home. To the officer, though a stripling, the soldier, though aged and battle-scarred, was always "My man," and he, in servile response, considered it a privilege if not an honor to black his master's boots. He was made to spend much time in acquiring a knowledge of the proper dress, manner, and deportment necessary to approach the presence of any one holding a commission. All this we inherited—much is unnecessarily perpetuated.

Until recently a similar unfortunate condition has confronted our army since its organization, in the fact that nine-tenths of it was compelled to abandon civilized association, going to the wilds to war with the North American savage, more dreadful than any with which the British Army has had to contend; only the poorest material could be induced to enlist, and the officers had at least a partial justification in maintaining the written and unwritten laws inherited from the British Army. But the cessation of these wars—now never to be resumed— and the transfer of the greater part of the army to the East, near the great cities, bringing both men and officers in contact with the people of the greatest civilization and also in direct association with the National Guards of States, who are directly from and with the people, has, within the last ten years, induced a great change in material of the enlisted men, so that now there can be no just reason why they should not be placed on a level as to pay, government, and promotion with other public employes in similar service, such as letter-carriers, city policemen, and others.

Right here it should be said, however, that the faults do not lie with the officers; as a rule they are blameless in these matters, as it is their sworn duty to maintain the unwritten laws, the customs of the service as they find them—which they have done, often knowing themselves to be the sufferers in alienation from the sympathies of the volunteers and the people in our greater wars—and at times impairing their usefulness for larger commands, by prejudices thus engendered. The material in officers is as good as any in the world, but there is little incentive to ambitious effort. The too certain tenure of office and the legal right to promotion by seniority are destructive of individuality and self-reliance (the distinctive characteristics of the American people) and subversive of ambitious efforts in time of peace, and in another decade the Army will degenerate into that state of imbecility and helplessness in which the great emergency of the Rebellion of 1861 found it. Neither is it the fault of the enlisted men.

Nothing, however, in our Republic, is so un-American as the great gulf that is maintained by laws, written and unwritten, between the commissioned and non-commissioned; a similar unfortunate gulf has also heretofore separated the Regular Peace Establishment from the Militia. Neither was intended by the Constitution nor its framers. The fault lies with the legislators, who should have perceived that our Government, founded on principles the reverse of those cited above, without classes, save as graded by worth, required an essentially different organization and administration, and they should have provided it, but they did not and have not to this day. They have practically kept up a small Army, generally quali-fied, however, by declaring the purposes temporary, but never seriously attempting a remodeling of its organization and administration, as was done in all other branches of the Government. They had suffered so much from the British soldier in Colonial times and had been able to vanquish him in battle with their citizen soldiery on such memorable occasions as "Saratoga" and "Yorktown" that they had contempt and hatred for anything in his semblance, and afterwards probably feared a permanent organization as menacing to the liberties they had wrested with such great sacrifice from its like, and repudiated it in spirit.

There are, however, two other alleged reasons which may have had a leading part in preventing politicians and statesmen from entering upon the necessary legislation. The first is the hazard or imagined peril to the safety of the Republic from "The Man on Horseback," a military leader placed officially at the head of a large body of well organized troops. This might be briefly answered with the truthful statement that at least two such men—Washington and Grant, and perhaps a third, Jackson—have had it clearly within their power to become dictators, and that the Republic as long as it survives will always regard them as the very safest of the many custodians of its liberties, while other leaders in the forum have attempted in vain their destruction.

The second is the great and lapsing question of "State's Rights," which at first had much force and reason, but is now fast losing all possibility of maintenance, and must eventually give way to the changed conditions and the much greater mutual interests of the States involved.

This doctrine had much right and reason in the earlier days of the Republic, because the States then, by reason of the comparative non-migration of their citizens and the transportation of products and commodities from one to the other, and the distinct characteristics of their people in habits and customs of business, might almost be said to differ from each other as did the baronies of Scotland in the Middle Ages, and required almost as autonomous laws for their government.

But gradually their wonderfully increased population, the unparalleled advances in steam transportation, the great multiplication of their products and commodities (in one part or another of the Republic almost everything useful being produced) have so stimulated travel and commerce that they have so far lost their original individuality, that the individual citizen of each State in his daily wants and affairs, is quite as much interested in the laws, customs and business of other States, as in those of his own. Judging by the past, within the next half century the Republic will contain over 200,000,000 people and scores of cities of over a million inhabitants; greater and broader-tracked railroads with easier grades and curves and swifter speed, interchanging swiftly and cheaply the commodities of Florida with Alaska, and California with Maine; great ocean ship-canals with single locks connecting the Great Lakes with the ocean via the Hudson and Mississippi rivers.

The humblest citizen of the Republic will then have a daily interest in the protection of these great properties and the lives of the men who maintain them in operation, which can only be accomplished by a strong, united and well-sustained Federal force supported by the States.

The Regular Army is now smaller in proportion to the population and wealth of the nation than it has ever been at any period since the organization of the Government; the number of the lawless, the facility for their organization, armament and concentration has on the other hand largely increased, with greater power to do harm by reason of the newly invented destructive and terrible explosives.

An organization and administration after the skeleton plan which is briefly outlined below would modify much that is evil and bring the military in harmony with the other democratic institutions of the Republic:

PROJECT FOR A PERMANENT MILITARY ESTABLISHMENT FOR THE
UNITED STATES

1. That the permanent Line of the Regular Army shall consist of one company for each district represented in the lower House of Congress, and one company for each Senator in the upper House, to be organized into regiments and corps as nearly as practicable as now authorized by law. Companies may be expanded to double their strength in time of war, at the discretion of the President.

2. That the permanent Line of the Militia of the United States (in the several States) shall consist of one regiment for each district represented in the lower House of Congress, and one regiment for each Senator in the upper House, a company of the Regular Army, when requested of the President by the Governor of the State, to be one of the companies of the Militia regiment, the captain its lieutenant colonel, the second lieutenant its adjutant, and the first sergeant its sergeant major; the regiment to be otherwise organized, armed and equipped as the Regular regiment to which the Regular company belongs. In the assignment of the Regular companies to these Militia regiments, to avoid sectional prejudices as far as practicable, but one company of any regiment shall be assigned to any one State.

3. That whenever there may be money appropriated for that purpose by Congress, the President may, at the request of the Governor, order the Regular company to join its Militia regiment, and report to the Governor, for mutual familiarization, instruction, and discipline, under his command for a period not exceeding two months annually.

4. That upon application by the Governor, the President may order the Regular company to join its Militia regiment, for the suppression of riots and insurrections within his State, under his command, and the President may upon proper application call the Militia regiment "into the actual service of the United States," with or without its Regular company, to "execute the Laws of the Union, suppress Insurrection, or repel Invasion" within or without the State to which it belongs.

5. That on request of the Governor, on the recommendation of a board of officers of the Militia regiment, the President may order a lieutenant of the Militia regiment to duty with its Regular company, for a period not exceeding two years, to receive, after taking the oath, the rank, pay and allowances of his grade in the Army, during his service for that period; *Provided,* That but one officer in the regiment is so assigned, at the same time, and that while so assigned, one of the lieutenants of the Regular company may, on the application of the Governor, be assigned to duty with its Militia regiment, by the President.

6. That it shall hereafter be the duty of Regular officers detailed to inspect Militia regiments to report the four officers in each regiment who are, in their judgment, best qualified for court-martial duty, and thereafter they may be detailed on courts for the trial of Regular officers; no court, however, to have over twenty per cent of its members of such

Militia officers so recommended; the Militia officers so detailed to have the rank, pay, and emoluments of their grade in the Army while serving on such detail.

7. That it shall hereafter be the duty of colonels of regiments of the Regular Army to report annually six of the sergeants of their respective regiments in their judgment best qualified for service on courts martial, and that thereafter they may be detailed on courts martial convened for the trial of enlisted men of the Regular Army; no court, however, to have over twenty per cent of its members of such sergeants so recommended.

8. That hereafter the finding and sentence of courts martial shall be publicly announced, in open court, to the accused, immediately after its determination.

9. That it be the duty hereafter of the committees on Military Affairs in both the Senate and House of Representatives, to send a sub-committee, the Chairman of the Senate sub-committee to have, during this duty, the temporary rank of Major General, and that of the House Brigadier General, and each sub-committee to have an officer of the Inspector General's Department for its Recorder, to visit and inspect, as far as practicable during the recess of each session of Congress, the principal points of interest, both in the Regular Army and the Militia, and submit their reports with recommendations—the Senate Committee through the Senate to the President for his information, and the House Committee to the Speaker for the information of the House.

10. That hereafter there shall be ordered before examining boards for examination for commissions as second lieutenants in the Regular Army, a number of enlisted men then having served at least two years (if there be so many applicants), equal to one-half the vacancies created in the Army during the preceding year, and if they pass the required physical, mental, and moral qualifications, they shall be commissioned; the other half of the annual vacancies to be filled from the graduates of the Military Academy.

11. That in each Congressional District where a Militia regiment may be organized, the cadet to the Military Academy from that District shall be selected from the members of the regiment including the Regular company, within the prescribed age, who have served in it at least one year, at a competitive examination, of all who choose to enter, by a board of officers of the regiment, convened for that purpose by the Governor.

12. That hereafter each alternate vacancy in each grade of each Regular regiment shall be filled by competitive examinations of such officers in the next grade below as may choose to enter the lists; the examinations to be made annually during the months of June and July at such places as it may be practicable to convene summer encampments of at least a brigade, embracing all arms of the service, and that (in addition to the present methods) each candidate be required to handle tactically

company, battalion, and brigade in presence of the board, and, if a foot officer, to march with his proper command (using for a reasonable part of the distance each of the prescribed gaits) a distance of fifteen miles in six hours, each day, for three consecutive days; if a mounted officer, the distance to be twenty miles; the examination to include field officers. The judgment of such boards to be final and determinate in each case.

13. That the monthly pay of the enlisted men of the Line of the Regular Army shall hereafter be as follows:

Regimental Sergeant Major and Quartermaster Sergeant, $90, less the actual cost of his subsistence and clothing.

First Sergeant, $75, less the actual cost of subsistence and clothing.

Sergeant, $50, less the actual cost of subsistence and clothing.

Corporal, $40, less the actual cost of subsistence and clothing.

Private, $30, less the actual cost of subsistence and clothing.

Wagoner, Artificer, Blacksmith, and Saddler, the pay of Corporal.

As the aggregate number of Senators and Representatives is 447, this project would create that many regiments of Militia (or National Guardsmen) which, allowing for the increased number of companies in Artillery and Infantry, would constitute an Army on a war footing of about 500,000 men; an added third battalion would increase it to 750,000, and then again if the number of enlisted men in each company in time of war was increased to, say, 200 men, would give us an Army of 1,500,000 men (all that the country is likely to need under any emergency) which would quickly blend and assimilate, Regulars and Volunteers, in one harmonious whole.

The present pay of the officer is ample but none too great, while the pay of the men is too niggardly to entice any one into any kind of employment in this country, save the unfortunate or the idle and vicious, seeking temporary relief from suffering for food, shelter and raiment.

The number and monthly pay on first entrance in the different grades (omitting musicians, artificers, etc.) of the Line of the Army, are as follows:

40 Colonels	....	$291.67

40 Colonels $291.67
40 Lieutenant Colonels 250.00
70 Majors 208.33
430 Captains ....Foot, $150.00....Mounted... 166.67
530 First Lieutenants..... "   125.00....   "   ... 133.33
430 Second Lieutenants .. "   116.67....   "   ... 125.00

Mark here the great gulf between officers and men in the gradation of pay, uniformity above and uniformity below:

	Pay	Rations	Clothing		
40 Sergeant Majors...	$23	$4.00	$3.83	Total,	$30.83
430 First Sergeants....	25	4.00	3.81	"	32.81
1,860 Sergeants	18	4.00	3.73	"	25.73
1,720 Corporals	15	4.00	3.71	"	22.71
17,264 Privates	13	4.00	3.34	"	20.34

Perhaps the police of our great cities, in the character of duties and the ends to be accomplished, bear a greater resemblance to the Army than any one other public organization in the country, and it may not be unfair to compare their pay, organization and administration (in the 454 largest cities there are about 36,000 policemen). The following represents the grades, numbers, salaries, etc., in the three representative cities of the Republic, New York, Chicago, and San Francisco, omitting surgeons, detectives, clerks, etc.:

New York

Number	Grade	Monthly Salary
1	Superintendent	$500.00
1	Chief Inspector	416.66
3	Inspectors	291.66
35	Captains	229.66
197	Sergeants	166.66
166	Roundsmen	108.33
2,548	Patrolmen—First Grade	100.00
287	Patrolmen—Second Grade	91.66
251	Patrolmen—Third Grade	83.33

CHICAGO

1	Superintendent	$416.66
2	Assistant Superintendents	250.00
5	Inspectors	233.33
14	Captains	187.91
35	Lieutenants	125.00
55	Patrol Sergeants	100.00
1,738	Patrolmen—First Class	83.33
525	Patrolmen—Second Class	60.00

SAN FRANCISCO

1	Chief of Police	$333.33
5	Captains	150.00
38	Sergeants	125.00
336	Patrolmen	102.00

Mark the uniformity in gradation of pay throughout! Their average hours of duty are nine. The only articles they furnish themselves which the soldier does not are quarters, subsistence, clothing, and equipments. The average cost of clothing and equipments per month in New York is $5.42. San Francisco has a retired list on half pay after twenty years' service at sixty years of age.

In 1891 there were employed in the Post Office Department in the 454 largest cities in the United States, 10,443 letter-carriers (nearly half the number of enlisted men in the Army) with monthly pay as follows: 1st class, $83.33; 2d class, $66.66; 3d class, $50.00; the average monthly pay being $73.00 per month, or a total annual pay of $9,161,137.00, nearly one-third more than the total pay and allowances of the 25,000 enlisted men in the Army.

On the breaking out of the Civil War in the early part of 1861, there were borne on the rolls of the Regular Army 1,083 commissioned officers and 15,367 enlisted men. These officers and men had been maintained by the Government, under the long existing organization and administration before referred to, for the main purpose of preparing them for the emergency that was then suddenly thrust upon them, as a nucleus for the large army then organizing.

Let us see how well they were prepared for that serious business: 282 of the officers abandoned their flag, leaving 801, with almost the full number of enlisted men remaining loyal. These, under a proper organization and administration, should have completely officered, with abundance to spare, the entire 2,000 volunteer regiments called into the Federal Army, but when they came in contact with them, there arose great distrust and want of confidence, the volunteers alleging that the Regular Officer was supercilious and determined to enforce upon them discipline which they deemed degrading and dishonorable. On the contrary, the Regular Officers asserted that the volunteers were ignorant, insubordinate, and unappreciative of the great trials that were set before them, and it came to pass that by long isolation on the plains and martinetism the Regular Army had become so alienated from the sympathies and confidence of the people that even as late as April 1, 1863, but 112 of the 801 had attained the rank of General, and comparatively few of these were successful. On the contrary, there were some 175 officers who had ceased to belong to the Army —most of them having discarded it, but some having been discarded by it—who had for years mingled with the people, becoming known to them and in sympathy with them. Of these, 45 had become general officers by the same date, and a remarkable proportion of them successful ones. But here again comes the remarkably instructive fact that for 23 years after the retirement of General Scott in November, 1861, the Army was commanded exclusively from this latter class— McClellan for 1 year, Halleck for 2 years, Grant for 5 years, and Sherman for 14 years; the only officers borne on the list of the Army at the breaking out of the war who succeeded to command it being Generals Sheridan and Schofield, and these latter not until long after the war had closed.

Then comes the additional instructive fact that of the 18

most distinguished Army and Corps commanders during the war, 12—Grant, Sherman, McClellan, Halleck, Fremont, Rosecrans, Hooker, Burnside, Meade, Dix, Curtis, and Slocum (two-thirds), came from the same class of ex-officers while only 6 —Hancock, Thomas, Buell, Pope, McDowell, and Sheridan (one-third) were from continuous service in the Army.

The only plausible explanation that can be given for these remarkable facts is that after 5 or 10 years' service in the Army, in time of peace, under its present organization and administration, ambition, grasp, individuality, and self-reliance are dwarfed, as compared with the school of the ex-officer who enters the list of civil pursuits on the lines of "The survival of the fittest."

As to the 15,000 enlisted men above referred to, from whom such great service was reasonably expected, they—by reason of the great gulf that had been placed between them and their officers—had lost much of their self-reliance, and personal pride, and made small figure in this four years' terrible war.

To illustrate what unwise and unjust discriminations are brought about by our present Army organization, where the enlisted men have so little voice and influence, here is a possible case, an extreme one it is true, but possible—many of its incidents often occurring.

First Sergeant Jones, sixty years of age, has forty years' continuous service; receives for his services in pay and allowances $32.81 per month; his grandson, Smith, with no other merit than the personal preferment of his Congressman, at the age of sixteen receives his education and $45 per month for four years while at West Point, at the expiration of which time he joins his grandfather, who is now sixty-four, and assumes command of the company, his pay jumping to $125 per month, but his grandfather's remaining the same. If they should both be killed the next day in battle (see paragraphs 85 and 162, Army Regulations) Sergeant Jones, the grandfather, may be buried but at an expense not exceeding $15; Lieutenant Smith, the grandson, may be buried by the Government at an expense not exceeding $75.

If they should both be disabled by wounds or otherwise and retired, Jones, the grandfather, receives $27 per month, while Smith, the grandson, receives $93.75.

If Smith, the grandson, approaches a guard in command of his company under arms, the guard will turn out and salute. If Jones, the grandfather, in command of the same company under arms, approaches the same guard, neither the company nor its commander will be honored.

If both these officers are ordered from San Francisco to New York as witnesses before a court martial, and travel on the same train throughout the distance, the grandfather, Jones, receives the actual cost of his ticket and $7.50 only for commutation during the journey. Smith, the grandson, receives the actual cost of his ticket and $156.64 as mileage, etc.

If the Sergeant desert en route, he is advertised with a reward; if apprehended, confined and tried as a felon. If the Lieutenant should do so (as some 24 have done since the Civil War), he would probably not be pursued, as none of the 24 referred to have been.

Article 66 of the Articles of War reads as follows:

"Soldiers charged with crimes shall be confined until tried by court martial, or released by proper authority."

Any other authorities of the Government would interpret the word "crimes," as here used, to cover only acts known as felonies or threats of violence, where the danger to law and order was too great to allow the accused to run at large, yet for over a hundred years Army officers, under the unwritten laws handed down from the Middle Ages, have interpreted this word to embrace every trifling offense for which a soldier is triable by court martial, even neglects and omissions, such as "Failure to attend roll-call" and "Neglect to clean arms"; that the article was mandatory—that no soldier could be tried by court martial until first confined in the guard-house, and grave and serious courts have refused to enter upon the trial of such enlisted men unless previously confined. The disgrace of the accused and the presumption of guilt were at once established by the commencement of punishment, and in hundreds of cases prisoners were held for weeks on trivial charges awaiting courts for their trial, when the scarcity of officers and the remoteness of their stations rendered it impracticable to promptly convene them.

The Adjutant General of the Army, in his report to the General commanding for the year 1891, reports "From January, 1867, to June 30, 1891 (24½ years), the number of desertions from the Army was 88,475," over one-third the number that enlisted during that period; he estimates the loss to the Government by their desertion and the necessary enlistments to replace them at $23,003,500, and further states that during that period 16,000 deserters were apprehended or surrendered, and estimates the expense for rewards of apprehension, transportation, and trials by court martial of these 16,000 at $2,500,000, making an aggregate pecuniary loss to the Government by desertion for this period of $25,503,500, or an annual loss from deserters alone of over $1,000,000.

If the pay of the enlisted men be increased and uniformly graded down from the commissioned officers as proposed in the project for a permanent military establishment, it would increase the cost of the Army but a little over four million dollars per annum; thereafter it is fair to presume desertion would be almost as infrequent in the Army as it now is in the police of the large cities or the letter-carriers of the Federal Government. If so, this saving of one million per annum would repay one-fourth of this additional expense, but the betterment only begins here. A large percentage of the force of each garrison is constantly in the guard-house for other offenses than desertion. This, and their frequent trials by court martial (in some years aggregating almost the total number of enlisted men), it is fair to presume, would almost totally disappear, and there would be another great saving in the expense, and an equally valuable gain in the efficiency of the Army.

The project referred to would bring a large per cent of the younger officers constantly in contact with citizens and the National Guard, and they would thus soon become imbued with the spirit and desires of the people and gain their sympathy and confidence in the same degree that the ex-officers in civil pursuits have done before them.

On the other hand, the National Guard would soon learn to appreciate the excellence of Regular Army methods—which in the main are valuable—so that should another occasion occur for the nation again to organize a vast Army, Regulars and Volunteers would soon harmoniously unite.

During the four long years of sturdy war, in which was developed the grandest, most intelligent, patriotic and chivalrous army that ever trod the face of the earth, save perhaps that which it overcame but was too magnanimous to subjugate, the Regulars were compelled by force of intelligent reason to abandon more of their idiosyncrasies than the Volunteers were of theirs—courts martial and confinements were comparatively rarely known. The soldier, both in the Regulars and Volunteers, had attained an individuality and self-reliance not before known in our Army or that of any other nation. But on separation from contact with the Volunteers and people, by isolation in the West, the Regulars, under old methods of organization and administration, soon lapsed into former conditions. Without remedies, like emergencies will produce like results in the future.

At the beginning of the war, the War Department issued the following order:

"War Department, Adjutant-General's Office,
"Washington, *November 20, 1861.*

"General Orders
    No. 101.

"The intention of the Government, in reserving the original vacancies of Second Lieutenants for the most deserving among the non-commissioned officers of the new regular regiments, was twofold: to secure the services of brave, intelligent, and energetic officers, by appointing only those who had fully proved themselves to be such, after a fair competition with all who chose to enter the lists against them, and to give to the young men of the country—those especially who were poor, unknown, and without any social or political influence—an equal opportunity with the most favored. In General Orders No. 16, of May 4, 1861, this intention was publicly announced. It is now reaffirmed, and commanding officers of the new regiments will see that it is carried out in good faith.

    "By order,

"L. Thomas,
"Adjutant-General."

Immediately the newly enlisted men of the Regulars became inspired with ambitious hope and self-reliance; promotion from the ranks was the rule, and the recipients of that period have ever since proved equal to those commissioned from other sources.

It may be said that the proposed change of giving one-half the vacancies to the enlisted men would be a hardship to the graduates of the Academy when there are now barely sufficient vacancies in the Army to give them all commissions, but it can hardly be considered a hardship to a young man favored with an appointment there and graduated free of expense to himself and family, when if thrown upon the world he would be better qualified than almost any of his fellows to fight the battle of life, and in case of war would prove, like the ex-officers before referred to, most valuable to this country. If it should be a hardship, it would be no greater than would befall the hundreds of enlisted men who under this project would doubtless qualify themselves quite as well for commissions as the graduates, and for whom, likewise, there would be an insufficiency of vacancies.

No one will assail the excellence of the Military Academy, though the present course there seems too severe in the higher mathematics and directed mostly to the production of engineer officers rather than officers for the command of men; for the former there should be an extended course, as in the military schools of other nations, but while admitting the excellence of this course for a portion of the officers of the Army, from long and varied contact with the people of almost every State and Territory, I know that he misjudges them seriously who thinks there is no other method equally good by which at least a portion of them can be supplied. No profession can maintain a healthy status where its members are derived solely from one source.

It ought to be understood by the law-makers in dealing with the Army, as it is in relation to every other service, public or private, that the Nation is but a joint stock company of seventy million holders, each with a certain amount of stock; that they require but 2,000 Army Officers; that commissions, as far as practicable, should be open to all competitors; that the best qualified may win on original entrance, promotion thereafter to be on lines of merit which can not be the case under present methods.

John Stuart Mill says:

"The despotism of custom is everywhere the standing hindrance to human advancement, being in unceasing antagonism to that disposition to aim at something better than customary, which is called, according to circumstances, the spirit of liberty, or that of progress or improvement. The spirit of improvement is not always a spirit of liberty, for it may aim at forcing improvements on an unwilling people; and the spirit of liberty, in so far as it resists such attempts, may ally itself locally and temporarily with the opponents of improvement; but the only unfailing and permanent source of improvement is liberty, since by it there are as many possible independent centers of improvement as there are individuals. The progressive principle, however, in either shape, whether as the love of liberty or of improvement, is antagonistic to the sway of custom, involving at least emancipation from that yoke; and the contest between the two constitutes the chief interest of the history of mankind. The greater part of the world has, properly speaking, no history, because the despotism of custom is complete."

For the reasons above, so clearly expressed, there is little hope for the reform before advocated to emanate successfully from the Army itself, which would be the greater beneficiary. Its officers have little power in political influence and it is to be regretted that the efforts they have made to use it have been principally directed to increasing their own number, rank, tenure of office and pay, or the establishing of such pernicious vested rights as "lineal promotion." That is to say, that Tom, who graduated in 1882, shall in no case be Captain before Dick, who graduated in 1881.

If any change for the betterment come, in this direction, the greater hope is with the National Guard of the States, who have not been so long hampered by imperious custom and who are more in contact with the legislative authorities. Eventually something in this direction must come about.

382

ADDRESS BEFORE THE SOCIETY OF THE ARMY OF THE CUMBERLAND

September 15, 1913

Mr. President: We survivors of the Army of the Cumberland with our guests are met here on the semi-centennial of its greatest battle to do honor to the glorious achievements of its members, living and dead, in the most sanguinary and yet the most chivalrous war ever waged in all the tide of time; a war, too, that had more significance at the time it was waged, and has had since, and will continue to have for the betterment of mankind, than any other war of recorded history.

If, indeed, "it needs be that wars must come," it seems we should all be thankful to High Providence that it fell to our lot to participate in this war for the Union rather than any other of which we have knowledge, and, further, from our knowledge of the past history of mankind, we should be thankful that it fell to our lot to live in our generation, race, and country, with all its blood and tears.

In fact, we of our generation who are still alive have witnessed more and greater progress for betterment physically, mentally, and morally, than all that had gone before.

But to revert to our text, "The Army of the Cumberland," and the war itself. My theme is to inspire just but long-belated honors to the Confederate soldiers in arms.

The nucleus from which sprang the new race and nation of thirty millions of unmilitary and unwarlike Americans called suddenly to form the mighty hosts of over three million Confederate and Union warriors, was the Puritans and Cavaliers of Northern Europe, who for conscience's sake exiled themselves from religious, social and political persecution over two hundred years ago to the American wilderness where they hoped, untrammeled by the imperious custom of ages, to raise a new people self-reliant and of universal common interests where all should be schooled in the same ethics politically, socially and morally.

For over a hundred years they kept faith in their purpose in a self-reliant way never known before, being almost wholly self-supporting, having no public factories, each trade making and repairing its own tools and implements, each rural family raising its own flax, wool and cotton and almost universally spinning and weaving its own fabric for clothing. This brought the rearing of children to the mother's fireside, where the moral training of the mother is more pure, effective and lasting than all other methods, including schools and colleges.

They kept this faith until they had increased to a population of three millions of the most earnest, sturdy and conscientious people on the globe, when the principal mother country beginning insidiously to re-establish over them the very evils from which they had fled into exile, they again in 1776 engaged to free themselves, this time in a war for independence and government of their own. In this they succeeded, and by the time of the adoption of the Constitution in 1787 they had established a government more unique in all its leading characteristics than any known to history, its leading feature being that "all just powers of government must be derived from the consent of the governed."

This Constitution erased from existence all vestige or semblance of a personal and despotic government, such as titles of nobility, established church, primogeniture and entailment of estates, all of which had played so great a part in upholding the cruel and despotic governments of the great nations of civilization, and substituted in their stead a complicated yet symmetrical government with executive, legislative and judicial powers blending—both Federal and State—in one harmonious whole, which amazed the world and set it doubting whether such liberties could long endure.

For 74 years its creators kept the faith of their professions, continuing their Colonial simplicity, universal industry and frugality. In these 74 years the new nation had risen to a population of 30 millions as resourceful, self-reliant, contented and prosperous people as ever lived under one flag. Their labor-saving machinery and devices had led all the rest of the world, so that the genius of the ceaseless and tireless mental workers had by mechanical appliances and organized labor in large factories relieved man's brawn and muscle from perhaps 30 per cent of its arduous toil in the struggle for existence.

But meanwhile political fanatics and moral agitators began to set up strife between the sections North and South concerning an alleged discriminating tariff against the South on cotton goods, with threats of nullification, and later in the recriminating discussion against slavery and its extension and the execution of the Fugitive Slave Law, until in the fifties a small portion of the people, mostly well meant but ill informed, had arrayed the political parties in great bitterness against each other.

So that in 1860 on the election of Mr. Lincoln to the Presidency the Northern agitators claimed it as foretelling forceful abolition and those of the South claimed it foretold the destruction of the rights of the Southern States. Both these classes busied themselves in embittering the sections by raising armed companies of emigrants to the new Territory of Kansas, where they inaugurated a miniature civil war.

The Mayor of New York City called the City Council and proposed an ordinance declaring New York an independent city, which in the temporary frenzy of the time came near passing, giving encouragement to those very few in the South who contemplated secession. In Boston it was declared in public speech "The Union must be dissolved."

Then there was the mob's resistance to the execution of the Fugitive Slave Law, the armed expedition to Harpers Ferry to incite the ignorant slaves to rise in domestic insurrection, and the declaration of a few fanatical orators that our flag represented "A covenant with death and a league with hell."

But in spite of all there were probably not ten per cent of the men North and South who afterward became soldiers for or against the Union who had any sympathy with the fanatical agitators on either side.

Mr. Lincoln had declared his purpose to "Maintain the Union, the Constitution and the laws, regardless of slavery," and in the border slave States—in fact, in all the slave States, public sentiment admitted that slavery was wrong, but as far as they were concerned an inherited wrong which they saw no practical way to remedy, as where slaves were held in large numbers they would be as helpless as children to care for themselves if freed.

In the border mountain States, however, Maryland, Virginia, North Carolina, Tennessee, Kentucky and Missouri, where families held only a few slaves, their close environments enabled the slaves to acquire such individual character in habits of morality, industry and responsibility as would enable them to make a living for themselves and become comparatively good citizens, and in hundreds of such cases their masters manumitted them, and these manumitted men were setting an example to others and making an incentive which they had not had before. So that by this time if there had been no war or senseless fanatical interference, a great majority of the slaves would be free and would have become citizens well qualified for all duties, including the franchise, and those still in bondage, if any, would have been honestly striving to emulate the example set before them by the more progressive and competent.

I have said that we were fortunate in living in our day and generation, but we have many other things to be thankful for.

We should be thankful that we for the Union had for our leader from start to finish one whom we, his contemporaries, believe to have been the greatest of the human kind; one who spent his early life in loneliness, poverty and toil, and whose after lot fell to lead our mighty hosts; yet with these extreme vicissitudes he was always the same great, good and lovable spirit, "with malice toward none and charity for all."

We should be thankful, too, that our adversaries had for their leader perhaps the greatest man and patriot next to Lincoln in this greatest of wars of history. This is no disparagement to Grant, Jackson (Stonewall), Sherman or Johnston (J. E.), for Lee had the most difficult part: it is easier to be great when triumphant than to be great when vanquished. Lee showed his patriotism from the day of his surrender to the day of his death by becoming a humble, useful and law-abiding citizen, setting an example to many of his more turbulent countrymen that was of untold value in the rehabilitation of the Union as it is today; another and greater Cincinnatus because he had the moral force and patriotism to guide his millions of vanquished but unconquered followers back to the flag—to a loyal obedience and support of the laws of those who vanquished them—thus doing perhaps more than any other to bring about Whittier's beautifully expressed hope that

> "The North and South together brought
> Shall own the same electric thought,
> In peace a common flag salute,
> And side by side in labor's free
> And unresentful rivalry,
> Harvest the fields wherein they fought."

We should be thankful, too, that we had such valiant and chivalrous adversaries as the Confederate soldiers proved to be. Had they been craven or of evil purpose, as many political warriors claimed them to be, and we had more lightly overcome them, it would have been natural to try and subjugate and exploit them, and surely the sequel would have then been different. The Unionists in arms respected the Confederates in arms and vice versa, neither practiced the water cure nor any such kindred barbarisms; they were patriots all fighting heroically and chivalrously, each for what they believed the right as it had been given them to see the right.

And last but not least we should be thankful that the nation had those brave soldiers, Union and Confederate, of border States, the true Highlanders of America, of the Appalachian Range and west to Texas, men

"Who feared not to put it to the touch
And win or lose it all."

None fled their country to escape the draft, but boldly took up arms according to conviction, son against father, brother against brother.

In this connection I overheard soon after the war a dispute between two Congressmen from Indiana and Massachusetts as to which of their two States had furnished the greatest proportion of soldiers without draft. General Tom Crittenden, of the Regular Army, late a Major General in the Union Army, whose brother had been a Major General in the Confederate Army, sitting near, interposed, saying: "Gentlemen, you should be ashamed to admit that you submitted to any draft at all. Kentucky furnished her full quota to both sides without drafting."

Companions of the Army of the Cumberland, I have mentioned these incidents attending the beginning of the war for the Union, not for your enlightenment, for they are well known to you, but to lay the foundation for convincing our children and grandchildren who do not know: that the country at large does not yet appreciate the patriotism, chivalry, heroism and fortitude of the Confederate soldier.

It seems that we, while yet alive, should rise and testify to them of what we have seen and known, for we soldiers of the Union have had ample praise and honor to the ends of the earth: but they have been comparatively forsaken even by their selfish and perfidious professed friends in Europe who once encouraged them.

After Appomattox high officials in England who had first urged them to war, and the English press, which had encouraged it by constant agitation and misrepresentation, now turned against them in their adversity.

The London *Dispatch* of June 10, 1865, used, among much else that was false, the following language:

"It was clear that a people who had not heart enough to

destroy their property that they might defend their rights were neither fit to fight, nor worthy of any fate but that of submission to oppression, that they were not soldiers, that they were wholly unworthy of their cause, and that they were only fit subjects to tyranny."

To which the late Confederate General, Robert H. Anderson, of Georgia, replied in the public press, proving by statistics that the whole Confederate army had lost more in killed and wounded in four years' war than the entire British army of the whole British Empire had lost in the wars of the preceding one hundred years.

But here was a terrible war where the combatants on neither side had any purpose of conquest, subjugation or exploitation, and to our successors it is hard to explain how it came about. It may probably be better explained by the fable of the two knights traveling in opposite directions who met opposite a road sign painted black on one side and white on the other. After salutations the knight on the black side remarked the strangeness of painting a sign black, whereupon he on the other, ever ready to correct errors, informed his new acquaintance that the sign was not black, but white. After disputation they decided to settle the question by combat, so after jousting about for a while their positions became so changed that black was white and white was black, when each glancing at the sign, one said to the other: "What are we fighting about?" "Well, you said the sign was black." "Why, so I did, and it did look black to me then, but now I see that you were right and it is white."

And so with the Union and Confederate soldiers.

The die was cast for war by political and fanatical agitators, and millions of the best men in the world rose to arms, nearly one-half of them minors, ready to sacrifice their lives as patriots for what they believed their rights assailed and likely to be lost; but after jousting about for four long and bloody years they found that each was jousting for the same object; that the Confederates had formed their Confederacy, their Constitution and their laws almost identical with those of the Union.

Shortly after the war in a conversation with Mr. Lanham, a member of Congress from Texas and a warm personal friend, he told me in discussing our different parts in the war that his father and mother and neighbors taught him the war was a holy and righteous one; so that at the age of fourteen he enlisted, believing religiously in what he had been taught, until he came to a halt in Pickett's charge at Gettysburg and saw a Union soldier about his own age, a bright-faced boy who asked for water from his canteen. Asking how badly he was hurt, the boy replied:

"I am mortally wounded, but thank God I am dying in a good cause."

From that hour Lanham said he saw there were two sides to the question. He years afterwards told the same story from the floor of the House.

Incidents like this, but more than all Lincoln's address at Gettysburg, led the soldiers of both armies to the conclusion that all were fighting for the same end, which made it easier for the Appomattox surrender and the greatest fraternal reconciliation of which the world has history.

I have said that nine-tenths of the native Americans who afterwards became soldiers in the war had no part or interest in the crimination and recrimination that brought it about and only took part after the die was cast and war was on, and as this is even at this day a broad statement, it may not be immodest in me to relate some of my exceptional opportunities for forming this and other opinions stated in this address.

I was born in the border State of Indiana, partially educated at West Point, a citizen of another border State, Texas, for four years prior to the war. There I studied law under Colonel Waddell, a former member of Congress from Kentucky, then a district judge, and had charge of his plantation with thirty slaves while he was on his circuit court, and as a surveyor and engineer became fairly well acquainted with its people, who I know were satisfied and contented with the Union as it was. But when the die was cast and war was practically on I went to Washington, asked and was given a commission in the regular army, and had a sword made with this sentiment inscribed thereon:

"No abolition, no secession, no compromise, no reconstruction, the Union as it was from Maine to Texas—Anson Mills, 1st Lieutenant, 18th U. S. Infantry, May 14, 1861."

This sword I carried throughout the war and have it still in my possession.

I served in the field with my regiment for the full term of the war without sickness or on leave, and participated in all its battles, serving with the regular brigade, First Division, Fourteenth Army Corps, Army of the Cumberland.

To illustrate how easy it sometimes is for a small number of political agitators and fanatical reformers in any community or nation to compromise the whole to a policy farthest from the thoughts of nine out of ten, I will take my own State, Texas; the methods there used being more familiar to me, but in all other States that claimed to secede similar methods to circumvent the comparatively dormant wishes of the great majority were employed.

These fanatics and demagogues knew that Governor Houston would not call the Legislature in behalf of secession, and even if he did that the Legislature would not pass such an act, so they resorted to that cure-all now so popular with present-day fanatical reformers, the "initiative, referendum and recall."

Circulars were sent to men in each district known to be violent agitators, stating that a crisis had arisen which could not be dealt with by ordinary methods and inviting them to nominate suitable men to assemble in the Capital to consider the question of secession. In a short time they met and passed a resolution which they asked the Governor to approve. When he declined they passed another, declaring the office of Governor vacant and authorized the Lieutenant Governor (Lubbock) to assume the duties of Governor, appointing a committee to accompany Lubbock to demand the keys to the office from the Governor. Houston declared their action unlawful, saying that were he a younger man he would see the State drenched in blood before he would submit, but turning over the keys to Lubbock and beating the dust from his feet on the door sill, said: "Governor Lubbock, I hope you may leave this office as unsullied as I leave it today."

Although two of his sons became Confederate soldiers, one being killed in battle, he took no part in the affairs of the war save on one occasion near the end when one of the last regiments raised was assembled in Austin, Lubbock invited Houston to review the regiment before it marched to battle.

He accepted and when the regiment was presented to him, gave only these two commands:

"Soldiers, eyes right. Do you see Governor Lubbock equipped for war? No, you do not see him.

"Soldiers, eyes left. Do you see Governor Lubbock equipped for war? No, you do not see him. He is a warrior in peace, but no warrior in war."

Houston being the most venerated man in Texas, his sarcasm weakened the faith of its Confederates in arms.

In March, 1861, when I arrived in Washington I met Lieutenant William R. Terrill of the artillery from Virginia, who had been my instructor at West Point, and asked him to recommend me for service in the army, which he did, remarking there would probably be a terrible war forced upon the people unnecessarily and it was the duty of all to fight for their convictions.

He was an earnest, faithful soldier and Christian gentleman and rose rapidly to the rank of Brigadier General of Union Volunteers, and was killed at the battle of Perryville, Ky., Oct. 8, 1862.

Meanwhile his brother, James B. Terrill, had attained the rank of Brigadier General in the Confederate army and was killed at the battle of Bethesda Church, Virginia, May 30, 1864.

After Appomattox, their father had their bodies brought back to their home in Virginia and buried them in the same grave, erecting a monument over it and a brief record of their lives and deaths, placing below in his despair:

"This monument erected by their father. God alone knows which was right."

But now that the passions of war are past, shall we not all and every one exclaim that they were both right and there can not in justice be any distinction as to the patriotism, chivalry and honor of these two brothers, and so with all of the combative force.

"No culprits they, though ire and pride
Had laid their better mood aside."

Now let us try to point a moral to this our experience: Notwithstanding the fact that the tireless and ceaseless thinkers and doers have by devices and combinations reduced the toil of brawn and muscle by perhaps sixty per cent and increased food, shelter and raiment many-fold, both in quantity and quality, so there is abundance for all who are willing to pay the price in mild and easy effort: unrest is again abroad in the land and the fanatical and political agitators are teaching that the do-less, shiftless and thriftless should share equally with the ceaseless and tireless doers in everything that is produced under pain of the stoppage of all progress unless granted, no rewards and no forfeits.

Let us implore our children and grandchildren to study well these questions lest they in turn be led to the misconceived belief that there is pending an irrepressible conflict, a feud that naught but blood can atone; and in conclusion commend to them the admonition of Doctor Lyman Beecher, of three generations past, who evidently had in view our present condition, of which here is an extract:

"We must educate! We must educate! Or we must perish by our own prosperity. If we do not, short will be our race from the cradle to the grave. If in our haste to be rich and mighty, we outrun our literary and religious institutions, they will never overtake us: or only come up after the battle of liberty is fought and lost, as spoils to grace the victory, and as resources of inexorable despotism for the perpetuity of our bondage.

"We did not, in the darkest hour, believe that God had brought our fathers to this goodly land to lay the foundation of religious liberty, and wrought such wonders in their preservation, and raised their descendants to such heights of civil and religious liberty, only to reverse the analogy of His providence, and abandon His work.

"No punishments of Heaven are so severe as those for mercies abused: and no instrumentality employed in their infliction is so dreadful as the wrath of man. No spasms are like the spasms of expiring liberty, and no wailing such as her convulsions extort.

"It took Rome three hundred years to die; and our death, if we perish, will be as much more terrific as our intelligence and free institutions have given us more bone, sinew and vitality. May God hide from me the day when the dying agonies of my country shall begin! O thou beloved land, bound together by the ties of brotherhood, and common interest, and perils, live forever—one and undivided."

ADDRESS BEFORE THE ORDER OF INDIAN WARS, ON "THE BATTLE OF THE ROSEBUD"

MARCH 2, 1917

Mr. Commander, companions and guests: I have been requested to describe to you my recollections this evening of the Battle of the Rosebud. General Godfrey last year gave you a description of the Battle of the Little Big Horn most excellently. I hope I can approach him in my efforts tonight.

I speak without notes from memory only, after a lapse of forty years, and will doubtless be incorrect in many things, but several officers of my regiment who engaged in the battle are present and may correct me, particularly Colonel Lemly, then a Lieutenant, who wrote a detailed account immediately after the battle which I have never seen; it would be interesting if he would read it so you may compare it with my recollection after forty years.

As the Battle of the Rosebud was so different, although second in importance in the Sioux war to the Battle of the Little Big Horn (in that it only occupied about four and a half hours), I am going to ask you to indulge me a few minutes to tell you some of the happenings which led up to this fight with the Sioux Indians.

First I want to say I have had a great deal of experience with wild animals and wild Indians, and so far as I know the buffalo were the only wild animals wholly nomadic, having no habitation or home, and their companions, the Sioux Indians, are the only humans that were entirely nomadic.

Coronado tells us of his great explorations through northern "New Spain," of the movement of the Indian cows, as the Spaniards called them, and their companions, the Indians, in his marches northward from the Pecos River (where the Indians had never before seen horses, they using dogs for their pack animals, and the Spaniards had never before seen buffalo and so called them cows), with the buffalo and Indians to the Platte River near what is now McPherson, Nebraska, so that to understand our discussion, with the relations that the Army had to the Sioux, we ought to understand that they were confirmed nomads as much as the buffalo that furnished their supplies. I have seen the whole face of the earth covered with buffalo moving at from four to six miles an hour.

In 1857-58 I traveled twice back and forth through Kansas, Indian Territory and Texas to the Pecos River (the buffalo never went west or south of the Pecos River), and encountered the buffalo and Indians moving back and forth; the buffalo in such great numbers that I felt the earth tremble under their movement, and we were obliged to stop our vehicles and turn the animals' heads in the direction of the buffaloes' flight, firing our pistols to scare them away.

In 1865, after the surrender of Appomattox, my regiment, the 18th U. S. Infantry, was ordered from Fort Leavenworth to Fort McPherson, Nebr. The Union Pacific Railroad was just then being commenced from Omaha, and it was not known then what route we ought to take to the Pacific, so the government ordered Colonel Carrington (in my reference to officers to avoid confusion with higher brevet rank, I will use only their actual rank at the time) to open a road through the Northwestern Territory, and he proceeded to obey that order with his twenty-four company regiment, building the new forts of Fetterman, Reno, Phil. Kearny and C. F. Smith, a march of about fifteen hundred miles through the then State of Nebraska and Territories of Wyoming, Dakota and Montana.

Colonel Carrington established these posts with the greatest expense, carrying all kinds of necessary material, saw mills, hardware, and everything essential to building first-class posts.

This was done without the consent of the Indians, who then generally occupied the wild country. After the establishment of the posts the Indians immediately began to annoy and harass them, and finally after they had assaulted the forts several times, the largest, Phil. Kearny, was unsuccessfully attacked, and a detachment of over one hundred men under Captain Fetterman was sent out by Colonel Carrington to attack the Indians, who, after their manner ambushed and surrounded them, and killed all the officers and men before any rescue could be made from the post.

Finally the Government became alarmed and withdrew the soldiers from these posts so suddenly that they were unable to take with them the valuable stores, munitions, furniture and supplies, leaving everything to be destroyed by the Indians. I was one of the captains of that regiment.

The Indians then demanded that all the troops be permanently withdrawn from their country, and a Commission was organized consisting of Generals Harney, Sherman, Terry and others, they formulating a treaty in 1868 by which they gave the Sioux in perpetuity all these lands, and agreed that they would never be dispossessed without the agreement of three-fourths of the Indians.

Time passed on. I was transferred to the cavalry, and strangely enough in 1872, I was ordered back to the command of North Platte Station, a sub-post of Fort McPherson, where my regiment, under Carrington, was in '65.

The Union Pacific Railroad had then been completed, though the Indians and buffalo were making their annual pilgrimage across the road as before, to the north in the summer, and the south in the winter, accompanied by the nine confederated tribes of the Sioux—Brulés, Ogallalas, Minneconjous, Uncapapas, Two Kettle, San Arcs, Lower Brulés, Yanktons and Gantees, associated with them were also the Northern Cheyennes and Northern Arapahoes.

As the Indians were entirely dependent upon the buffalo for subsistence, the buffalo became the controlling factor in the change that then took place, by refusing to longer cross the road, and the buffalo took up their permanent abode north of the Platte River, the last of the buffalo passing in 1874.

There were different ideas as to what impelled the buffalo to come to this conclusion, but most probably the smoke and noise, and the terrible appearance of the engine, resembling huge monster animals, prevented the buffalo from attempting to cross, and consequently they never returned south after their northern trip in '74. The Indians, of course, for obvious reasons, following permanently.

There can be no reasonable doubt but that the forebears of these Indians and these buffalo were the companions of Coronado in his wonderful exploration (for that day), from the Pecos to the Platte (over four hundred years ago) at the great forks near the present city of North Platte and these Indians were the adversaries we were to meet at Rosebud.

Here at North Platte, while the buffalo were hesitating to go north permanently, I often met and became well acquainted with Spotted Tail, Chief of the Brulés, the greatest and best chief I ever knew.

Spotted Tail, with a great portion of his Ogallalas, remained around North Platte until some time in 1873, when his agency was established on the headwaters of the White River, on a branch called Bear Creek, near the boundary between Nebraska and Dakota. Here he assembled all his tribe, some four thousand.

In the winter of 1874-5 General Crook directed me to follow Spotted Tail and build at his agency a five-company post, to be called Camp Sheridan (three cavalry and two infantry companies), in which Lieutenant Lemly assisted.

Like Carrington, we were furnished with everything necessary: soldier labor, saw, shingle and lath mills, hardware and some thirty skilled artisans, and as we were in a pine forest, many trees were felled, and the lumber from them placed in the building on the same day. There were no contracts, no delays in construction, and it was probably the cheapest, most satisfactory, and most rapidly constructed post ever built by the Army.

Shortly after this Lieutenant Colonel Custer, with an expedition including engineers, mining experts, and geologists, had been ordered to make an exploration of the Black Hills. Custer returned, reporting gold in the hills, which excited the western people so they began to move in from all directions.

This again aroused the Indians, and it became apparent that there would be trouble. General Sheridan issued orders to myself and adjacent commanders to prevent the whites from violating the Indian non-intercourse law by arresting and destroying outfits for that purpose.

I, together with a co-operative detachment from Fort Randall, commanded by Captain Fergus Walker, on May 21st, destroyed by fire a wagon train with mining equipment destined for the Black Hills, under the command of one Major Gordon, at a point now known as Gordon City, returning the party, which numbered about seventy-five people, to Fort Randall, confining Gordon at Camp Sheridan.

The Indians at my agency, and I presume at the others, were constantly forming war parties to go out against these trespassing miners, and Spotted Tail, realizing the critical status, made a confidant of me, and frequently reported as near as he could the probable time and number of warriors that were leaving his agency, suggesting that I intercept them by sending out soldiers to head them off, which I often did.

As they were acting in violation of his orders, it was difficult for him and the other Sioux chiefs to know where they went, and for what purpose, but he did his very best to suppress the insurrection which was then before him.

The War Department has kindly furnished us with two large photographic maps, to which I call your attention. The first represents a portion of the States of Colorado and Nebraska, and the Territories of Wyoming, Dakota and Montana. On this map I have indicated Carrington's route from Kearny to C. F. Smith in green ink, and underscored Forts McPherson, Laramie, Fetterman, Reno, Phil. Kearny and C. F. Smith, the last four being built by Carrington. I have also indicated in red squares the seven principal engagements during the Sioux war, Powder River, Little Big Horn, Tongue River, Rosebud, Slim Buttes, McKenzie's Fight, and later Miles' Battle of Wolfe Mountain. The Camp on Goose Creek is marked with a red circle.

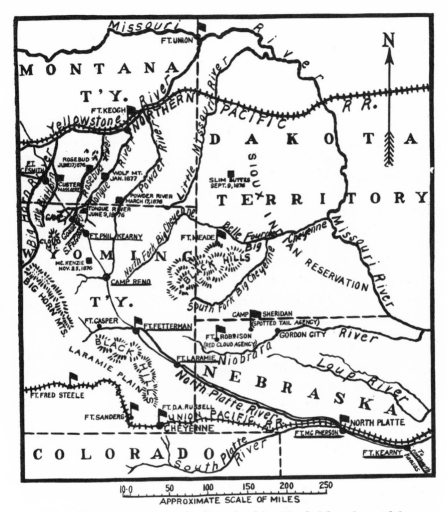

APPROXIMATE SCALE OF MILES

The other map covers the Rosebud battle-field, enlarged from one in *Cyrus Townsend Brady's* book. In my further remarks I will refer to those maps by names and letters.

The roving bands of Indians from the nine Sioux agencies continued their resentful depredations during the fall of '75, and finally a hostile party attacked Fort Fred Steele in considerable numbers, entering the parade ground and killing five or six soldiers right in the presence of the officers and men of the command. About the same time a similar attack was made on Fort Fetterman, and the Indians pinned one of the soldiers they had killed to the ground with sticks in sight of the troops.

In March of '76 the War Department ordered General Crook to send a force from Fort Fetterman to chastise any of these roving bands wherever found. General Crook commanded this expedition which left Fort Fetterman, and proceeded by the Carrington route to the Tongue River, then down the Tongue River, crossing over and attacking a large force of Indians at Powder River. Through some misunderstanding it did not turn out very favorably, and it was considered advisable for the troops to return to the vicinity of Fort Fetterman.

The War Department and the Interior Department then concluded to make general war on these hostile Indians in the field, and General Terry and General Crook were directed to organize armies, the former at the mouth of Powder River, and the latter at Fort Fetterman.

The aggregate number of the nine Sioux agencies was supposed to be about sixty to sixty-five thousand souls, the Minneconjous being the greatest in number, and the most hostile, but it was not known by any one how many Indians had left each of the agencies, or where they had gone; however, it was supposed that they would follow the buffalo wherever they might be, so Terry was to assail them from the north and Crook from the south.

Crook had to do everything hastily, and a more incongruous army could hardly be conceived of; packers, guides, teamsters, and camp followers of all kinds, were assembled together with regular troops from different parts of the country.

Finally we started from Fort Fetterman on May 29th, with twenty companies of regular troops, fifteen of cavalry and five of infantry, amounting to over one thousand soldiers. We followed Carrington's route but before we reached Fort Reno, communication with our base was forbidden because of the danger from the surrounding hostile Indians, and we could neither receive supplies nor return our sick and disabled.

It might add a little spice to my story to relate some of the humorous incidents that occurred on this very somber and serious expedition.

In organizing the wagon train at Fort Fetterman, the wagon-master had unintentionally employed a female teamster, but she was not discovered until we neared Fort Reno, when she was suddenly arrested, and placed in improvised female attire under guard. I knew nothing of this, but being the senior Captain of Cavalry, having served as a Captain for sixteen years, and being of an inquisitive turn of mind, I had become somewhat notorious (for better or worse).

The day she was discovered and placed under guard, unconscious of the fact, I was going through the wagon-master's outfit when she sprang up, calling out "There is Colonel Mills, he knows me," when everybody began to laugh, much to my astonishment and chagrin, being married.

It was not many hours until every man in the camp knew of the professed familiarity of "Calamity Jane" (as she was known) with me, and for several days my particular friends pulled me aside, and asked me "who is 'Calamity Jane'?" I, of course, denied any knowledge of her or her calling, but no one believed me then, and I doubt very much whether they all do yet.

We carried her along until a force was organized to carry our helpless back, with which she was sent, but she afterwards turned out to be a national character, and was a woman of no mean ability and force even from the standard of men. I learned later that she had been a resident of North Platte, and that she knew many of my soldiers, some of whom had probably betrayed her. Later she had employed herself as a cook for my next-door neighbor, Lieutenant Johnson, and had seen me often in his house, I presume.

When we arrived at Fort Phil. Kearny the whole command went into camp near that ruined post on the headwaters of Goose Creek, between its two forks, almost under the shadow of Cloud Peak of the Big Horn Mountains, where General

Crook had made arrangements to meet 250 friendly Indians, Shoshones, Crows and Snakes.

The wagons, supplies, and animals were parked for defense by the teamsters and civilian employes and we made ready to proceed against the Sioux as soon as joined by the Indians.

The friendly Indians having arrived on the morning of June 16th, we started out to find the Sioux. I did not think that General Crook knew where they were, and I did not think our friendly Indians knew where they were, and no one conceived we would find them in the great force we did.

General Crook ordered his classmate, Major Chambers, to select from the one thousand mules a sufficient number on which to mount his infantry soldiers. Chambers and his officers protested, but Crook was obdurate and compelled him to do so suddenly but very reluctantly.

Captain Stanton was our engineer officer, and in order to make good in his scientific profession, equipped himself with a two-wheeled gig, drawn by a mule, which he ornamented with odometers, thermometers, barometers, and other ometers, not forgetting some creature comforts, visible to the men as they passed and repassed. The road was extremely rough even for the cavalry, there being no trail, and as the soldiers were required to carry, each one on his person, four days' simple rations, the sight of his wheeled conveyance aroused their jealousy and envy, and whenever he appeared they would cry out, "Mother's Pies, Mother's Cakes," etc., making life a burden to him. After he had progressed a few miles the gig broke down and he reluctantly abandoned it, where I presume it lies today (but for illness he would be here), and I have promised to explain that he did not ride the gig, but a horse.

We marched thirty-five miles the first day until we came to a lake or swamp of about five hundred yards diameter, the headwaters of the Rosebud, which I have marked on the small map. We left Chambers' command several miles in the rear, and when we had bivouacked our camp on three sides of the lake, leaving the fourth side of the rectangle for Chambers

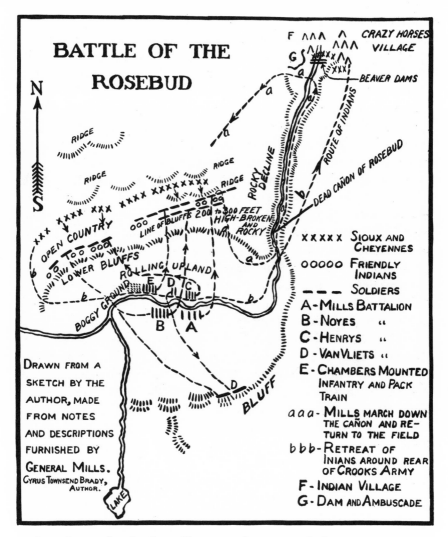

BATTLE OF THE
ROSEBUD

N

S

CRAZY HORSES
VILLAGE

BEAVER DAMS

ROUTE OF INDIANS

DEAD CAÑON OF ROSEBUD

RIDGE

RIDGE

RIDGE

RIDGE

ROCKY DECLINE

200 to 300 FEET
HIGH-BROKEN
AND ROCKY

LINE OF BLUFFS

OPEN COUNTRY

LOWER BLUFFS

ROLLING UPLAND

BOGGY GROUND

E D C

B A

BLUFF

D

LAKE

x x x x x SIOUX AND
CHEYENNES

o o o o o FRIENDLY
INDIANS

— — — SOLDIERS

A - MILLS BATTALION
B - NOYES "
C - HENRYS "
D - VAN VLIETS "
E - CHAMBERS MOUNTED
INFANTRY AND PACK
TRAIN

a a a - MILLS MARCH DOWN
THE CAÑON AND RE-
TURN TO THE FIELD

b b b - RETREAT OF
INIANS AROUND REAR
OF CROOKS ARMY

F - INDIAN VILLAGE
G - DAM AND AMBUSCADE

DRAWN FROM A
SKETCH BY THE
AUTHOR, MADE
FROM NOTES
AND DESCRIPTIONS
FURNISHED BY
GENERAL MILLS.
CYRUS TOWNSEND BRADY,
AUTHOR.

when he arrived, the officers and many of the men walked over to observe the military movements of the "mule brigade," as it was called.

Chambers was proud and ambitious to do his duty, however humiliating and disagreeable, as well as he could, so when the leading company came near the line designated, he gave the command, "Left front into line" in military style, and the first company came into line, but no sooner had the mules halted when, after their custom, they began to bray as loud as they could, making extra effort in accord with the extra effort they had made to carry their strange burden into camp. The cavalry officers began to laugh and roar. As the other companies began to halt, Chambers lost courage and with oaths and every evidence of anger, threw his sword down on the ground and left the command to take care of itself as best it could.

We remained there that night. There were no buffalo, and we could not learn anything from the friendlies about the enemy. The next morning, the 17th, at sunrise we started on our march down the Rosebud, without any indication of danger. General Crook had previously to do only with the semi-nomadic tribes, and from conversations with him I felt he did not realize the prowess of the Sioux, though it was hard to think that he was not well informed by his numerous guides, scouts and especially the 250 friendly Indians.

About 9.30 or 10 o'clock, General Crook being with Captain Henry's squadron marked "C" on the left bank, signalled a halt. Van Vliet's squadron "D" was in the rear of Henry, and Chambers' battalion marked "E" was in the rear of Van Vliet, and the packers were in the rear of Chambers. My squadron of four troops of the Third was in the advance on the right bank marked "A," followed by Captain Noyes with five companies of the Second marked "B." Everything was quiet, the day was beautiful, clear and very warm. All had unbridled and were grazing for perhaps half to three-quarters of an hour, when my colored servant observed he heard shouting, and knowing that his ears were better than mine, I advanced up the hill towards "D" until I got to a high piece of ground, when, looking north, I saw on the crest of the horizon about two miles distant, great numbers of moving objects, looking somewhat like distant crows silhouetted on the clear sky above the horizon. I soon came to the conclusion that they were Indians in great numbers.

The friendly Indians were supposed to be in advance to find the enemy for us. General Crook and the troops on the left bank of the river were prevented from seeing anything to the north by the rising bluffs between them and the approaching Indians. I am satisfied that I was the first person to observe the coming hostiles.

They were, when I first saw them, from two to three miles distant, coming at full speed towards us and cheering. I immediately sounded the alarm, directing some of my squadron to mount, and calling out to General Crook, who was playing cards with some of his officers, that the Sioux were rapidly approaching.

He ordered me to report to him with my squadron at once. When I met him after crossing the stream, which was very boggy, I told him we were about to be attacked by a large force, and that the Indians were coming from due north. He told me to march rapidly and as soon as I got to higher ground to take the bluffs and hold them. I did so. What orders he gave to others I have never known. There are members of the Third Cavalry here, and they would probably correct me if I made mistakes. In all of this fight I do not remember to have received a single order except from General Crook personally or his Adjutant, Major Nickerson.

I marched as rapidly as I could through the rough and broken rocks, and as soon as I got on smoother ground gave the command "front into line," and sounded the charge.

There were two prominent rocky ridges, the first about a half mile from where I met General Crook, and the second probably about a half mile further on. When I reached the first ridge the leading Indians were there but gave way. There were large boulders at its foot, some large enough to cover the sets of four horses. I dismounted and directed the horse holders to protect them behind these rocks, advancing the men to the top of the ridge where the boulders were smaller, but of a size to protect one or two soldiers, and appeared to be just what we wanted to fight behind. We met the Indians at the foot of this ridge, and charged right in and through them, driving them back to the top of the ridge. These Indians were most hideous, every one being painted in most hideous colors and designs, stark naked, except their moccasins, breech clouts and head gear, the latter consisting of feathers and horns; some of the horses being also painted, and the Indians proved then and there that they were the best cavalry soldiers on earth. In charging up towards us they exposed little of their person, hanging on with one arm around the neck and one leg over the horse, firing and lancing from underneath the horses' necks, so that there was no part of the Indian at which we could aim.

Their shouting and personal appearance was so hideous that it terrified the horses more than our men and rendered them almost uncontrollable before we dismounted and placed them behind the rocks.

The Indians came not in a line but in flocks or herds like the buffalo, and they piled in upon us until I think there must have been one thousand or fifteen hundred in our immediate front, but they refused to fight when they found us secured behind the rocks, and bore off to our left. I then charged the second ridge, and took it in the same manner and fortified myself with the horses protected behind the larger boulders and the men behind the smaller ones.

These Indians lived with their horses, were unsurfeited with food, shelter, raiment or equipment, then the best cavalry in the world; their like will never be seen again. Our friendlies were worthless against them; we would have been better off without them.

In the second charge my trumpeter, Elmer Snow's horse became unmanageable, and he could not halt him but continued through the Indians, receiving a wound shattering the bones of both forearms, but guiding his horse with legs only he described a circle of several hundred yards, returning to us and throwing himself on the ground.

On our right we were absolutely protected by the jagged and

rough places down to the Rosebud Canyon, so we were most fortunate in securing this position.

On examining my front after taking the first ridge, I found that one of my troops, Captain Andrews, was missing, and learned that Colonel Royal had cut him off and directed that he report to him, as he was moving to the left with Captain Henry's squadron. We could see little of the left, as the ground depressed and the rough rocks obscured vision of what was going on by either the Indians or Henry's, Van Vliet's and Royal's commands.

I observed about this time two troops which I afterwards learned were Van Vliet's, going to "D" on the south bluff, and later saw them proceed in a northwesterly direction towards where we could hear firing from Henry's and Royal's commands.

Soon after I took the first bluff the infantry took position on my left and Captain Noyes with his five troops arrived, and was placed in reserve by General Crook in our rear and left, and the infantry joined on the ground lying on my left. General Crook held his position near my squadron between my squadron and Noyes' during the entire battle, but I had little communication with him save when he came to me to give orders, and I knew little of what was going on until finally most of the Indians left my front. About 12.30 he ordered me to take my command of three troops and ordered Captain Noyes with his five troops to report to me, and proceed with the eight down the canyon and take the village, which he said he had been reliably informed was about six miles down the canyon.

Henry, who was one of the best cavalry officers I ever knew, moved off as indicated on the map.

This canyon was about six miles long. I was directed to follow it until I came to the village, and take it, and hold it until he came to my support with the rest of the command. I obeyed the order until I reached the vicinity of the village, when I heard a voice calling me to halt, and Major Nickerson,

the Adjutant General, directed me to return at once to General
Crook. Some of the officers advised not. "We have the village," they said, "and can hold it." Nickerson then came
across the stream. I asked him, "Are you sure he wants me to
go back?" He replied he was.

The canyon had opened here so I found I could climb the
rocks and get out, as indicated on the map.

I returned about 2.30 and found General Crook in about the
same position I had left him, and said, "General, why did you
recall me? I had the village and could have held it." I never
saw a man more dejected. He replied, "Well, Colonel, I found
it a more serious engagement than I thought. We have lost
about fifty killed and wounded, and the doctors refused to
remain with the wounded unless I left the infantry and one of
the squadrons with them." He said, "I knew I could not keep
my promise to support you with the remainder of the force."

The General had assembled the hospital around him and
the infantry, also two battalions near him. In visiting my
wounded, Captain Henry heard my voice and called me. I
did not know until then that he had been wounded, and going
to him, found his breast all covered with clotted blood, his
eyes swollen so he could not see, and a ghastly wound through
both cheeks under the eyes. I said, "Henry, are you badly
wounded?" and he replied, "The doctors have just told me
that I must die, but I will not." And he did not, although nine
out of ten under such circumstances would have died. Henry
and I were rival captains in the same regiment, but always
friends.

Though the Third Cavalry had less than one-half of the soldiers engaged, their loss in killed and wounded was about
four-fifths, principally of Henry's and Van Vliet's squadrons
and Andrews' company of mine, that of Vroom's company
being the greatest in proportion, this owing to their isolated
exposure on level ground where the Indians could pass through
them.

The officers then mingled and talked over the fight. I

learned that Royal, with Henry's and Van Vliet's squadrons and my troop E had gone to the extreme left, where the ground was open, and that when the 1,000 or 1,500 Indians had refused to fight in the rocks they had swung around and overwhelmed them, charging bodily and rapidly through the soldiers, knocking them from their horses with lances and knives, dismounting and killing them, cutting the arms of several off at the elbows in the midst of the fight and carrying them away.

They then swung around and passed over the halting ground we had made at 9.30 in the morning, capturing some horses and killing an Indian boy left there. We then all realized for the first time that while we were lucky not to have been entirely vanquished, we had been most humiliatingly defeated, and that the village which Custer was to meet only seven days later, fourteen miles west on the Little Big Horn, contained probably 15,000 or 20,000 souls, perhaps 4,000 or 5,000 warriors, and that perhaps only half of them had met us in battle, and that had my command remained at the village not one of us would have returned.

In fact, I, with General Crook, visited this village site in our fall campaign, and he told me I ought to have been thankful to him for returning me from that canyon as they were as well or better equipped to destroy me as they were to destroy Custer and his command, and here I want to pay a tribute to both Colonel Custer and Captain Henry. I knew both as long as' they lived, and have been acquainted with nearly all prominent cavalry officers during my service, and they were always in my mind typical cavalry soldiers of the U. S. Army. I always resented criticisms that were made against Custer by men from General Terry down, who had little or no knowledge of Indian warfare. While a good man, Terry was not familiar with Indian warfare.

The next day we returned to our camp on Goose Creek, where General Crook and all of us made very brief reports of the battle, having little pride in our achievement. General Crook asked for reinforcements, and went into camp awaiting them, meanwhile we amused ourselves by hunting and fishing in the Big Horn Mountains, both General Crook and I being very fond of hunting. We spent much time in the mountains, and some two days later, after the Custer engagement, I and my Lieutenant, Schwatka, went to the peak of the Big Horn Mountains, the northernmost point, thinking we might observe something in that direction, it being about thirty-five or forty miles to the Rosebud. About 2 p.m. we observed a great smoke, and realized that there had been a fight. Returning to camp in the night, we reported to General Crook. About June 30th, I, with my squadron, being the outpost on the lower Goose Creek, observed at sunrise some smoke which created suspicion, and looking down the valley I saw three mounted men coming toward me, which I first thought were Indians, but later discovered that they were white men on mules, Privates James Bell, William Evans, and Benj. F. Stewart, Company "E," 7th Infantry (who were awarded medals on December 2, 1876), and I rode to them. They handed me a dispatch from General Terry to General Crook, stating that Custer and his command had been massacred and that they had been sent by General Terry to carry his message to General Crook. Crook was in the mountains hunting. I carried the dispatch to Colonel Royal, commanding the camp, who opened it, and read the dispatch, which horrified the assembled officers.

He ordered me with my full company to carry it as rapidly as I could to General Crook, and after climbing about eighteen miles in the mountains I found him returning with his pack mules loaded down with elk, deer and big horn sheep. He read the dispatch, and while all of us were horrified and oppressed with mortification and sympathy for the dead and wounded, there was with all, particularly in General Crook's expression, a feeling that the country would realize that there were others who had underrated the valor and numbers of the Sioux.

While General Crook was a cold, gray-eyed and somewhat cold-blooded warrior, treating his men perhaps too practically in war time, there yet ran through us a feeling of profound sympathy for his great misfortune, while at the same time we had a still more profound sympathy for the other gallant and more sympathetic Custer—at least, most of us. There were some there, I regret to say, who had ranked him and over whom he was promoted, that would insinuate, "I told you so," and for these sentiments the majority of us had no respect.

Finally, we were joined by General Merritt and the entire Fifth Cavalry, and the fall campaign ensued. After its termination I was returned to the command of Camp Sheridan, my former post, and was directed by General Crook to enter into communication with Chief Touch the Clouds of the Minneconjous, whose tribe still remained hostile, and I proposed to approach him through Spotted Tail and try to induce him to surrender. He approved, and I fitted up Spotted Tail with about thirty of his friendly Indians, rations and pack mules, and he proceeded to the camp of Touch the Clouds, and after some protracted negotiations induced him to return and surrender at a given time, about thirty days in advance, stipulating, however, that he was to be received with honors when he joined Spotted Tail's band. This reception, according to Indian tradition, consisted of the following program:

When a hostile band agrees to return to peace and join its former friends, the hosts are supposed to be captured by them; the tribe to be joined is notified when the tribe joining will approach; the approaching tribe is drawn up in war paint in apparent hostile array, and with great shouts and whooping, charge through the receiving village, who stand out receiving them with cheers, apparently of joy; the charging Indians firing their pieces in every direction save toward their supposed make-believe enemies. After charging fully through the village they return again, dismounting, and shake hands with their newly-made friends, and direct their squaws to pitch their tepees around those of the village. Chief Touch the Clouds sent in word that he would like to make a formal surrender, and if General Crook and his staff would appear on the parade ground of the military post, he, with his principal chiefs—about thirty in number—would gallop in, mounted as with hostile intent, and when arrived within a few yards of the General, would cast their arms on the ground. And this ceremony was actually gone through by General Crook and his staff officers. The arms they threw down were pieces of no value.

It will be observed that the ethics of the North American Indians did not differ materially from the ethics of the barbarians now fighting in Europe, in that they wanted no peace without victory.

Touch the Clouds surrendered about 1,500 Minneconjous, which increased Spotted Tail's tribe to nearly 6,000.